Sisters of Salome

SISTERS
OF
SALOME

□ □ □ □ □

Toni Bentley

Yale University Press   New Haven & London

"Light as a Breeze," by Leonard Cohen, Copyright © 1992 Sony/ATV Songs
LLC. All rights administered by Sony/ATV Music Publishing, 8 Music Square
West, Nashville, TN 37203. All rights reserved. Used by permission.

"Waiting for the Miracle," by Leonard Cohen, Copyright © 1992 Sony/ATV
Songs LLC, Robinhill Music, Universal-MCA Music Publishing and Geffen
Music. All rights on behalf of Sony/ATV Songs LLC administered by
Sony/ATV Music Publishing, 8 Music Square West, Nashville, TN 37203.
All rights reserved. Used by permission.

Designed by James J. Johnson and set in Cochin Roman types
by The Composing Room of Michigan, Inc., Grand Rapids, Michigan.
Printed in the United States of America by R. R. Donnelley and Sons,
Harrisonburg, Virginia.

Library of Congress Cataloging-in-Publication Data

Bentley, Toni.
   Sisters of Salome / Toni Bentley.
      p.   cm.
Includes bibliographical references (p.) and index.
   ISBN 0-300-09039-0 (alk. paper)

   1. Women dancers — Biography.   2. Feminism and dance.   3. Salome
(Biblical figure)   I. Title.
   GV1785.A1 B47   2002
   792.8′092′2 — dc21

                                                    2001005243

A catalogue record for this book is available from the British Library.

The paper in this book meets the guidelines for permanence and durability
of the Committee on Production Guidelines for Book Longevity of the
Council on Library Resources.

10   9   8   7   6   5   4   3   2   1

For L.K.

The Dance?
Believe what you care to.
Picture it any way you want to.
All the world knows
truth is best revealed
by gradual deception.
It was a striptease pure and simple.

—George Garrett, "Salome" (1963)

The significance of the femme fatale lies not in her gender
but in her freedom.

—Angela Carter, *Shaking a Leg: Collected Writings* (1998)

Contents

Acknowledgments

I wish to thank the late Lincoln Kirstein and Lloyd Fonvielle for their initial encouragement and belief in this project.

To Alix Freedman, whose invaluable time, help and good faith made this book possible, I am deeply grateful.

Marc Kristal's editorial notes and consistent good humor helped this book in numerous ways.

I am also indebted to the following for various suggestions and guidance — Christopher d'Amboise, Jeff d'Avanzo, Peter Bentley, Beverly Berg, Laurence Frank, Anne Freedgood, Maxine Groffsky, Jay Grove, Michael Hacker, Kenneth P. Norwick, Michael Schrage, Jonathan Shikora, Bob Tzudiker and Noni White, J. B. White, and Michael Wolf; for translations, Laura Blum, Betty Maetz, and Marvin J. Ward, Ph.D.; and my terrific agents Glen Hartley and Lynn Chu.

At Yale University Press I extend many thanks to the following for a very civilized publication process — Jim Johnson, Susan Laity, Amy Steffen, and especially Harry Haskell for overseeing the entire publication process, as well as Noreen O'Connor for editing, and Marcia Carlson for indexing.

As this book comprises the lives of four real women and one mythical one, the sources were voluminous, and I wish to acknowledge the following writers for their invaluable research that preceded my own. For Salome, Richard Bizot; for Maud Allan, Felix Cherniavsky and Michael Kettle; for Mata Hari, Russell Warren Howe, Julia Keay, Erika Ostrovsky, Sam Waagenaar, and Julie Wheelwright; for Ida Rubinstein, Michael de Cossart, Jacques Depaulis, and Lynn Garafola; and for Colette, Claude Francis and Fernande Gontier, Herbert Lottman, Yvonne Mitchell, Michèle Sarde, and Judith Thurman.

For help finding and reproducing the photographs I would like to thank Karin Bentley, Whitney Chadwick, Lynn Garafola, Paul Kolnik, Joe Lucchesi, David Hirshey, Michèle Le Pavec, Tom Rodgers, Mikael Salazar, and the Crazy Horse, Paris. At the Dance and Theatre Collections of the New York Public Library, Andrea Felder, Phil Karg, Jeremy Megraw, Monica Moseley, and Madeleine Nichols were extremely helpful.

I wish to thank the following for their kind permission to use or reprint photographs: Richard Bizot (fig. 11); Mlle Samia Bordji, Collection Jouvenel, Musée Colette, Saint-Sauveur-en-Puisaye, dans l'Yonne (figs. 1 and 21); Marcel Dekker, Inc., to reprint from Felix Cherniavsky, "Maud Allan: Part II," *Dance Chronicle*, 6, no. 3 (1983): 204 (fig. 9); Dover Publications to reprint from *The Decorative Art of Léon Bakst*, 1972 (fig. 19).

Also, I wish to thank the following institutions: Bibliothèque de France, Paris; Musée National des Arts Asiatiques-Guimet, Paris; Bibliothèque de l'Opéra, Paris; and the Library of Performing Arts, New York Public Library, New York.

Introduction: Colette's Breast

The personal quest that led me to this book began years ago with a single image of Sidonie Gabrielle Colette's left breast. I was eighteen when I discovered the French writer's novels, and while interest quickly became obsession, I devoured as many of them as I could find in fast succession. I fell completely in love with this woman who seemed to speak the unspeakable about the pursuit of love, the pain of desire, and the tenderness that binds the two. Then I saw the photograph of my heroine that I would never forget (fig. 1). She was posing in profile on a stage set, her short, curly hair a thick halo about her head, and her right arm raised softly before her uplifted face, her palm facing up and away. Her steady gaze looked expectantly into the distant horizon beyond her hand while, paradoxically, shielding herself from its onslaught. It was a lyrical and yearning gesture that, as a young Balanchine dancer, I recognized from the opening of his ballet *Serenade,* made almost thirty years later. Colette looked fabulous, and I was thrilled to see that brains and beauty could indeed coexist in one woman.

But it got even better — she was dressed in a torn slip of white linen, her left breast exposed and aiming at the camera lens with shameless pride. The nakedness continued down the left side, revealing a rounded, expertly posed thigh that ended its length in a slipper tied with suggestive black laces. She offered her bosom with a demure gesture of surrender tempered by the grace of an aristocrat.

Her breast was beautiful, and the woman of words suddenly became flesh and blood — and curiously naughty. "Colette's Breast," as I came to think of the image, symbolized for me something that I wanted for my-

FIG. 1. Colette in *La Chair*, ca. 1907. "Poor unhappy little left breast," she wrote more than twenty-five years later, "when I say poor not so poor, not so *unhappy*, not so *little* as that!" (Collection Jouvenel, Musée Colette)

self, though I was not sure exactly what that was. Did I want the power of her pen? Or the power of her bosom? Her assertive intellect? Or her alluring magnetism? My search was furthered by a second vision that came a few years later. George Balanchine, my boss at the time, led me to it.

I was dancing with the New York City Ballet in Paris. We were performing at the historic Théâtre des Champs-Elysées on the avenue Montaigne, where Stravinsky's *Rite of Spring* had premiered in 1913 to a barrage of protest and tomatoes and where Josephine Baker had first conquered the Parisians with her wicked belt of bouncing bananas. Things were quieter in 1980; we were simply dancing one Balanchine masterpiece after another to sold-out audiences, rave reviews, and the unquestionable knowledge that Balanchine was a genius and his company was at its pinnacle.

Contrary to the usual easy-come, easy-go backstage policy, this theater was small, and visitors were forbidden backstage — there was no room in the wings. Until the night that Mr. B broke his own rule. We were warming up for Stravinsky's *Symphony in Three Movements*. As leg-warmers were tossed off, toe-shoe ribbons were secured, and the stage manager called "Places, please," we lined up in the epic diagonal that spans the stage as the curtain rises on sixteen women wearing the bare essentials — white leotards, pink tights, toe shoes, and high ponytails. Mr. B, in his usual dapper outfit with silk cravat, suddenly appeared, escorting several glamorous young ladies in very short skirts into the front wing, his wing, the wing where no one else dared to stand. The curtain rose, the orchestra began, and we were off, Balanchine thoroughbreds moving with total precision and breakneck speed through the sacred space created by Stravinsky's sound and Balanchine's shapes. And the short-skirted girls watched. When the curtain came down, Mr. B led the women away. He sniffed and looked pleased.

Anything Balanchine did was, naturally, of great interest to us, and word got around that these were dancers from the Crazy Horse Saloon, the most elegant strip show in Paris, perhaps the world. My interest deepened when I found out that after watching our performances Mr. B would sometimes walk, often with a favorite ballerina, the few blocks from the avenue Montaigne to the fashionable avenue George V and descend into the plush, red velvet underworld of the Crazy Horse for its midnight show.

"Mr. B at a strip show!" I thought, half shocked, half impressed, and very curious. Why was one of the great artists of the twentieth century watching nude women strut their stuff? Was it just prurient interest, a sign that he really was human after all (we who danced for him were never entirely sure), or was it something else? He was friendly with the owner and founder of the Crazy Horse, Alain Bernardin, and I was soon to see why. One night I decided to investigate, and spent sixty dollars of my per diem on a ticket to the show.

The twinkling, purple curtains parted on a small stage, revealing a black space with a single prop in its center: a six-foot-high, blue neon outline of a sarcophagus. The number was called "Adagio d'Oltre Tombe" — "Adagio from Beyond the Grave." To mournful, slow music, naked women, wearing only a sequined rope about their midriffs, posed on a moving stage belt and were carried to the center of the space, behind the coffin door. One by one they passed ceremoniously through, the neon adding a velvet glow to their luminous skin as they emerged in the afterworld, the other world. As one dancer paused before the gateway, her eyes caught the light and flashed, and while her beautiful breasts pointed upward, her black pubic triangle radiated the eternal mystery of what one of Casanova's lovers called the "fatal vault."[1] This creature, in that moment, was to me the most powerful woman in the world.

In her youth and brazen nakedness she was more powerful than a rich woman, a married woman, a titled woman, or a woman with degrees, diplomas, or awards. She manifested a quality that transcended the public world — the intangible allure of sexuality, of vulnerability, of grace. She was an icon of desirability. She presented the external image of internal revelation. In her nudity and anonymity she had what so many women want: power and safety within her own circumscribed world. This image burned itself into my mind's eye and became its master (fig. 2).

The connection between Bernardin, the king of naked dancing, and Balanchine, the great ballet choreographer, became clear as I experienced an astonishing moment of self-recognition: this glamorous, slim, athletic woman was a Balanchine dancer without her leotard — and I was she. The striptease at the Crazy Horse gave new meaning to my years spent in tights, tutus, and tiaras. Partial, simulated, decorated, and disguised nudity is part of the appeal of a ballerina. Ballet wear is theatrical underwear — silk, satin, velvet, and chiffon their common coverings.

FIG. 2. "Adagio d'Oltre Tombe," Crazy Horse, Paris, 1991
(Courtesy of the Crazy Horse, Paris)

Stilettos are toe shoes with a stabilizing training heel; both elongate the female leg to its erotic pinnacle. What are boned tutu bodices but skintight corsets and push-up bras? What are pink tights but warm naked legs? The figure-forming beauty inherent in ballet costumes and footwear is erotically related to the bondage element of classic strip lingerie: breath is shortened, visibility heightened.

In dancing Balanchine we were dancing naked (if we were dancing well) — not only in showing every delineation of a highly trained body, but in "turning out," classical ballet's guiding force, where hips, legs, and feet are literally opened outward, away from each other. What is revealed is the sexual core. In attempting this unnatural vertical physical split, encounters with one's moral and spiritual bodies are inevitable; it is deep and dangerous exposure.

The overlap of so-called high and low art intrigued me. Both Balanchine and Bernardin had devoted their lives to their respective images of woman, using their talents to present that image to the world — pared down for the maximum visual effect. They had each devised worlds where women appeared as mythical queens and sexual madonnas — both forever out of reach. The physical similarities between Bernardin's and Balanchine's girls were uncanny — long, lean, energized bodies and concentrated, youthful faces, all shaped by a distinct discipline. But it was on another, paradoxically invisible, level that the likeness taught me about myself and why I so loved and wanted to dance for Balanchine in the way that he wanted.

The Crazy Horse dancers' nudity perfectly mirrored and symbolized for me what Balanchine really asked of us — complete and total surrender of the ego that served only to conceal the deeper levels of being that his art was all about. In his world, it was through movement of the physical body that we could hope to find and illuminate the spiritual realm for an audience and for ourselves. Balanchine hated "acting," "emoting," "Gisellitis," or any other show of "soulfulness" — those were garments behind which one could hide. The transcendence that could be felt in dancing a Balanchine ballet was to be found through elimination: elimination of sets, costumes, stories, and one's own stubborn vanity, elimination of all but the inevitable. Dancing Balanchine was about removing our self-directed will in order to reveal the unseen, the unspoken, the feared, and the desired — what he referred to as the "Real World." The dancers at the Crazy Horse illustrated this visually, and viscerally, with their literal nudity.

From that first moment of self-recognition at the Crazy Horse Saloon in Paris, the idea was born. Watching those dancers' stylized, witty performance, I rapidly developed a consuming fantasy of my own. I didn't want to just admire their beauty, I wanted to be in their lineup, to be that vulnerable, publicly. Would being the center of such an unconventional display be as powerful an internal experience as I imagined from the other side of the footlights? Could I become the object of my own fantasy? One day in class Balanchine had remarked, "You can see Paradise — but you can't get in." I wondered if I could.

I proceeded first with a safe, secondary approach. In my journalistic persona I would investigate the Crazy Horse Saloon and its founder; I would penetrate the performance and infiltrate backstage. Bernardin, despite carefully controlling publicity, invited me into his naked harem as one of Balanchine's girls. I spent a week in Paris, interviewing him, his assistants, and many of the dancers.

Alain Bernardin was a man who, as a teenager, had had an epiphany one night while looking at a naked woman. In her limbs, her lines, her aura, and her pointed nipples he saw not only his destiny; he saw the world. And the Crazy Horse was indeed a world unto itself, a multimillion-dollar enterprise founded, developed, and overseen entirely by one man's sacred, horny vision of beautiful young women. Security was high, access backstage was almost impossible, but once behind the stage door I saw the intricate product of Bernardin's investment. The carpets and walls lined in red velvet suggested a high-class bordello-convent run by a strict but benevolent dictator. There was no prostitution here; in fact, should any girl have any contact, even outside the club, with a patron, she was fired. Money, flowers, and jewelry sent backstage were promptly returned to their smitten senders. There were even white lines painted in the wings to separate the performers from the male production staff. The dancers were well paid — more than I earned at the New York City Ballet — had pension plans, and were escorted by guards each evening to waiting cars to carry them home. These dancers were Bernardin's stable of thoroughbreds, just as I was one of Balanchine's.

I came away with two souvenirs of the Crazy Horse — a heavy glass bottle of Dior No. 004 stage makeup and black Leichner pancake makeup in a round plastic case. The girls covered their flesh head to toe each night with the thick Dior to achieve a sisterhood of similarity and a creamy gleam under the spotlights.

The black Leichner was pubic paint. With her hair trimmed to a minimum, each girl would take a small brush and paint an equilateral triangle with four-inch sides onto her mound of venus. This brilliant innovation was the solution to Bernardin's quest. As a connoisseur of his territory he was frustrated with the requisite "cache-sex," or G-string, and in 1970 he invented what has become the club's trademark. "Like a painting, like a Modigliani, everyone the same," he explained, drawing a trian-

gle on a piece of paper. "You cannot have a girl with eye makeup and lipstick and not have makeup there. She looks unfinished. Having a black
sex makes her beautiful, like a painting."[2] A man who would devise such
a novel sexual image could only remind me of Balanchine fussing over a
ballerina's eye makeup, tiara, or chignon. Both men were fetishistically
obsessed with the details of female beauty — heterosexual male lesbians.

I left Paris with my Dior and Leichner souvenirs and wrote an article about the Crazy Horse for *Allure* magazine, but still my personal curiosity was unsatiated. I too wanted a Modigliani triangle. The next move
in my voyage of modest exhibitionism was to pose for nude photographs
by a lovely French photographer, Marie-Claire Montenari. For several
thousand dollars she shot numerous soft-focus black and whites while I
posed on a small antique couch with gauzy veils. After I chose my favorites from a contact sheet, she mounted them in a discreet gray portfo-
lio for posterity or framing.

Ostensibly for my husband at the time — they were of course for
me — the images were startling. I liked the ones that did not include my
face, which understandably looked pensive and somewhat strained under the circumstances. I had never taken off my clothes for a stranger before, and shyness was, once again, the enemy. But my overall aim was accomplished; I wanted a visual record of my lean dancer's body before it
aged, something permanent to counteract my impermanent self. The
driving theme of gathering evidence of my very existence was leading me
along the path to self-revelation. Again turning journalist, I wrote a brief
article for *New York Newsday* about the experience of being photographed
in the nude, but stopped short of allowing the newspaper to actually print
one of the images.

But the static photos were still not enough. As they gathered dust, I
still wanted an audience for my body, not just for my words about my
body. I had by now stopped dancing professionally for the New York
City Ballet because of a hip injury that would not heal — years of turning
out had finally, ironically, left me unable to turn in, and walking became
more difficult than dancing. My desire to strip was surely due in part to
the loss of a theatrical outlet and the daily physical challenge, though it is
certainly not the aim of every ballerina who has been grounded.

This quest coincided with the last two years of my marriage. In fact,
it became a testing ground for my increasing dissatisfaction. As my sexual life inevitably decreased, my need to strip increased — exponentially.

I did not want to have sex with anyone else, but I sure did want to know whether I could be both sexually brazen and alluring. This is a performer's version of adultery.

I sent Bernardin at the Crazy Horse my nude photos, asking to perform, even if only once, on his stage. The answer was no — he was not about to allow an outside dancer, especially one who writes, onto his stage for a brief interlude; his operation was too professional to accommodate my personal fantasy. Disappointed, I shelved the idea temporarily while my marriage dissolved completely. Until late one rainy Saturday night in New York City.

The Blue Angel was no Parisian music hall, and it was hard to find. The first phone query to information produced a number, but the annoyed voice at the end of the line indicated that this was definitely not the strip club. A second plea to the operator produced another number. Someone actually answered the phone and offered an address. After grabbing a cab in torrential rain, a few friends and I arrived on Walker Street — and walked. Located in Manhattan's deep downtown Tribeca, the short block was dark, empty, and, with the rain still pelting down, there was not a soul in sight. Was the address wrong? Was this club available only to some elite membership and ordinary mortals couldn't find it? As the mystery grew, so did our determination, and we prowled the block, door to door, looking for an indication of civilization.

A pale blue bulb barely illuminated a dark and ominous staircase that led down below street level. This must be the place. In a small alcove inside the door we each paid fifteen dollars and were cautioned that no alcohol was served inside. The absence of alcohol in New York State strip clubs is the trade-off for no nipple pasties and no G-strings. Full nudity must be taken sober. Once inside it was clear why.

After passing a very alert bouncer, who lent a much-appreciated air of safety to the joint, and a cozy but empty lap-dance room, we entered the cabaret. Two tiny raised platforms, one in front and one to the right, marked the sites. There they were, one by one, young women of all colors and sizes, making entrances and exits on these stages, doing the most astonishing things. Each had a gimmick — Gypsy Rose Lee was right about that: one presented a James Bond girl in black jacket, dark glasses, and daunting high heels, one burlesqued a vaudeville queen with twirling, tasseled nipples, another played a schoolgirl in a kilt and knee highs, one dripped candle wax on her breasts and belly, while yet another ate fire from the most inconvenient positions. And each one got very, very naked, more naked than you ever thought a woman could get — Casanova's "church squares" were opened to the public.[3] I had never seen the female body — certainly not my own — from such angles, and, while the Blue Angel was clearly of a very different demeanor from the Crazy Horse Saloon, that same overwhelming sensation of female beauty, power, and mystery flooded my system. The time had come.

I was in town for the publication party for my book *Costumes by Karinska,* a lush tome of text and photos about Balanchine's closest costume collaborator, the woman who changed the way his dancers looked by her exquisite rendering of tutus, taffeta, and tiaras. I wanted to celebrate the end of the costume project by taking off my own.

For the next frantic few days a dear friend and old City Ballet cohort, Christopher d'Amboise, conspired with me on my dance. I knew the music I wanted to dance to, and my outfit was culled from my suitcase — my gown was the one I wore for the book party.

I returned to the Blue Angel two days later to fulfill, tongue planted seriously in my cheek, that desire for self-exposure and vulnerability that Balanchine had desired but that I had never done; youthful fear and apologetic modesty had prevented me. Being literally naked would dramatize my purpose; I would not miss my own experience this time.

"She stands before you naked, you can see it, you can taste it, but she comes to you light as the breeze," Leonard Cohen growled over the loudspeakers as I grasped the sides of my black velvet gown with red lacquered nails, sliding it gently, slowly over my bare hips, my ass, my thighs, my knees, my calves, my ankles, my high, high heels. "Then she dances so graceful," Cohen crooned, "and your heart's hard and hateful and she's naked but that's just a tease." As I peeled my body to the skin my legs remained straight and, with my chin now at my feet, I was folded in two equal halves, like a circus acrobat, like Flaubert's Salome.

Cohen's raspy voice filled the small, smoky club with its bittersweet lament. Unfolding myself, I stood upright and stepped carefully out of the pool of soft velvet now circling my feet. I made my way slowly to the tip of the tiny stage and, bathed in the spotlight, back arched, chest and face thrust forward, hands reaching upward, I thought of the Winged

Victory of Samothrace. I was naked — as God and Balanchine had shaped me — in front of fifty paying strangers.

I didn't move too quickly or too much at this point; it would have been vulgar. I wore steep black suede pumps, black fishnet lace-top stockings, a black satin choker fashioned out of a toe shoe ribbon from *Western Symphony*, deep red matte lipstick, and nothing else. The last time I had been onstage was uptown at Lincoln Center as a member of the New York City Ballet. I wore the pastel blue bodice and translucent tulle of a Karinska tutu in Balanchine's *Serenade*. My lipstick was pale pink.

As I returned the very apparent "male gaze" in the audience at the Blue Angel, I knew we shared a unity of purpose. That much-maligned male instinct to look was allowing my fantasy to fly. There was no victimization on either side of these footlights. I locked eyes with a solitary fellow seated just below the stage. I'd never felt such attention in all my life. His eyes lowered to my breasts and belly and then returned to my eyes with a look of shyness, shame, and excitement. His desire burned into my own gaze, showing me with a clarity I had not experienced before the power of my own body. I then knew what triumph felt like. In that moment, that nameless man, who was every man, was entirely mine. Transient power, perhaps, but overwhelming in its force, it fused into my conscious memory and resides there still as a moment of victory over my own inhibitions and every man who wanted to possess me. I was now in full possession of my self. My anonymous admirer quickly took his place on the list of men who have affected my life as a sexual woman.

"I dreamed about you, Baby, it was just the other night," Cohen croons in "Waiting for the Miracle." "Most of you was naked but some of you was light." As I bathed in the soft red neon at the Blue Angel, the real revelation was not my flesh. I was unmasked and, for a miraculous minute, thrilled in my body, unafraid of my life. I was in — for me — Paradise.

Wrapping a black lace shawl about my hips, I cruised the audience for tips with a crystal goblet held out before me. The bowl quickly filled with green bills and my amusement turned into a silent cackle. I felt a sudden affinity with my eccentric Viennese great-grandmother, whose daily massages, obsession with handbags, and drawing-room recitations had made her the only theatrical person in my known ancestry. And now

I, her namesake, was collecting money for a striptease at a downtown dive.

The solitary fellow in the front row gave me a twenty and offered to buy me a Coke. I told him this was my first public strip, my audition, and he promptly encouraged the boss behind the bar to hire me. Ah, male enthusiasm, it felt fantastic. They gave me a job but I passed on the Coke.

This was my first flesh-for-cash transaction, and the sensation was overwhelmingly immediate — never had cash come so quickly, so easily, for seven slow, ecstatic minutes of work. I'd made money for my ballet dancing and for my writing, but this felt the most just of all — money for my simple naked body and the ability to move with a combination of grace and lewd intention. I made eighty-nine dollars for that dance, more than I was ever paid for a single *Concerto Barocco* or *Symphony in C*. To this day I keep that cash in a paper clip in my bedside drawer on top of a small black Bible. I smile each time I open the drawer . . . and remember my humble search for Colette's Breast and Balanchine's Paradise. I hear them both, in Paradise, laughing.

My Blue Angel strip was a profoundly symbolic act for me — a move out of an identity that no longer pleased me, that no longer served me emotionally, physically, or aesthetically. Along with my clothes I shed my past lives — my European upper-middle-class upbringing, my classical ballerina tutu, my marital allegiance, my good little girl status, the only one I'd ever known. I gained the freedom to be whoever I might have the courage and imagination to be. I broke my own image in my own eyes and breathed new air. The shell of my old identity now cracked, and the light came pouring in.

I knew that my urge to strip in public was an archetypal will to power, and I could not be alone. Turning writer again, I looked to the past to find my sisters, to find out why other women had chosen to remove their robes. I became fascinated with the ancient ritual of naked dancing that still endures despite continuous attempts by the keepers of public morality to exorcise it.

Beginning in 1066 with Lady Godiva, history has revealed numerous notable women who have taken off their clothes to considerable acclaim — from Josephine Bonaparte, Lady Emma Hamilton, and Lola Montez to Adah Isaacs Menken, Isadora Duncan, Josephine Baker, and Madonna. Here was a small but significant group of women who had used their bodies and their beauty to achieve just about anything and everything they might want: fame, fortune, sex, matrimony, political change. Then there were the purists who just did it for fun and provocation. None met with indifference.

My survey narrowed itself to an unmistakable congregation of women who, at the turn of the twentieth century — and all within two years of one another — found stripping in some exotic manner to be a very attractive endeavor. Four of these women — Maud Allan, the Canadian modern dancer; Mata Hari, the Dutch spy; Ida Rubinstein, the Russian performance artist; and Sidonie Gabrielle Colette, the French writer — are the heroines of this book.

Why did these women dance naked? Was there coercion? Financial or sexual reward? Or was it by choice, some subliminal erotic instinct, some recessive Salome gene that led to a kind of power in societies where women were mostly mute? Ever since Eve arrived in Adam's world, throwing off one's clothing in public has always had the magical effect of clearing a little room of one's own, though it is not, perhaps, the method Virginia Woolf had in mind. These women subverted the existing rules to search out a new identity. They recognized, without moral constraint or fear, that the body is basic, and men through the ages have shown a negotiable weakness for it, even when they've shown little for other forms of appeal.

These are women who created themselves and re-created themselves over and over, sometimes with success, often with disaster. Bold, beautiful, and defiant, each found her own form of liberation in a culture far more stratified than our own, not by directly pursuing equality with men or by competing with them, but rather by searching out and expanding her own unique spirit, fantasy, and physique.

Predictably, their paths toward self-definition were long and uneven in societies designed for wives who stayed at home, bore children, and stood by their more significant husbands. These rebels broke every rule of acceptable female behavior, and each had more than one moment center stage. These were women who did not seek liberation by doing the work of men but rather used the very suppression that had imprisoned them to free themselves. They did not change or even protest those rules; they simply transcended them with diverting flamboyance. Their stories happily celebrate the undeniable lure of glamour-as-anarchy. They succeeded not by succumbing to men's fear of their sexuality, but by using it.

As Carole Lombard succinctly stated, "I live by a man's code designed to fit a man's world, yet at the same time I always remember that a woman's first job is to choose the right shade of lipstick."[4]

These women — Maud Allan, Mata Hari, Ida Rubinstein, and Colette — are the illustrious sisters of an unorganized but distinguished subset of the female population who fulfill in fact what is commonly recognized as fantasy — a male fantasy. But, more significant and less comfortably acknowledged, especially by women, is that the prospect of revealing one's nude body to a roomful of riveted voyeurs is a common female scenario. Nancy Friday's collections of real women's sexual fantasies underscore Nora Ephron's confession that "in my sex fantasy, nobody ever loves me for my mind."[5] It is undoubtedly a male fantasy to look — but it is also a female fantasy to show.

"Yolando" in Friday's *Women on Top* shyly admits that she wants to be "one of the strippers," but she doesn't know how and yearns to be taught "how to move, dress and dance," by professionals. "Roxanne" states unabashedly, "I'd love to perform a strip act which culminated in me fucking the whole damn male audience. I'd like to masturbate . . . and drive men to distraction." "Fanny" reveals the desire to affect both sexes — the world — by her graphic display: "One of my fantasies now is that I'm onstage in front of a room filled with men and only about a dozen women. I come out and strip to the music, then I walk back and forth . . . bending over. . . . By now, the men are screaming, 'Come on, baby,' and the women are in shock."[6]

These women are pleasing themselves. Stripping is both defiant and seductive, an autoerotic metaphor for female arousal where foreplay is central, not peripheral, and the art of the tease is the path to pleasure.

The fact that these scenarios employ a theatrical device where the woman is physically separated from her audience is of central importance to these fantasies, just as it was for the women in this book and for my own brief display. The performance setting provides the artificial boundaries, the protection, needed to overcome the fear that accompanies vulnerability. Paradoxically, the separation frees them for the intimate exposure they yearn for. Because they retain control over the entire event, they can abandon control within it and thereby satisfy their own erotic desires. For them, as for most performers, it is often far easier, and safer, to expose oneself, physically or emotionally, to a crowd than to one other human being. Numerous eyes and ears blend to form an impersonal safety net.

"Two thousand people were nobody," said Josephine Baker of her sittings for Paul Colin, the artist, "but undressing in front of a single man? The mere sight of my jacket lying on Monsieur Colin's footstool made me feel faint." She also, however, confessed that it was with Colin, in her state of undress, that "for the first time in my life, I felt beautiful."[7] She did not feel exploited.

Public striptease as we know it today was invented a hundred years ago during a peak of social and intellectual misogyny, a time that also saw the first rumblings of feminism and the fight by women for equal rights. Was stripping a female accommodation to misogyny? Or a proclamation of autonomy?

All the women in this book risked prison, derision, and alienation — not just for taking off their clothes but throughout their lives. Indeed, there is a connection between their erotic boldness and other acts of bravery: Maud Allan challenged a member of the British Parliament in a courtroom; Mata Hari refused a blindfold before the firing squad; Ida Rubinstein defied the Russian Orthodox Church; Colette wrote the unwritten about love and sex.

Taking off one's clothes in public certainly serves as a willful act of separation from the rules and laws of others. These women also used their nude displays as a form of escape: Maud Allan from the shame of a criminal sibling; Ida Rubinstein from her rigid aristocratic destiny; Mata Hari and Colette from abusive husbands. They are unique because they enacted this fantasy in real life, although it is quite evident that their own sexual pleasure was not the central purpose of their dances, as in private fantasy. Their concerns centered on reality — the music, the lights, the veils — and their dances became sensual metaphors for something far greater than pleasure; they were declarations of sexual independence.

As dancers, these women were dilettantes — specialists in personality and their own headstrong ideas. They had no political agenda but sought only to display themselves. They fell into no acceptable category, and their legitimacy as performers was always questioned. But each wanted to be a woman of fatal attraction, to show her body to the world, and each found a way to do it with great style. Were these women victims of the male gaze that coveted them or rebels who returned that gaze to their audience, burning a pathway to power? They cared little themselves for such questions; they were the questions. Women in the cracks, they yearned only to be in the center of the light.

In her strip, each had dared to press her young body against social constraints and had witnessed the bendings, the twistings, and the primitive lurchings of society's awkward reactions . . . and all lead to Colette, the great naked intellectual, the woman who didn't think stripping was such a big deal and therefore gave it all the humor, charm, and gravity that the most provocative act in the world deserves.

These women are the sisters of Salome.

Two thousand years ago, Salome, the young daughter of Herodias, deviously initiated this symbolic will to power and became the first and most famous figure in historical legend to have reaped a sizable reward for baring her body, thereby setting a precedent for all her sex. In the unveiling of her limbs she revealed something far more mysterious than her glistening flesh: the violence of man's desire for it, his weakness for it, his fear of it. Salome unleashed what has been one of woman's most widely used weapons since Adam saw Eve and was tempted to travel the road from innocence to intercourse. John the Baptist's bloodied, severed head will forever symbolize the rage of a rejected child — and the triumph of a woman's erotic power.

PART I

Salome:
The Daughter of Iniquity

In her hands she carries ever
That sad charger, with the head of
John the Baptist, which she kisses:
Yes, the head with fervour kisses.

For, time was, she loved the Baptist —
'Tis not in the Bible written,
But there yet exists the legend
Of Herodias' bloody love —

Else there were no explanation
Of that lady's curious longing —
Would a woman want the head of
Any man she did not love?

— Heinrich Heine,
"Atta Troll"

Chapter One

The Wilde Story

FROM a few scant lines in the New Testament Gospels of Mark and Matthew — neither even call her by name — Salome's notorious reputation was born as the woman responsible for the death of John the Baptist, the prophet who preached the coming of Christ. This is a serious, albeit almost unbelievable, allegation against a nubile teenager — although Mark and Matthew do imply that Salome is a passive player manipulated by her angry mother. Flavius Josephus, Jewish historian of the ancient world, first named Salome as the daughter of Herodias in his histories, though he did not associate her with the death of the prophet. Historically, it is highly unlikely that a young girl would have held so much sway over such mighty matters, but Salome's value as an archetype of the castrating woman was born and still thrives today.

Salome's story is a fascinating blend of Roman gossip told in cautionary tales by Seneca, Livy, Cicero, and Plutarch,[1] New Testament Gospel, medieval legend, and Oriental Romanticism, all based on a dash of actual truth. As a creature of legend she has never been herself but always in bondage, serving men's ideas, desires, and fears about the erotic woman. She has been portrayed in virtually every style of art through the ages — Greek, Eastern, Byzantine, Gothic, and Baroque — and in every medium from illuminated manuscripts to miracle plays, from frescoes and mosaics to engravings and oils. During the Middle Ages she was an androgynous acrobat, during the Renaissance an exemplar of virgin beauty, and to clerics throughout the centuries, she demonstrated the evil that ensues from a woman who dances. Always defined by male sensibilities, Salome had yet to find her feet as the subject of her own life.

Between the seventeenth and nineteenth centuries, Salome went into artistic hibernation, perhaps preparing, phoenix-like, for her greatest entrance in history, at the turn of the twentieth century, when as a raging seductress, an inescapable siren, she left the holy man in the wings and finally took center stage for herself. It was none other than Oscar Wilde, in his 1893 play *Salome*, who gave this woman a voice and a dance, and she exalted in her freedom. The tale as told by Wilde — and further popularized by Richard Strauss in his opera that used the Wilde play as its libretto in 1905 — has become the definitive portrait of Salome to date.

The play begins one hot summer night two thousand years ago in Galilee. King Herod is hosting a banquet for his birthday, and with all the local notables and representatives of Rome in attendance, he is in a mood to celebrate. Herod has recently married his sister-in-law, Herodias, after imprisoning, and then executing, her husband, Herod Philip, who was also his own half-brother. Herod was now not only incestuously wed to his sister-in-law but was stepfather to his niece, Salome. Herodias is growing a bit shrill for his taste, but her teenage daughter, Salome, is a delight to behold.

Since Salome's father had vacated the underground cistern, its chains were employed holding down another illustrious prisoner. John the Baptist had been making quite a stir in the land by baptizing men and women and predicting the coming of the Messiah. While hundreds congregated at his baptismal waters, the Romans were suspicious of his message and his charismatic powers. Who was this "Jesus" of whom he spoke?

John the Baptist was also fond of condemning the marriage of Herod to Herodias as unlawful, preaching to the public of its iniquity and its bloody beginnings. Herodias, livid at being reminded of her crime, insisted that John be silenced, and so Herod had him imprisoned. But he would not execute the Baptist, as Herodias wished; he thought he might indeed be a prophet from God, and he dared not risk his soul to please his wife. And so, as John the Baptist howled the word of God from his cavernous jail, the birthday banquet proceeded.

Herod, drunk on wine, power, and pleasure, asks young Salome to dance for him. Bored with his demanding spouse, he longs for this Lolita to stir his loins. She refuses, and her mother applauds her decision. "You look too much upon my daughter," she berates Herod, seeing his lascivious eye. Herod insists and negotiates. He offers Salome magnificent rewards, even the mantle of the high priest and the veil of the sanctuary. When the teenager still refuses, trapped in his lust, he offers half of his kingdom, whatever she desires as payment. Salome now agrees to dance; she has a reward in mind.

Salome prepares. She removes the slippers from her dainty feet and is dressed in seven veils of seven hues. As she dances, she removes her veils, one by one, from her face, from her shoulders, then her waist, her legs, her breasts, and finally, in the last shudders of her hypnotic display, she loses the last veil revealing all and sealing her deal.

Herod, thrilled with her dance, asks what her reward will be and the princess stills the air with her request — "I want the head of John the Baptist on a silver charger!"

Herod is horrified. He begs her to accept any number of other beautiful and rare things: topazes pink as "the eyes of a wood-pigeon," opals that "make sad men's minds," onyxes like the "eyeballs of a dead woman," and one hundred white peacocks with gilded beaks. "I will give thee all that is mine, save only the life of one man." Encouraged now by her mother, Salome is adamant. But why does the young princess want John the Baptist dead?

Earlier that evening, Salome had heard the haunting voice of the Baptist crying in the night air and, intrigued, demanded to see the body of the plaintive voice. Upon seeing him, she is blinded by love. John abhors her. "I will not have her look at me. . . . Back! Daughter of Babylon! Come not near the chosen of the Lord."

But the princess of Judea has fallen in love and yearns for the holy man as only a virgin could. Her lusts are three — his body, his hair, his mouth — and each, in turn, is reviled by its inspiration. But obsession is a one-way dialogue, and Salome continues to voice her desperate longing. "Suffer me to kiss thy mouth," she begs. "Never! . . . Daughter of Sodom! Never!" replies the original unavailable man.

Realizing her utter rejection, she is filled with pain and the desire for revenge that is its natural balm. The ability to execute that revenge is acquired later that evening during her dance for Herod, wherein she witnesses the power of her own beauty over a king. In deciding to use this power she becomes a woman.

Herod, in attempting to divert Salome's request, explains to her,

"He is a holy man. He is a man who has seen God." When this appeal to the sacred fails, he tries the profane. "The head of a man that is cut from his body is ill to look upon, is it not?" Salome thinks not. After all, she craves that man; she wants his head.

Untempted by material or spiritual wealth, Salome remains steadfast. Her obsession is about possession at the expense of the possessed itself. Undone by his own oath, King Herod is rendered powerless, and John's severed head is produced on a bloody platter. Before her trophy, slave of her unrequited adoration, Salome delivers a magnificent ode of self-referential love: "Neither the floods nor the great waters can quench my passion. I was a princess, and thou didst scorn me. I was a virgin, and thou didst take my virginity from me. I was chaste, and thou didst fill my veins with fire. . . . The mystery of Love is greater than the mystery of Death."

In a lurid gesture of necrophilia she kisses the mouth of the Baptist's disembodied head. It is their first — and final — kiss. She comments on "a bitter taste on thy lips. Was it the taste of blood? . . . Nay; but perchance it was the taste of love."

Her victory is bittersweet indeed. Herod, revolted by Salome's perversion, tells Herodias, "She is monstrous, thy daughter. . . . In truth what she has done is a great crime. I am sure that it is a crime against some unknown God." In the last line of the play he cries, "Kill that woman!"

Salome meets her own bloody demise beneath the shields of Herod's guards.

Wilde, writing in the early 1890s, was a medium for the imagination and fears of the turn-of-the-century male psyche, all the more fascinating by his being the most famous, and persecuted, homosexual of his day. Wilde was not, however, writing in a vacuum. Salome was being examined in the late nineteenth century by a number of other notable artists, but before Wilde, they were all heterosexual and Salome became their favorite femme fatale. This fictional female, whose erotic allure leads men into danger, destruction, and even death, was created by the male masochistic mind, resolving his contradictory desire for sexual connection and his even deeper fear of castration and annihilation.

Fears about the sexual woman were especially prevalent in both Europe and America during the late 1800s as a "medical" preoccupation with the virus of female insatiability gathered momentum. A new breed of experts, the sexologists, began defining and labeling their subject, and suddenly "nymphomaniacs" were seen on every street corner in search of erections along with other aberrant women: the "masturbator," the "lesbian," and the masculine "androgyne." The unmarried "odd woman" was considered such a serious threat that one journalist suggested maintaining a social balance by rounding up single women and shipping them off to the colonies.[2]

The psychological climate in France during the late nineteenth century was rife with insecurity, fertile ground for Salome's insurrection. The devastating defeat in the Franco-Prussian war in 1870 and the divisive turmoil of the Dreyfus affair filled political life with confusion, shame, and loss. The rise of industrialization challenged the individual's place in the world, while both rampant venereal disease and the legalization of divorce in 1884 left women vulnerable as scapegoats. As issues of women's rights edged forward, so did male anxiety. The French diarist Edmond de Goncourt recorded an image of a "vagina dentata" that had terrorized his sleep: "I dreamt last night that I was at a party, in white tie. At that party, I saw a woman come in, and recognized her as an actress in a boulevard theatre, but without being able to put a name to her face. She was draped in a scarf, and I noticed only that she was completely naked when she hopped on the table. . . . Then she started to dance, and while she was dancing took steps that showed her private parts armed with the most terrible jaws one could imagine, opening and closing, exposing a set of teeth."[3]

However women were viewed, there remained a problem: both the highly sexed woman and the celibate woman might seek independence. This dilemma was synthesized in Salome, the oversexed virgin. With her nineteenth-century incarnation, the current gender debate came together in a single contradictory figure of icy allure — and sure death.

By the 1870s Salome was resurrected in an unprecedented glory of paint, poetry, and prose. This return to renown is inseparable from the prevailing passion for the Orient in late nineteenth-century Europe. Orientalism was the raging fashion in books, paintings, furnishings, and females. To Western minds, the East was ruled not by Christian morality and the Ten Commandments but by sun, sensuality, and opium. There were no "thou shalt nots" in the Sahara or the seraglio, only desires imagined and fulfilled and then preserved in a state of melancholy loss. The veiled woman stood at the center of this world of ageless pyramids — and

Salome would emerge as her paramount personification, her seven veils echoing her mystery, for behind them lay the world of sex — transcendent, rapturous, mind-bending sex.

Gustave Flaubert actually went east in 1850 to research his Oriental woman and found her in the form of Kutchuk Hanem, a gypsy entertainer who delighted him with her "Bee" dance, a striptease. She surfaced as the heroine of his novel *Salammbô*, and as the Queen of Sheba in *The Temptation of St. Anthony*, where she states unequivocally, "I am not a woman, I am a world." In the detailed, sensual evocation of her dance in his 1877 short story about Salome entitled "Herodias," Flaubert's dancer would be the muse for a whole generation of writers and painters, Wilde among them. "Opening wide her legs, without bending her knees, she bowed so low that her chin brushed the floor; and the nomads accustomed to abstinence, the Roman soldiers skilled in debauchery, the avaricious publicans, the old priests soured with controversy, all with flaring nostrils shivered with lust."[4]

The previous year, at the Paris Salon, Gustave Moreau, a middle-aged French painter, exhibited two startling images of Salome that took Paris by storm and drew over a half million spectators (fig. 3). *L'Apparition* depicted a semi-naked, bejeweled, and mystical Salome, a svelte dancer posing proudly in the center of a mammoth enchanted religious edifice. John the Baptist's head, levitating before her gaze, drips golden blood, a halo of sexual radioactivity.

Des Esseintes, the protagonist of Karl Joris Huysmans's 1884 novel *Against the Grain*, is obsessed with Moreau's Salome and stands mesmerized for hours before her image.

> No longer was she merely the dancing-girl who extorts a cry of lust and concupiscence from an old man by the lascivious contortions of her body; who breaks the will, masters the mind of a King by the spectacle of her quivering bosoms, heaving belly and tossing thighs; she was now revealed in a sense as the symbolic incarnation of world-old Vice, the goddess of immortal Hysteria, the Curse of Beauty supreme above all other beauties by the cataleptic spasm that stirs her flesh and steels her muscles, — a monstrous Beast of the Apocalypse, indifferent, irresponsible, insensible, poisoning.[5]

These fathers of Salome — Flaubert, Moreau, and Huysmans — demonstrated in their real lives a consistent and paradoxical pattern with

FIG. 3. Gustave Moreau, *L'Apparition*, oil on canvas, 1875
(Giraudon/Art Resource, New York)

women. While often indulging in sex with prostitutes — Flaubert, on occasion, liked to have his male friends watch his exploits — they never
married and remained curiously faithful only to their mothers. Is this co-
incidental? Or is it indicative of men who needed the fatal woman and so
created her?

Flaubert, after the death of his father and sister, lived with his mother
until her death. Moreau maintained a mysterious twenty-five-year relationship with a woman named Adélaïde-Alexandrine, who married
someone else during their liaison with his approval. He nevertheless

moved in with his mother at age thirty-six and remained with her until
her death twenty-two years later. Huysmans also never married, and his
only traceable female companion was a poor seamstress with whom he
had a brief relationship as a very young man.

No marital ties, sex with prostitutes, homosexual and narcissistic
leanings, and lifelong devotion to Mom — these men were in a cycle of
perpetual indulgence and retreat from their sexual obsession. Each artist
exhibited a combination of lust, followed by self-loathing, tempered by
intellectual and aesthetic pursuits, often about sex and prostitution. Sir-
ing no acknowledged children, these bachelors fathered the powerful fatal female of late nineteenth-century European culture — Salome was
their fear, their desire, their daughter. They were themselves Herods all,
lusting and losing, lusting and losing — wishing her in their bed while
wishing her dead.

Salome became so popular a lady in the last few decades of the nineteenth century that almost every poet or painter — English, Swiss, Russian, Portuguese, Spanish, Lithuanian, American, German, Polish, Irish,
but mostly French — wrote about her. One scholar claims that by 1912 no
fewer than 2,789 French poets had tried their lyrics on the daughter of
Herodias.[6] Much bad poetry was the result. It was left to Oscar Wilde —
who, acknowledging the prevailing French obsession, even wrote his play
in French — to give Salome a fame that would reach far beyond the elite
artistic and intellectual circles where she ruled from her distant pedestal.
Wilde's Salome would become a pop icon.

Irish, homosexual, married, father of two, Wilde was the anomaly
among the bachelor fathers of Salome. But he was the one who liberated
Salome onto the stage where, for the first time, real women added their
own ideas, not to mention their bodies, to the masochist's fantasy female.
Salome took on three dimensions and was publicly transformed — for the
first time in history — into a distinctly female fantasy. Almost two thousand years after her birth, the princess of Judea was released from the
underground cistern of male machinations and patriarchal control. Unleashed from the constraints of her admirers' prose and paint, Salome onstage went beyond their fantasy and became their nightmare: she became
a flesh-and-blood woman. And she had a dance to die for.

Chapter Two

The Dance of the Seven Veils

ALOME'S first scheduled public appearance in 1892 didn't happen: she was banned. The first sister of Salome who longed to portray Wilde's Oriental princess was none other than the most famous woman of her time, Sarah Bernhardt. She was forty-seven when she began rehearsing Wilde's play in June, and while he did not write the play for her, he was certainly enthusiastic about the great actress taking the role.

"What has age to do with acting?" he wrote to a friend. "The only person in the world who could act Salome is Sarah Bernhardt, that 'serpent of old Nile,' older than the Pyramids." When it was assumed that she would have someone else dance for her, she replied indignantly that she would not, and then when pressed further on her ideas for the dance she replied mysteriously, "Never you mind."[7]

The play, in its original French language, was to premiere in London. Wilde told designer Graham Robertson that he wanted "in place of an orchestra, braziers of perfume. Think — scented clouds rising and partly veiling the stage from time to time — a new perfume for each new emotion." To another friend he suggested Salome be naked. "Yes, totally naked, but draped with heavy and ringing necklaces made of jewels of every colour, warm with the fervour of her amber flesh."[8]

While scents, hues, and jewels were being debated in detail, the public licensor's office was making sure that a half-naked woman in jewels surrounded by scented clouds would not find her way into a theater. A centuries-old law initiated by the Protestants to suppress Catholic mystery plays prohibited the depiction of biblical subjects onstage, and Edward Pigott, the Examiner of Plays, found much in *Salome* to worry him. He forbade her entrance into London society.

"The whole affair is a great triumph for the Philistine," wrote Wilde of the banning, "but only a momentary one." It was not as momentary as he thought. Aside from several "private" performances — in 1905, 1906, 1911, and 1918 — *Salome* was not performed before a general public in England until three decades and a world war after its author's death in 1900.[9]

The play did, however, find its own serpentine life elsewhere. In

1893, eight months after the British ban, six hundred copies of *Salome* were published in France, and one year later, five hundred copies of an English translation were published by John Lane in London. Again there was an uproar. "The tragic daughter of passion appeared on Thursday last," wrote Wilde of the British publication, "and is now dancing for the head of the British public."[10]

This time the scandal was due, for the most part, to the accompanying erotic illustrations by a brilliant twenty-two-year-old British artist. The publisher had paid Aubrey Beardsley fifty pounds for ten full-page drawings and an endpiece. Sharp-lined, Japanese-style, in stark black and white, Beardsley's sketches were stunning and anarchic: they caricatured Wilde as both the man in the moon and Herod; Salome and John, both sporting Medusa-like tendrils and horns, had the same androgynous face, and every image was oozing with sexual innuendo. The British were not amused, and *The Times* called the images "fantastic, grotesque ... and so far as they are intelligible, repulsive." These "naughty scribbles," as Wilde affectionately called them, were, however, to become as infamous in their own right as Wilde's naughty play (fig. 4).[11]

Across the channel in Paris, in the land of Catholicism, confession, wine, and other sensual endeavors, Salome found her first stage. The great actor Aurélien-Marie Lugné-Poë directed the world premiere of the play on 10 February 1896 at the Théâtre de la Comédie Parisienne, while its author was in Reading Gaol convicted of sodomy. He was never to see his play performed, but word of its success did reach him and brought him unexpected solace.

The passive child Salome of the Bible had been converted by her nineteenth-century fathers into a classic femme fatale of knowing evil and vicious intent. In a key shift of emphasis from both these previous one-dimensional incarnations, Oscar Wilde gave Salome what she had heretofore lacked: a personality, a psychology all her own. Wilde transformed Salome from an object of male desire and fear into the subject of her own life. Wilde saw Salome from her own point of view and completed her evolution into a real woman with real motivations.

Wilde's Salome is a young woman overwhelmed by her first experience of sexual desire. She is driven more by the pain of unrequited love than by revenge. Lost in her lust, she gets her man the only way she can. The death of John the Baptist, according to Wilde, is not the result of Sa-

FIG. 4. Aubrey Beardsley, *The Dancer's Reward*, 1894
(Courtesy of the Fogg Art Museum, Harvard University Art Museums,
Bequest of Grenville L. Winthrop. Photo: Katya Kallsen.)

lome's vengeful soul but of her virgin pain. She is not evil; she is merely
amoral. Her desire for her beloved is so consuming that she must have
him, if not alive then dead.

John's death for Salome is not his punishment for rejecting her, the
act of a woman scorned, but simply the only way she can possess what
she must possess. As she confronts his bodiless head, she remains deeply
in her desire, retaining the egoism of a child at the center of her own
world. In Wilde's retelling, the tragedy of John the Baptist's murder is
matched only by the tragedy of Salome's own. The death of Salome is not
derived from the Gospels, which do not mention her fate, or history,
which proves her to have lived a long life with two notable husbands and
several children.[12] Salome's murder is Wilde's gory fiction. While other
male artists continued to perceive Salome as a conniving femme fatale,
Wilde tried on her veils himself and viewed her, radically, with compassion. He saw her, as perhaps only he could, from a woman's point of view.

Forever altering her legend, Wilde gave Salome the Dance of the
Seven Veils. In so doing he gave her — and her sisters-to-be — room to ma-
neuver, creating a movement larger in scale, surely, than even he might
have imagined. Instead of a gymnastic, circus dance on her hands, or a
gleeful, maiden dance with a ribboned tambourine as in her medieval ren-
ditions, Wilde assigned Salome nothing more — or less — than a striptease.

Witnessing Herod's insistence, Salome has learned the potency of
the sword she wields — her own young body. In her ability to display it —
and withhold it — lies her power, her only power. This dance was her liberation. Salome became feminist through Wilde, achieving her emancipation by embracing her own exploitation. She grasped her freedom
through irony, not tyranny, through manipulation of reality rather than
protest about reality. And more than a few sprightly women latched onto
this intriguing proposition.

In giving Salome a striptease, Wilde states, more overtly than anyone before him, that only a king swayed by uncontrolled lust would offer
a young girl anything as huge as half his kingdom, and that only when desire overtakes reason would such a gift be proffered with such devastating consequences. Wilde suggests that a striptease earned the murder of
a man of God, the man who baptized Christ himself, by a man, a king,
who is ruled by his flesh, not his faith. It is the triumph of sex over spirit,
of pagan over Christian, of profane over sacred. Oscar Wilde knew of

what he wrote; he conceived of this deadly dance just ten months after meeting Lord Alfred Douglas, the beautiful, blond Adonis who would be his own undoing.

Salome's dance is a display involving manipulation of things less visible than veils. It demonstrates the dual power of a woman to both reveal and conceal. In showing herself, she hides, in covering herself, she reveals. This is the paradox of eroticism — vulnerability desires exposure, but exposure desires protection; withholding desires release, but release desires withdrawal. In her dance, Salome enslaves the world while holding it at bay, the connection between desire and unavailability made visible.

In all the references throughout history to Salome and John the Baptist — religious and historical texts, medieval plays, poetry, painting, sculpture — since her birth two thousand years ago and until 1893 there is no mention of Salome's dance being called the Dance of the Seven Veils. Until Oscar Wilde.

He had contemplated having Salome "dance on her hands, as in Flaubert's story," after seeing a Romanian gypsy acrobat dance on her hands at the Moulin Rouge. Another evening, at Le Grand Café, he asked the orchestra to play music for "a woman dancing with her bare feet in the blood of a man she has craved for and slain."[13] But when it came to the text itself, Wilde gave no description of the dance, no hand dancing, no music, no style, just a descriptive name without even capitalization to distinguish it: "[Salome dances the dance of the seven veils.]"

Wilde's bracketed brevity allowed for a world of interpretation. Can the invention of striptease be traced to a single innocuous stage direction in a censored play that could barely find a theater or audience? Can Oscar Wilde be considered the unlikely father of modern striptease?

A hint at Wilde's idea of Salome's dance lies in the cryptic dedication he wrote in March 1893 to Aubrey Beardsley on a copy of the original French edition of the play: "For Aubrey: for the only artist who, besides myself, knows what the dance of the seven veils is, and can see that invisible dance."[14]

Shortly thereafter, when working on his illustrations for the British edition, Beardsley rendered an image of this "invisible dance." He chose to ignore the name Wilde assigned and called his representation simply "The Stomach Dance," and Salome, in a harem outfit, does indeed display a ripe belly. Just as the lack of detail on Salome herself in the Gospels of Mark and Matthew allowed for centuries of projections and additions by those for whom her story held fascination, so would the seven veils of Wilde be expanded on in the years following his play.

The great paradox of the veil — that which conceals yet invites revelation — is crucial to the meaning of Salome's dance. For a nun to "take the veil" is to choose her calling of chastity and devotion to God. Her veil is literally the draped part of her headdress that falls on the sides of her head to her shoulders, the article that signifies her vocation — and virginity.

In Islamic and Muslim culture, women's faces must be veiled in order to protect men from the distracting allure of the female face and form. It is a controlling mechanism for female sexuality, not unlike the concealing purpose of the nun's veil. In Christian marriage, the white veil signifies virginity and innocence, and in mourning the black veil covers heads and faces in humility and modesty before the unveiled face of death.

In Eastern harems, women are veiled like nuns while their bodies are receptacles for male desire. Veils conceal but are penetrable. Opaque, translucent, and diaphanous, they allow light to be filtered through the threads, building illusion while implying truth. They allow for fantasy and mystery and suggest the ultimate veiling — a naked woman still conceals the darkness where life begins. The hymen veils the womb, the womb veils the origin of life itself.

And then comes Wilde's Salome unveiling herself, in a defiant act of will, controlled not by others but by her own hand. It is in her dance that the veils of concealment — of chastity, of marriage, of mourning, of sex, of the harem — are discarded. Salome has broken through the male-imposed laws that attempt to hide the female object of desire. She is autonomous, and her dance is a profound tear in these veils of concealment.

Four thousand years ago, Ishtar, the great goddess of Babylon, performed the first documented striptease when she descended to the underworld to retrieve her lover-son-husband, the mortal Tammuz. In this death and resurrection myth, Ishtar must relinquish her jewels and robes at each of the seven gates to the underworld until she stands naked in the "land of no return." Oscar Wilde assigned this symbolic descent to the underworld of the unconscious, a ceremony that equates stripping naked to being in a state of truth, the ultimate unveiling, to Salome.

Chapter Three

The Salome Craze

WHEN Salome made her dramatic entrance on the European stage in the first years of the twentieth century, middle-class women were largely invisible and silent in public as sexual beings — they were either at home tending their domestic dominion, bedridden with neurasthenia (the chronic-fatigue syndrome of the day), or just trying to breathe between corset bones. A few artistically inclined rebels who painted or wrote on sexual themes were generally dismissed by the male legion. While some notable women nurtured the beginnings of feminism as we understand the term today — trying to get women the right to vote, divorce, and own their own property — the largest number of independent women earning a living for themselves were prostitutes who confirmed male dominance by literally selling their sexuality to male fantasy.

The women inside Salome's theater constituted a new female voice, and they were in the wings ready to perform. Though born of men, once onstage, in character, Salome became a woman's woman — her dance the Bride of Frankenstein's silent scream, Galatea's first breath. In her nakedness she became visible as no woman before her.

Just as nineteenth-century male masochists harbored fantasies of revenge on the femme fatale, women found that in playing the part, they too could exact revenge for their own social, physical, and sexual powerlessness. Salome was not only a misogynist, masochistic male fantasy but a heterosexual, sadistic female fantasy as well.

The fatal woman became a fashion, and while murder was the rare extreme in reality, she captured women's imaginations in less violent, more socially acceptable ways. Many society women at the turn of the century commissioned their portraits not as a pastel and pliable wife but as a seductive woman surrounded by furs and phallic-nosed dogs. They affected Mona Lisa smiles and cultivated the vampire look, with thin, androgynous bodies, blood-sucked pallors, and sunken black eyes. The vamp was born.

What is the appeal to women of the femme fatale, who is a creation of misogyny and male anxiety, a creature who is beautiful, manipulative, murdering, self-contained? Power. For women this power, deadly as it may be, is the antidote to being so long suppressed in so many ways. Preferring to be feared instead of ignored, these women grasped their sexual power and wielded it as both shield and sword — and they did this best before a paying audience.

Woman's erotic territory at the beginning of the twentieth century was on the stage. With Eleanora Duse and Sarah Bernhardt at the peak of their popularity, women surged onstage, where they could be heroines of mythical proportions without real-life consequences. Onstage they could even be men. With the separation of a proscenium, a woman, while remaining in her usual role of object, could enact a paradoxical transition: she became the author of her own objectification, and the dark anonymous audience became *her* object.

Once Salome hit the stage dancing, things changed for her. Here was the magic portal that offered women a chance to participate, to take charge of the notorious virgin themselves. For the first time, a woman's imprint was to be seen on this deadly archetypical female. Through the halls of male fear and purple prose, women wiggled onto the stage and made Salome their own. She became a modern woman and, for the first time, breathed again in a moment of real time. And how her sisters seized the day.

Female enthusiasm for Salome, reborn into her new skin, was profligate and unexpected. They slipped into her silky veils with one smooth move. Men offered her the power — sexual power — and the Salome woman simply said, "I'll take it," and proceeded to have herself a fine time, dancing, stripping, making a living, and displaying her sexuality. Female auto-eroticism, exhibitionism, even fetishism, for centuries under strict surveillance by Christian patriarchy, blossomed on stages in Europe and America.

Incarnating Salome, women gained a very particular forum for liberation, not through cries of victimization but, in the ultimate of ironies, by appearing to act in accordance with a misogynistic point of view. In accepting the premise, they subverted it. When a woman put on Salome's veils for herself, a magical transformation occurred for she then contained in her being both misogyny and feminism, thereby embodying, literally, the cultural debate of the time.

The dancing woman at the beginning of the twentieth century provided several functions for society as a whole: she allowed for male sexual fantasy to roam and provided a forum for female self-expression. Dancing provided a venue where her body would be seen. Performing on a stage she was indeed a world unto herself, sexual but unavailable. And Salome, the demon dancer from Herod's pagan court, was her prototype.

In 1903 the German composer Richard Strauss, inspired after seeing Max Reinhardt's enormously successful Berlin production of Wilde's play, decided to use the text as the libretto for his next opera. Cutting some of the repetitions but not altering the story, Strauss changed the languorous rhythms of the French language into stark, guttural Germanic tones, accentuating the brutality and aggression of the morbid tale. And he wrote nine minutes of music for the Dance of the Seven Veils. He indicated that the dance should be "thoroughly decent, as if it were being done on a prayer mat."[15] By 1905 Strauss's Salome was ready to perform — but not without the trail of censorship and scandal that had dogged Wilde's play.

Banned from premiering in Vienna, the opera debuted on 5 December in Dresden, and the problem of the dance arose immediately. Maria Wittich, in the title role, refused to perform the dance, declaring, "I am a decent woman."[16] A ballerina from the opera house was called in to perform the Dance of the Seven Veils. The opera was a huge sensation, critical protest of its degenerate subject only fueled its popularity, and within two years it had been performed in more than fifty German opera houses. In Berlin, however, at the insistence of Kaiser Wilhelm, a wildly incongruous Star of Bethlehem was to be found in the night sky in an attempt to lessen the offense of the pagan subject matter. Strauss became a rich man, and even the beleaguered estate of Oscar Wilde became solvent for the first time since his death.

Wilde had given Salome words, and Strauss gave her a voice and a very long dance. Together they set the scene for real women to add to the growing collage. The passive child of Matthew and Mark had been incubating for 1,900 years until Wilde and Strauss released her as a three-dimensional woman, introducing her to a vast public that reached far beyond the elite audience of her nineteenth-century fathers.

Salome would be silent no longer; in fact, Strauss fantasized that she would display the voice of a Wagnerian heroine and the body of a ballerina — an intriguing though unlikely composition. The resolution of these disparate requirements gave birth to the tradition of having a dancer per-

form the Dance of the Seven Veils. The subsequent Salome Craze owes
everything to this two-person solution. Salome the dancer was born, of
necessity, from Salome the soprano, and her subsequent life as a visual
icon soon competed with her life as an aural heroine. Salome's Dance of
the Seven Veils was, as Strauss himself stated, "the heart of the plot," and
so when the opera was banned in New York after one performance in
1907, "the heart of the plot" was not lost but simply went downtown to the
music hall.[17] Her way had been paved by the first American Salome, Little Egypt.

Twelve years prior to Strauss's opera, at the 1893 Chicago World's
Fair, a mysterious creature, who came to be called Little Egypt, performed in the Egyptian "Streets of Cairo" exhibit the "hootchy-kootchy,"
a dance of deeply unauthentic Eastern origins that centered around an
Oriental-flavored wiggle. This performance prompted a public protest
by the Board of Lady Managers, who attempted to shut down the Per-
sian Palace for indecency. The scandal stole newspaper headlines and
saved the Fair from its initial low attendance. The character of Little
Egypt emerged from this publicity, and several women claimed to be her.

One of these, a petite Algerian dancer named Ashea Wabe, greatly
popularized the name when she became the center of a New York City
scandal (fig. 5). Hired for a hundred dollars to perform "a dance and a
pose" at the 1897 bachelor party of one of P. T. Barnum's grandsons in a
fashionable Fifth Avenue establishment, she had performed her "dance"
but not her "pose" when the police raided the party. Both guests and
Wabe were called before the Board of Police Commissioners and a grand
jury for questioning. It was widely reported that Wabe had discarded
"her garments one at a time." When further questioned on her activities,
she explained to the courtroom, "Oh, Monsieur, just a little pose in the al-
together, a little Egyptian slave girl, comprenez-vous? . . . I do what is
proper for ar-r-r-t."[18]

No charges were filed, and Oscar Hammerstein I, who owned the
fabulous Olympia vaudeville theater, immediately hired Wabe at the
enormous fee of a thousand dollars a week to perform in a skit based on
the scandal. The Olympia received its biggest crowds to date. With Little
Egypt now starring on Broadway, ersatz Little Egypts starting popping
up everywhere with their hootchy-kootchies from Coney Island to

LITTLE EGYPT.
13 and 15 WEST 24ᵀᴴ ST. N.Y.
·MADISON SQUARE·

FIG. 5. Ashea Wabe, "Little Egypt," ca. 1897
(Harvard Theatre Collection, the Houghton Library)

vaudeville, from circus acts to carnival shows. Salome's blue-collar American sister was born.

As for Salome, her life in America during the 1800s had been obscure. Appropriated by several poets and novelists, she was usually a puritan, redeemed from her sins, converted to Christianity, and sent into quiet retirement in such disparate places as Miami Beach or a Wild West ranch, as two amusing versions outlined. The clergy also seized upon her story as a morality tale depicting the dangers of dancing, and as a result Salome was a pretty dull gal—until 1907 when she hit the Metropolitan Opera house with her sensational strip.[19]

Wilde's play, though published in America in 1894, did not premiere in a theater until 1905, when the Progressive Stage Society of New York produced it at the Berkeley Lyceum Theater in New York. It received little attention. Two years later, when Strauss put Salome on the most important opera stage in the country, people finally took notice of Wilde's heroine. While the censors and conservatives condemned her, the public could not get enough of her hootchy-kootchy.

The opera had its American premiere at the Metropolitan Opera in New York on 22 January 1907; it was a notable disaster. Olive Fremsted, at two hundred and fifty pounds, portrayed the adolescent temptress, while Bianca Froelich, the Metropolitan's prima ballerina, executed the Dance of the Seven Veils. "She spared the audience nothing in active and suggestive detail," wrote W. J. Henderson of Froelich's frolic, and the women in the audience covered their eyes with their programs. The visual discrepancy between Fremsted, the voice of Salome, and Froelich, the body of Salome, was so apparent that critic Franklin Foyles wrote that it was "as if some anti-fat remedy had worked wonders for a few minutes and then suddenly lost its potency."[20]

At the urging of his daughter, J. P. Morgan, who headed the company that owned the lease on the Metropolitan Opera House, had the opera banned after the single performance, and it did not reappear at the Metropolitan Opera for another twenty-seven years. After decades of literary prudery, America was unprepared for the salacious, unrepentant Salome of Wilde and Strauss. Froelich, however, was not about to waste her hard work. Banned from the legitimate stage, she simply took her show to the Lincoln Square Variety Theatre and thus initiated the craze of "Salomania." Once more, Wilde's Salome was crushed by censorship only to reemerge elsewhere. The lightweight, tongue-in-cheek tone of vaudeville eagerly embraced Salome's dance in a way that the prestigious, serious world of opera could not. Salome, in the hands of dancers, became a free agent. No amount of wiggles, flesh, or passionate, necrophiliac kisses was too excessive for her enthusiastic fans.

Fourteen years after Little Egypt, the operatic Salome descended to the very same stages, a vaudeville princess, and initiated a craze of her own that lasted for several years. "The red-light heroine," as she was termed by one magazine, celebrated her freedom with ferocious zest, and, adorned in thousands of fake pearls and silky veils, she shattered America's puritanical mirror.[21] This dance was Salome's salvation, and vulgarity tempered by sweetness was her style.

A few months after Froelich's great escape, the impresario Florenz Ziegfeld presented his first show, *The Follies of 1907*, at the "Jardin de Paris" of the New York Theatre. "Salome" was the show's most successful act. Mlle. Dazié — Daisy Peterkin from Detroit — performed Salome in a skit based on Aubrey Beardsley's designs. The number was so successful that Mlle. Dazié opened a school for Salomes for two hours each morning, teaching her pupils an assortment of seductive undulations in the "style" of Salome on the theater's roof garden. Mlle. Dazié's school produced no less than one hundred and fifty Salomes a month, glutting the aisles of American variety theaters with half-naked young women dancing with a mute, papier-mâché head. This woman was in complete control of her man, a radically unorthodox image for 1907.

Hammerstein, who had capitalized so expertly on the Little Egypt fad, now jumped on the Salome bandwagon. He sent Gertrude Hoffmann — Kitty Hayes from San Francisco — known for her comic imitations of Anna Held, Eddie Foy, and George M. Cohan, to London to learn her act from Maud Allan, the most popular European Salome of the day. Hoffmann premiered her Allan take-off, set to Strauss's "Dance of the Seven Veils," in New York on 9 July 1908 and was so successful that she toured the country with it for twenty-five weeks.

"Miss Hoffmann had on, above her waist," wrote the *Hartford Courant*, "first a black wig and a good makeup, second a lot of jewelry and chains and there is no third."[22] Outside New York, Hoffmann was frequently banned. Her appearance in Des Moines, Iowa, caused such a scandal that a law was passed that rendered it illegal for women to kick their legs higher than forty-five degrees off the floor. Apparently this heartland Salome had incorporated the can-can as part of her biblical ritual.

Salomania had broken out full force. In August 1908 there were four Salomes performing in New York alone; by October there were twenty-four. Eva Tanguay, the "I Don't Care Girl," topped her version by pouring a bottle of champagne over her head. Salome dances presaged burlesque, paving the way for the great striptease queens of the 1930s and 1940s.

By 1909 there was not a variety or vaudeville show in America that did not offer a Salome act as part of its entertainment. One can only imagine Wilde's surprise, and amusement, if he had known that his censored Salome had inspired hundreds of eager young women to bare their midriffs while seducing a saint. Salomania represents a jewel-like example of good old American enthusiasm grasping an icon of serious European art, stripping it of all pretense, and popularizing it for everyman — at least for every man who could get a ticket.

But while the men were lining up, their wives and other decent-minded matrons launched a full-scale protest. The counterattack received full play in the press, and the Salome problem was even debated in the presidential election of 1908. Ironically, it was mostly other women, not men, who protested these flagrant displays of sexuality. While the men enjoyed the show, their corseted wives hyperventilated at home and made valiant attempts to stop the stampede of flesh and pearls. It was understood that a decent woman's job was to control male sexuality, and Salome was the enemy.

The protest by the Lady Managers against Little Egypt at the 1893 Chicago Fair was now intensified by a renewed campaign against the Salome dancers. Julia Ward Howe, an early feminist and writer of "The Battle Hymn of the Republic," described Oriental dancing as "simply horrid, no touch of grace about it, only the most deforming movement of the whole abdominal and lumbar region."[23]

In August and September 1908 the *New York Times* alone ran four articles on the subject, this "alarming" decadence. Marie Cahill, a serious actress, heard the call and, single-handedly, decided to launch a political debate. Two years earlier, she had made a name for herself protesting against Broadway theater managers for forcing chorus girls to wear tights and excessively short skirts. But that was nothing compared to the slew of Salome dances around town.

Cahill wrote letters to President Theodore Roosevelt, the presidential and vice presidential candidates, and various other politicians asking that they denounce the "Salome Craze." Cahill called the Salome dances "such theatrical offerings as clothe pernicious subjects in a boasted artistic atmosphere, but which are really an excuse for the most vulgar exhibition that this country has ever been called on to tolerate."[24]

The press seized on a trend ripe for satire. "The management [at the New Amsterdam Theatre] has been exceptionally active in guarding against outbreaks of Salomania among members of the company," wrote the *New York Times*. "As soon as any chorus girl shows the very first symptoms of the disease she is at once enveloped in a fur coat — the most efficacious safeguard known against the Salome dance — and hurriedly isolated."[25]

Hammerstein, sponsor to both Little Egypt's display a decade earlier and Gertrude Hoffmann's recent act, knew the value of exploiting a fashion. With his help, Salome had become a very popular figure on the vaudeville circuit. Now he dared to present Strauss's opera in New York a mere two years after its initial ban at the Metropolitan Opera. He had just the woman for the role, and she wasn't a two-hundred-and-fifty-pound voice. In Mary Garden, Hammerstein had a slim, attractive, and able singer with a nose for publicity.

Garden, of Scottish birth, became the first singer since the opera's premiere in Dresden four years earlier to perform her own dance. She approached the opportunity with relish — but consummate good taste. "I want the Dance of the Seven Veils to be *drama* not Folies Bergère," she announced, and to underscore her high-class intentions, she traveled to Paris to study at the Paris Opera ballet to prepare for her debut.[26] The opera, with Garden as Salome, premiered at the Manhattan Opera House on 28 January 1909 and was an enormous success, touring to Philadelphia and Paris.

Despite Salome's resurrection on the legitimate stage, she retained her racy reputation. "Well, Miss Garden," one admirer commented in Chicago — where the opera was again banned — "we've heard that you rolled around like a cat in catnip and that you had very little on."[27] Here was a Salome for her time. In Mary Garden's hands the princess was an amalgam of the diva of German opera and the ballerina of the Paris Opera rounded out by a good dose of the hootchy-kootchy girl from American vaudeville.

Salome's incarnations, however, did not stop with opera and vaudeville. She was to feature prominently in the two new major art forms of the twentieth century — film and modern dance. Her operatic debut behind her, she was poised for her silver screen close-up.

Salome had, in fact, been rehearsing on single-reel shorts since the moving picture camera was invented. Little Egypt had been featured as far back as the late 1890s when, as "Dolorita," she performed a thirty-second hootchy-kootchy dressed in pantaloons with barely concealed breasts. Her brief routine involved wild hip and belly gyrations and ended with her pelvis thrust straight at the camera lens — Salome as porno queen. At the time of its release, this short held the record for peep show popularity on the boardwalk in Atlantic City and became one of the first films ever censored. With black and white bars painted across the frame, only Dolorita's head, not hips, could be clearly appreciated.

During the Salome Craze, Salome herself hit celluloid when three one-reelers of her dance were filmed within months of each other in America. Three more shorts were released in England in 1909 — *The Salome Dance Music* synchronized Strauss's dance music with the image on screen; *Salome Mad*, a chase film, has the description "Man chases windblown poster of 'Salome' under sea"; and yet another, a comedy, lampooned a man driven insane by his obsession with the Salome dance. So popular was the craze that would-be starlets who did not yet have an actual film on their resume often posed for publicity stills as Salome with serpentine tendrils, jeweled breastplates, and bare midriffs. Salome paved the way for the birth of the great screen femme fatale, the blood-hungry vamp, as personified by Theda Bara, Pola Negri, Barbara La Marr, and in the 1930s Marlene Dietrich as Lola in Josef von Sternberg's *The Blue Angel*.

In the first feature-length American movie, made in 1914 by D. W. Griffith, father of American film, the fatal Eastern woman starred in *Judith of Bethulia* in search of the head of Holofernes. A few years later, in Griffith's Babylonian epic *Intolerance*, multiple Salomes walked the parapets of the pyramids.

In 1922 Salome received her most beautiful and eerie film rendition to date in a silent movie of Wilde's play. The production, designed by Natasha Rambova, Rudolph Valentino's wife, was based on Beardsley's drawings and starred the Russian actress Alla Nazimova. More filmed pantomime than moving picture, Nazimova's work presents a delightfully nubile and graceful Salome with pouting lips and headstrong will. Nazimova, dressed in short, tight sparkling outfits, with exquisite ballerina legs and a short, curly black wig peppered with large pearls on wires that vibrated with her every move, is Salome as flapper — zany, impetuous, and alluring (fig. 6). The Dance of the Seven Veils finds her in a platinum halo of hair twirling beneath a huge, thin white veil of silk, a beam of spinning white light. It was an image worthy of Loie Fuller.

FIG. 6. Alla Nazimova in *Salome,* lobby card for the film, 1922. This production
was based on the Aubrey Beardsley drawings.
(Billy Rose Theatre Collection, The New York Public Library
for the Performing Arts, Astor, Lenox and Tilden Foundations)

Fuller was one of a small group of American solo dancers that included Ruth St. Denis and Isadora Duncan and who, in the early years of
the twentieth century, wanted their "art" to be taken seriously and fled to
Europe to reinvent themselves in a more sophisticated cultural atmosphere. They became the mothers of what today is called modern dance.
But even in the more rarefied air of this artistic pursuit, the Judean
princess was available to them, and they often used her as a vehicle for
exotic forays, Oriental aromas, magical lighting, and veils galore. Salome
was a modern dancer waiting to happen.

Ballet had never attracted Salome and for good reason. With the codified movement, strict hierarchy, and the romantic tales of love lost, found, and transformed into happily ever after, Salome clearly had no place. Toe shoes would have hurt her princess feet, and she was definitely not a team player. She did, however, uncannily incorporate the prerequisites of early modern dancers — barefoot, uncorseted, half-naked, uncompromising, and ruled by her need for self-expression. Hers was a solo act.

Loie Fuller holds a special place in the Salome canon for having presented one of the first versions of the story long before Salomania broke out. Born in Fullersburg, Illinois, in 1862, Fuller began her performing career as a child temperance lecturer, graduating to vaudeville, where she found a lifelong partner in a long silk scarf. With bigamy, divorce, and disgrace behind her, she sailed to Europe in 1892 and made her debut at the Folies-Bergère in November and rapidly became the toast of Paris with her fantastic displays of veils and lights. She epitomized the age of Art Nouveau and became the most imitated performer of her day.

In March 1895 Fuller presented her first *Salome* at the Comédie-Parisienne showcasing a rather benign, biblically inclined Salome (fig. 7). It flopped. Jean Lorraine, the dandy poet with a wicked tongue, referred to Fuller as "a laundress misusing her paddle . . . with the gestures of an English boxer and the physique of Mr. Oscar Wilde, this is a Salome for Yankee drunkards."[28]

Twelve years later, while Salomania flourished in America, Fuller, now forty-five years old, once again donned her veils as the princess, this time as a woman more in keeping with the alluring Salome of Wilde. Presented at the Théâtre des Arts in Paris, *La Tragédie de Salome* featured a score by Florent Schmitt dedicated to Igor Stravinsky and a libretto by Robert d'Humières, friend of Proust and translator of Kipling. The production was sensational. Her feather costume comprised 4,500 real feathers, and she used 650 lamps and fifteen projectors to turn the entire stage into a sea of blood when John is decapitated. This was a Salome light show worthy of a World's Fair — and there, among the amperes, was the shadow of Loie Fuller, naked.

Mythologizing one's existence was the similar goal of Ruth St. Denis, who saw in Orientalism her religion and pursued it throughout a seventy-year career on the stage. No one examined the life of the veils as persistently as this farm girl from New Jersey. Born in 1877, St. Denis made her debut at the age of sixteen performing cartwheels, backbends, and "flourishes" in a gig at the Worth Museum in New York. She joined

FIG. 7. Loie Fuller in *Salome* ("The Flower Dance"), Paris, 1895
(Jerome Robbins Dance Division, The New York Public Library
for the Performing Arts, Astor, Lenox and Tilden Foundations)

David Belasco's acting troupe, and while on tour in Buffalo, New York, in 1904 she experienced her Oriental epiphany. While drinking soda pop in a drugstore with a friend, she glanced up to see a poster for Egyptian Deities, a cigarette, which featured the goddess Isis seated on her throne, naked to the waist, scepter in hand. "I identified in a flash with that figure of Isis," wrote St. Denis, "and my destiny as a dancer had sprung alive in that moment."[29] She sent her friend back to the drugstore to purchase the poster and proceeded to have herself photographed as Isis on her throne. Her transformation from farm girl to goddess had begun.

After Oscar Hammerstein rejected her dances for New York — they weren't racy enough — she traveled to Europe for three years where she was applauded by the most respected artists and audiences as a sacred Oriental dancer and was even asked by Max Reinhardt to take the role of Salome in Wilde's play for his German production. While she did not perform the role, she did embark on lengthy discussions with Hugo von Hofmannsthal, librettist for Richard Strauss, on producing her own *Salome*. This project did not come to fruition until years later when she performed Strauss's "Dance of the Seven Veils" with the New York Philharmonic-Symphony, and in the 1930s she played Wilde's heroine in a staging of his play in Asheville, North Carolina.

St. Denis returned from Europe to a long career in her native country where she completed her goddess cycle: *Radha*, the Hindu Shiva; *Egypta*, the Egyptian Isis; *Ishtar of the Seven Gates*, the Babylonian goddess; and the *White Madonna*, the Christian Virgin — veiled goddesses all. But for St. Denis, a virgin until the age of thirty-seven, her body, naked or draped, was a sacred place. This celibate Salome once again redeemed the daughter of Herodias to decency from the pagan extravagances of the Salome craze.

Since 1900 Wilde's Salome has moved smoothly between high art and low, from the spotlight of the elite opera stage, film, and modern dance to the dark backrooms of private late-night clubs, vaudeville, and burlesque. She carries in her wake the snob, the educated, the aesthete, and the artist right alongside the blue-collar worker, the peep-show addict, and the married man with a roving eye — and behind them all the protesting wife waves her fist while her conservative allies scribble new laws in the attempt to control the situation. Salome is subversive. She threatens the social order, civilized behavior, monogamy. She is every woman who has ever dreamed of stripping for a lover — or an audience — and she is every woman who has.

PART II

Maud Allan:
The Cult of the Clitoris

A fluke and no clothes made her name.
— Mischel Cherniavsky

Chapter Four

The Crime

AUD Allan, the Canadian dancer who ten years earlier had been the toast of London society, was on the witness stand in the Number 1 Courtroom of London's Old Bailey. It was May 1918. Though she was the plaintiff in the libel suit, her accuser now had her on the defensive. Referring to the startling title of the article in his weekly political broadsheet, *The Vigilante*, Noel Pemberton-Billing, an Independent M.P., asked Maud whether she understood the term *clitoris*. She answered in the affirmative, and the courtroom tittered. Maud had incriminated herself. Wasn't knowing the name of her own sexual center proof that she was a lesbian? Pemberton-Billing went on to explain that the term was a medical one that only students, doctors, and perverts would recognize. Furthermore, he explained that in his own casual investigation of the matter he found only one in twenty-four people surveyed knew the term, and that one man was a barrister. Maud, not being a student, doctor, or lawyer, must then be a pervert, or, as Pemberton-Billing referred to it, one of "the initiated."[1]

In early 1918 Germany appeared to be winning the Great War. It was time for a distracting scandal, and what better target than a foreign woman, an unmarried woman, and a dancing woman, who had begun her career in Germany and had a long personal history with Salome, Oscar Wilde's decadent princess? Maud's trial, however, for all of Salome's acknowledged depravities — incest, lust, murder, sadism, necrophilia — marked the first time she had ever been accused of lesbianism. It was, ironically, about the only perversion not present in Wilde's play. According to the repressed sexual mores of the day, if perversion was your game, you indulged all and any, without discrimination. If high heels moved you, then masochism, sodomy, and androgyny were sure to follow.

Pemberton-Billing had found a landmine of salacious material, and Maud Allan's libel suit proved to be the ideal ground to resurrect the long-dead Oscar Wilde and, in his guaranteed absence, retry him for his poetry, his sexual inversion, and, specifically, his play *Salome*.

Maud, realizing her mistake in acknowledging the clitoris, was at the point of losing her composure, not to mention her reputation — the very thing she had come to court to preserve. She had spent her whole life creating respectability for herself; she prized it above all else. This was not the first legal trial she had endured, and it was at the first, some twenty years earlier in San Francisco, that she had inherited the shame that was to define her life. She had with great skill and imagination managed to re-create herself, change her name, and distance herself from that legacy, and now, in the cruelest of ironies, while defending her honor, she had it thrown back in her face in one swift flash, in a public trial that garnered front-page headlines.

Just prior to his query about her clitoral knowledge, Pemberton-Billing had completely disarmed Maud by handing her a book entitled *Celebrated Criminal Cases of America* and asking her if she knew the person identified in a photograph as Theodore Durrant. Maud's face froze in horror; she had not expected this. She would never have pressed charges against the M.P. had she known he would be so ruthless in his own defense.

"Was your brother executed in San Francisco for murdering two young girls," asked Pemberton-Billing, "and outraging them after death?" The pain, long hidden but never healed, was uncovered for all to see. As Salome dancing, Maud had revealed her body and a range of emotions for John the Baptist, but in that revelation she had been able to hide, from herself and her public, the true horror of her family's secret. Pemberton-Billing, she declared, was "the worst man that ever was."[2]

Maud Allan's career as the "Salome Dancer" outlines a tale of a woman escaping herself, her past, her family. When she declared, "No one knows my feelings and no one ever shall," she spoke, most succinctly, about herself.[3] Salome, for Maud, provided refuge from her own aching and lonely self. As the Judean princess, Maud, perhaps more than any other Salome of the time, could best express publicly, with ironic anonymity, the pain of her own life. Maud harbored Salome's potent ambivalence, adoring a man who was dead, "decapitated" by the hangman's noose, and yet also repulsed by him. And at the center of the family closet of crime and passion was Isabella, Maud's very own Herodial mother, overbearing, strong-willed, controlling. There were even strong intimations of incest between the smothering mother and the murderous son. The Durrant family, who had migrated from Toronto, where Maud was born on 27 August 1873, to the West Coast in 1879, was as twisted and tormented as was the house of Herod where Salome dwelt. It was no accident that Maud chose to go on the stages of Europe, briefly clad, as her biblical sister incarnate; she had much to hide behind those veils. It all began in San Francisco.

On 3 April 1895, Blanche Lamont, age twenty-one, was reported missing. Her whereabouts were not discovered until the body of Minnie Williams, age twenty-three, turned up in the Emmanuel Baptist Church library ten days later. Blanche was then found in the church belfry, dead, naked, and laid out as if for medical examination, an anatomical Venus. "Besides a suit of undergarments with an extra pair of black equestrienne tights," reported the *San Francisco Examiner*, "there was a corset waist, a pair of corset covers, a black sateen combination petticoat and waist, and a pair of stockings discovered in the rafters."[4] The murderer had performed a careful and lengthy stripping, probably after death.

Minnie had not been treated with such respect. She, like Blanche, was naked, but instead of an eerie scene of clean deliberation, Minnie was a mess. She had been hacked to death and lay in a pool of blood. Slashed three times in the heart and ribs, she had been sliced open from her forehead to her nose and her wrists were cut to the bone. She had been strangled, and a piece of her clothing was stuffed down her throat. A broken knife was buried in one breast. The *San Francisco Examiner* called the case "the Crime of a Century."[5]

Emmanuel Baptist Church had never known such a nightmare, nor the San Francisco press such a sensational story. Maud, aged twenty-two, missed it all: she had left her family residence in San Francisco only seven weeks prior to the murders to pursue fame and fortune as a pianist in Berlin. The Durrant family — William Allan, the shoemaker father; Isabella, the domineering mother; Theo, the medical student brother; Maud, the budding pianist — were all devoted members of the congregation at Emmanuel Baptist Church. Theo was the assistant Sunday School superintendent and had keys to the church. Maud knew both Blanche and Minnie. She knew the murderer better.

Maud and Theo, born only a year and half apart, were very close, best friends, constant companions. Theo wrote to Maud the day of Blanche's disappearance, reporting the news and enclosing the press reports. He had advised the police to search the local brothels for Blanche. Did he think this young woman was a prostitute? He was, at the time of the murders, engaged to be married to yet another young woman. The marriage did not take place.

Theo had suggested to Blanche that she could borrow a book, *The Newcomes* by Thackeray, from the church collection. He had just catalogued it, and, conveniently, he had the key to the library. Blanche accepted his offer and was not seen again. Ten days later, Theo and Minnie were identified going inside the church at 8:30 P.M. Later that night, as secretary for the Christian Endeavour Society, Theo arrived at a Good Friday meeting an hour late, disheveled and sweating, explaining that he had been corralling horses and got his hands dirty. Minnie, also expected at the gathering, never arrived. Theo was arrested within twenty-four hours of the discovery of the two bodies, and the press deemed him guilty from that day on.

Theo entered a plea of not guilty and refused to even consider a plea of insanity, which was surely closer to the truth. There were some lines the Durrant family would not cross, and they definitely had no insanity in the closet. Respectability had to be maintained at all costs. Besides, to prove insanity, previous episodes would have to be established and none were forthcoming.

Although Theo sat without emotion throughout three months of trial proceedings, he gloried outside the courtroom in his newfound fame and notoriety. He was repeatedly photographed, gave numerous interviews to the press (who compared him to Jack the Ripper), and engineered phonograph recordings of his speeches. The *San Francisco Examiner* even published excerpts from a crude novel he had penned called *Azora*, in which his sister Maud was the heroine. Finally, he was attracting greater attention than his multitalented sister.

Seven months after the murders, Theo was pronounced guilty of murder in the first degree with no recommendation for mercy. The jury had deliberated for fifteen minutes. He was hanged three years later, on 7

January 1898, at San Quentin prison with all the melodrama worthy of his lurid case.

Two hundred guests were invited to witness his execution, and although the law did not permit his mother to be present, Isabella insisted. In her last interaction with her living son, she placed a locket with a picture of Maud about his neck, the neck which was then broken by the noose. When his body was delivered to Isabella, she kissed Theo's lips and talked to him for hours — just as Salome communed with the dead John the Baptist. There were both private and public hints of an unnatural intimacy between Theo and his mother, and, years later, family friends destroyed letters from Theo that referred to this intimacy. Isabella was called "the Mother of the Century" by her proud husband; the phrase echoed ominously.[6]

Maud had departed for Berlin on Valentine's Day 1895 with Isabella and Theo expected to follow shortly, mother as adviser, brother as protector. In early summer of 1899, they arrived as planned, after a four-year delay, with Isabella carrying Theo's ashes in an urn at her breast. She carried them everywhere, advising Maud that "When you have had your success we will build a monument in Southern California and then lay them to rest, won't we? Then I shall be content and not until then."[7]

At the time it was not unusual for talented young ladies to travel to Europe to finish their education, as did Maud. But the plan was usually to get that European touch and return to the homeland. Maud would not. Arriving in Berlin after a long journey by land and sea, she established herself in safe lodgings and began her studies at the musical conservatory. On 17 April there was a knock at her door. It was the police informing her that Theo had been taken into custody. Her lifelong cover-up commenced.

Telling no one in Berlin of her circumstances, Maud followed Theo's fate through numerous letters from Isabella, a few girlfriends, and Theo himself. She also made weekly visits, incognito, to local library reading rooms where she followed the case in the American press. By 21 May, she wrote in her diary, "I can see no one." Self-reinvention for Maud, racked by shame and secrecy, was a matter not of vanity but survival.

There was also her guilt. She wrote to her mother in great anguish that if only she had not left for Europe, this horror would not have happened. "Why was I not at home to be with him those fatal days?"[8] Between the lines, in both Maud's and Isabella's letters, Theo's guilt was acknowledged. But this unmentionable fact was never stated. Denial was to be enforced as they waged the long — and futile — struggle to save his neck from the gallows.

Maud wanted to return home to help but was swiftly turned away. "Do not come back under *any* circumstances now," wrote Isabella, "as it would only make Theo feel he was the cause of blighting your prospects. . . . I think it is the most fortunate stroke of luck that you were away."[9]

The pressure on Maud to succeed in the world was increased by the family tragedy. It was up to her to make money for a monument, to bring back some semblance of pride, and to recoup financially the ruinous cost of Theo's trial and execution. "Oh dear, if I only had the money," she confessed to her diary, "to relieve them and be at the same time my own supporter."[10] Like a good daughter, Maud took the disaster upon herself, family pain being the impetus of many a successful career. And a stage mother doesn't hurt — the career, that is. Isabella had no shortage of advice for Maud on how to behave. Her letters were filled with directives on how to dress, stand, sit, speak, and curl her hair like a proper young lady.

After Theo's execution, Isabella tightened the reins and gave Maud her full attention. Having lost a son to the noose, Isabella wasn't about to lose Maud to marriage and persuaded her to refuse the several proposals that came her way. With power established, Isabella declared war: "You must make a name for yourself if you wish to gladden our last days, for nothing else will make up for our loss but showing the world that you as well as he were ambitious. Now, my dear, close your teeth tight and say I WILL, even if it takes every minute of my time, I will, I shall I MUST and NOTHING will prevent it!"[11] And then build the monument to Theo.

The ambitious mother, the vague father, the dead brother — Maud's identity was in shambles. Her diary reveals her conflict: "I must rouse myself and be somebody. Why am I so afraid of people? . . . I have a duty to perform and I must do it, or die in the attempt." Later she weakens: "How I long to be free of the chains that are binding me. I want to fly away from my surroundings, away, away."[12]

Maud tried to proceed with her studies despite increasing emotional and financial difficulties. The money she arrived with to establish herself soon was gone, and owing to the huge cost of Theo's defense, no more was forthcoming from home. She could give piano lessons, but was too afraid to teach Americans lest she be recognized as the sister of the notorious Theodore Durrant.

Industrious and bright, not to mention rather desperate, she embarked on two imaginative moneymaking endeavors. She began a corset business, designing, measuring, sewing, and even modeling her constructions. By 1898 she was applying for a patent. The other project to which she applied her artistic talents also involved the female anatomy — a commission to illustrate a two-volume German sex manual for women entitled *Illustriertes Konversations-Lexikon der Frau* (Illustrated dictionary of the woman), published in 1900. If she did not know before, surely here Maud learned about that damnable "clitoris" — she was drawing them, no less — that would bring her so much trouble twenty years later at the Old Bailey. She did well in the courtroom to conceal the fact that she had illustrated a German sex manual. How Pemberton-Billing would have pounced on that as evidence of her depravity. It is not an incidental footnote to Maud's later dancing career that her artistic talents at this time were focused on the female anatomy and its possibilities in shape, sexuality, and exposure.

Maud also found more socially acceptable financial help from a German-American patroness, as well as a monthly allowance from Artur Bock, a young sculptor, her fiancé. Despite Bock's passion for her, Maud wrote in her diary the day after Theo's execution that "as a brother I could love him, but not as a ——."[13] The engagement was broken. Bock proceeded to become the most famous sculptor in Hamburg, and in a prescient portrait, he made a sculpture of Maud as one of the most popular women of the day, Salome. She is posed bare-breasted, kneeling before the head of John the Baptist, her arms engulfing him, her mouth poised to pounce. The sculpture was completed a year before Maud's debut as the Salome dancer. Maud also posed naked, again as a laughing Salome, for another German painter, Franz von Stuck, whose three oil paintings of her have become well-recognized images of Salome dancing beside her trophy head (fig. 8).

Maud would indeed have her public fame, as Isabella wanted; she would "show the world" all right. The shy, frightened girl who was afraid to see anyone would now show everyone, not her fingers on the ivories, but her whole body. This was not exactly what Mamma had envisioned, but it would have to do. What better way for Maud to divert attention from her guilt, inadequacy, and secret — and to both acquiesce and yet

FIG. 8. Franz von Stuck, *Salome,* 1906. Maud Allan was the model. (Jerome Robbins Dance Division, The New York Public Library for the Performing Arts, Astor, Lenox and Tilden Foundations)

rebel against Isabella — than to expose her outer self as a femme fatale in a rather questionable profession?

Chapter Five

The Vision

WITH attention, respect, and money as her priorities, Maud reflected on her options and concluded that a career as a concert pianist, despite her musical talents, would not satisfy her requirements. With an eye to being an opera diva, Maud decided to become a singer and pursued lessons with vigorous determination, studying with six teachers in the course of five years. Her inability to carry a tune soon put an end to this particular ambition. Classical music and opera, both arts with age-old traditions and numerous more-talented performers, had little room for ambitious newcomers. Dance, however, did.

Maud was twenty-seven years old in 1900, and once she turned her attention to dance as a possible venue, it is no surprise that she did not choose ballet: she was twenty years too late to begin the necessary training. But there was a new form of dance that came to be called modern dance, which was just beginning to find devotees at this time. Not only were late starters welcome, but, with no tradition behind it, this new art form was, by definition, begun by dilettantes with big ideas. So-called self-expression was its raison d'être, and this notion provided a catch-all into which any flaws — lack of training, imperfect proportions — could be incorporated with impunity.

At the turn of the century, as modern dance was finding its first, barefoot hold, this concept was a brilliant tool, allowing its first practitioners the freedom to experiment, fumble, fail, and succeed without condemnation at every attempt. An amateur like Maud could be not only a pioneer in this newfound profession but a leader. And there was very little competition, with the formidable exception of a certain Isadora Duncan, a fellow San Franciscan who had already been peddling her dances to a European audience for several years.

Maud's only preparation for her dance career had consisted of participating in static poses in a few "living picture" tableaux at informal festivities in both San Francisco and Berlin, as well as posing for various painters, sculptors, and photographers. The first performance in which she incorporated movement between poses took place at an evening gathering of her teacher, the great Italian pianist and composer Ferruccio Busoni, who directed the Meisterschule in Weimar. With Busoni himself at the piano and a shawl borrowed from his wife, Maud improvised a dance and was received with great success. The seed was planted.

Having decided on her career, she gave up the piano and singing, and spent two years preparing for her debut. She attended no dance classes but rather researched classical poses in libraries and museums and experimented in front of a mirror. Her musical training and innate musicality were her greatest assets. And, of course, she had her body, her face, and that horrible secret to distinguish her.

With thick, wavy, dark hair, blue-green eyes, pale skin, and full lips, Maud had a feminine face with a figure to match. Her body was large but curvaceous, bosomy and graceful, with beautifully articulated arms and hands. Her smile was open and bright — she was a sexy woman. Fearing her competition, she acknowledged no influence from other dancers, but rather from the two great actresses of the day, Eleonora Duse and Sarah Bernhardt. Both Isadora Duncan and Loie Fuller had helped Maud during the early years of her career, but, at the suggestion of Isabella, Maud kept the associations secret and later denied them outright.

Maud's debut took place on Christmas Eve 1903 at the Theater Hall of Vienna's prestigious Conservatory of Music. Taking her father's middle name in place of the wretched Durrant, "Miss Maudie Gwendolyn Allan" performed various pieces, including Mendelssohn's "Spring Song," Schubert's "Ave Maria," and Rubinstein's "Valse caprice." In Chopin's "Marche funèbre," Maud mourned the dead with great conviction. It was a sentiment she knew all too well. With mostly favorable reviews, Maud, at age thirty, was off to a promising, if quiet, start as an "aesthetic dancer."

Immediately, however, her state of undress began a public dialogue on the subject. "The human body has forgotten how to move in the nude," wrote one critic. "Miss Allan is no doubt the least dressed dancer of our time — and seeing such a slender body glide by wrapped in veils, and moving beneath veils, one might deplore the lack of aesthetic cultivation of the nude."[14]

The attention Maud garnered cheered her mother, and the letters came fast and furiously. First, Isabella sought the advice of a family friend, a Dr. Thrasher, to bolster Maud's single-minded dedication. "Dr. Thrasher says it would be better not to get married," counseled Isabella. "Of course you could, but the ideal purity of your work is so much better portrayed by a virgin than by one who has been contaminated by man." On the flip side she stated, "I would not care to have you do this work if married — any other work but dancing for a married woman." Isabella then went to work on taking down Maud's prospective competition. "I wonder how Miss Duncan likes to have a rival, or did she know you were preparing to be her rival? . . . The longer you wait the more time it will give Miss Duncan to give you trouble."[15] As history has noted, the success that Isabella so wanted for her daughter became Isadora Duncan's forever, while Maud Allan's name now resides in relative obscurity.

Maud made another appearance in Brussels at the end of 1904, but drew little attention. Something more was needed to put Maud in the spotlight; her name was Salome. The timing was excellent. By 1906 exotic solo dancers were the rage, and Vienna lent them prestige and opened doors — both the American Ruth St. Denis and the Dutch Mata Hari were performing in town at the same time (fig. 9). But Maud, the Canadian, was the only one doing Salome, and her version, set to music by Marcel Remy and entitled "The Vision of Salome," became the first notable dance rendition independent of Wilde's play and Strauss's opera. Her ensuing fame was to rest entirely on this one twenty-minute dance.

Maud made her debut as the daughter of Herodias on 26 December 1906 in Vienna at the Carl-Theater before an invited audience of one hundred guests. The effect was immediate. "One moment her dancing is hot, barbaric, lawless," wrote one witness a few years later, "the next, grotesque, sinister, repulsive; one moment she enervates, with a gliding sweetness; the next she stabs with a terrible attitude. She kisses the head and frenzy comes upon her. . . . The wonder of it all is that throughout this fantastic mockery, this enchanting insistence upon the flesh, nothing is extravagant, nothing discordant. . . . It is of a magical beauty. But the beauty is magic; and the magic is black and insidious."[16]

Max Beerbohm, writing for the *Saturday Review*, gave his own, more concise, summary of Maud's drama: "Miss Allan performs a wild quasi-Oriental dance, the head of the Baptist appears on the cistern, the dancer . . . sets it in the middle of the stage. . . . [She] overcomes her repugnance,

FIG. 9. Front page of *Illustriertes Wiener Extrablatt,* entitled "Exotic Dancers in Vienna,"
18 December 1906, featuring caricatures of Maud Allan and Mata Hari,
who were both appearing in the city at the time
(Jerome Robbins Dance Division, The New York Public Library
for the Performing Arts, Astor, Lenox and Tilden Foundations)

hears someone coming, puts the head behind her, pops it back in the cistern, dances again, and finally repeats the swoon she did in the 'Valse
Caprice'" (fig. 10).[17]

Maud's own description in her book *My Life and Dancing* offers an interesting psychological explanation of Salome's predicament. She asserts,
more in accordance with Mark and Matthew than with Wilde, that Salome was merely an innocent child who is conned by her vengeful mother

FIG. 10. Maud Allan in "The Vision of Salome," ca. 1908
(Jerome Robbins Dance Division, The New York Public Library
for the Performing Arts, Astor, Lenox and Tilden Foundations)

to ask for John's head — the daughter is sullied by her mother's evil. Her dance offers salvation for "the atonement of her mother's awful sin!"[18]

But what was this "mother's awful sin" of which Maud had such personal knowledge? Isabella's incest with Theo? Stage mother superior to Maud? In kissing John was Maud kissing her beloved Theo, canonized in death? Maud was using her triangular family tragedy not only to great artistic advantage in her dance, but also for her own catharsis. As Salome she was no longer the sister of Theodore Durrant, the murderer, but an exotic, alluring woman. This was Maud's "monument" to Theo, the only one he would ever have.

What Maud smoothly leaves out of her written description, however, is precisely what her audience actually saw: the raw sexuality of her dance. She wrote one thing, but she performed another. To ward off any public excoriation of sexual exhibitionism, Maud pleaded an innocence verging on religious sacrifice in a newspaper interview:

> It takes tremendous courage . . . to come out on the stage before hundreds with feet bare, with little dress. . . . Every time I appear, until the spirit gets

into me, it is as though I were about to undergo martyrdom. Don't you
think that is courage — to fight down and go out and face the thing you
dread? . . . Hundreds peering at you from a darkened house. Eyes of men,
eyes of women. In how many are there other lights of contempt — of desire? Each time I dance I think of it and I dread it.[19]

Dreading their desire? Here is Maud's ambivalence: she was desperate
for recognition, but terrified of it. She walked the fine line between pro-
priety and vulgarity with poise, and this was her victory.

For her Salome dance, Maud wore a stunning costume of her own
devious devising: an elaborate bikini where more of her body was naked
than not (fig. 11). The bra-like top consisted of two spheres saturated in
circles of pearls and jewels that dripped in chains onto her bare belly.
Slung low on her hips was another ornate assembly of pearls and jewels
in both circular and linear shapes, a chastity belt of glittering stones. Between her thighs hung more strings of pearls doing little to conceal her
bare legs and feet beneath the ankle-length transparent skirt. Each wrist
and ankle sported a Houdini-like cuff of beads and pearls. She was
chained up — for all to see all. She wore a crown of rhinestones about her
forehead over her gathered dark hair, with long loops of pearl beading
hanging down by each ear. The overall pointillistic effect was uncannily
reminiscent of one of Gustave Moreau's tattooed Salomes. Maud's home-
spun costume was an exemplary three-dimensional display of the Western idea of an Oriental belly dancer and one of the first such concoctions
to reach the public's attention.

Attention is precisely what Maud got. Ten days before her debut,
the Vienna paper *Illustriertes Wiener Extrablatt* reported the first of many
scandals surrounding her "Vision of Salome." An "unnamed princess"
who was a great supporter of the Court Opera had attended a dress rehearsal and, deeply offended at Maud's lack of dress, registered a complaint. To placate their patron, the director of the Opera and his staff
scheduled a second rehearsal to preview the offending costume. The director was none other than Gustav Mahler, and, being a great supporter
of Strauss's opera *Salome,* he suggested a few extra veils and approved
Maud's exhibition. Here is Maud's account: "He [Mahler] was delighted. . . . Then the police brought up some moral questions. They said
my dance was immodest . . . they decided I had to wear a leotard. Never!
I chose rather to leave. I do not make compromises. No! Never!"[20]

The prima donna in Maud had surfaced. She was learning how to

FIG. 11. Maud Allan in her Salome costume, ca. 1908
(Jerome Robbins Dance Division, The New York Public Library
for the Performing Arts, Astor, Lenox and Tilden Foundations)

manipulate the press, her old family enemy, to her own advantage. Within six months of her debut as Salome, Maud's fame traveled across the Atlantic, where America was in the throes of the Salome Craze. With the tabloid headline "The American Girl Who Danced Salome with a Real Head," the *Herald* of Augusta, Georgia, breathlessly reported that a prankster had exchanged her papier-mâché John with a real man's head, dripping blood and brains, whereupon Maud had fainted onstage.

Touring across Europe, Maud cleverly arranged her Paris debut of the "Vision" within days of the Paris premiere of Strauss's *Salome*. Performing at the Théâtre des Variétés, she received reviews praising her grace, mime, and modesty, though Strauss stole the big headlines. She had been performing her Salome dance for nearly a year without the kind of superstardom she really desired. She remained a touring gypsy with a one-gimmick act. Something more was needed. Fate was about to provide.

In September 1907 King Edward VII, son of Queen Victoria, was staying at the Hotel Weimar while taking the cure at Marienbad. A couple of notable society women arranged for Maud to perform her "Vision of Salome" in a private audience for the king of England. The opportunity to be a little after-dinner entertainment for royalty was Maud's ticket to the top. With an audience of twenty-five friends and attendants, Maud donned her pearlized bikini and, to a piano accompaniment, made love to John the Baptist's head before the happy king — an amusing recreation of Salome's dance for King Herod.

Sir Frederick Ponsonby, at the time private secretary to the king, had voiced concern about Maud's display. "The King expressed a wish to see her dance," he recalled in his memoirs, "but I was rather doubtful as to whether it would be right for his Majesty to do so. I had been told that she danced more or less naked, and I was afraid the English press might get hold of this and make up some wild story. . . . I had heard that Miss Allan danced with only two oyster shells and a five franc piece."[21]

In 1907 English women were still being strapped into their constricting corsets and high-necked bodices, whereas "Salome's heavily Oriental dress seemed to concentrate about the wrists and ankles," wrote the eyewitness at the keyboard, "for there seemed to be nothing much anywhere else. She wore a diminutive bra, doubtless intended for Mrs. Tom Thumb, and ditto a G-string of diamonds, designed for a midget's baby."[22]

The important reaction, of course, was that of King Edward, and it did not apparently concentrate on Maud's lack of undress. He praised her artistry and asked why she had not performed yet in London, to which the ready reply was, "Only, Sir, because I've never been asked."[23] Within weeks, Sir Alfred Butt, London's most powerful theatrical impresario, had invited Maud to present her dances at London's preeminent variety theater, the Palace. This was more what Isabella had in mind for her daughter. The enterprise, sanctioned by British royalty itself, oozed respectability.

With her beaded crown, pearl and rhinestone two-piece, a couple of veils, and John's carefully packed head in hand, Maud set out to conquer the British capital, the home of teatime, charity matinees, and birch-in-the-boudoir sex.

In February 1908, after fulfilling previous engagements in Prague, Bucharest, and Leipzig, Maud arrived in London for a two-week engagement. Sir Alfred Butt now added the Canadian dancer to the list of luminaries he introduced to London: Anna Pavlova, Adele and Fred Astaire, Maurice Chevalier, Paul Robeson, and now Miss Maud Allan. Butt, like any good presenter, sought to stir interest in Maud prior to her debut and produced a lavish, illustrated pamphlet, which launched a huge publicity campaign. Since Maud's real life was far too scandalous for a star-in-the-making, Butt simply dissected her face and figure in purple prose: "Her skin is satin smooth, crossed only by the pale tracery of delicate veins that lace the ivory of her round bosom. . . . Her lovely face has the small pointed nose with sensitive nostrils, while her mouth is full lipped and ripe as a pomegranate fruit, and as passionate in its ardent curves as Venus herself."[24]

Butt succeeded in turning Maud into a sex goddess for the Edwardian era, one enjoyed by the king himself. The campaign worked. Introduced first at an exclusive invitation-only matinee on 6 March 1908, Maud's Salome debuted at the Palace on a program that featured the "Juggling McBans," "Belle Davis and her Southern Piccaninies," and "Princess Trixie, the only animal in the world known to be possessed of responsive intelligence." The theater was packed, the reviews unanimous in praise, and Maud's two-week engagement turned into a year and a half run. These eighteen months saw the biggest box-office receipts in the history of the Palace, and, thanks to Maud's popularity, its shareholders received a 33 percent dividend.

In an ironic revisitation of history, the Palace was the very theater where Oscar Wilde's drama *Salome* was to have premiered with Sarah Bernhardt in the title role before the Lord Chamberlain had banned it in 1892. Sixteen years later, Maud Allan put Salome on its stage, but the Lord Chamberlain registered no protest as Buckingham Palace had already approved the subject and its biblical matter. Because Maud's sexuality was wrapped in grace and elegance, two ideals of Edwardian England, she could proceed, with dignity, to unveil herself night after night.

Within months Maud Allan became a popular household name. "She was the Marilyn Monroe of my youth," remarked Sir Herbert Read, the British critic and poet.[25] Londoners purchased Salome flowerpot statues molded in her image, while sandals, bare legs, painted toenails, and even jeweled breastplates became the rage — and often outrage — in polite society, while Maud herself dressed, offstage, only in impeccable ladylike attire. Cartoons, monographs, sonnets, essays, interviews, burlesques, and satires surfaced, all featuring Maud as Salome. A photograph of her in costume, seated and pensive, became a popular greeting card of the day, its caption reading, "Thinking of you." Maud enjoyed at least one royal liaison, with the duke of Westminster, one of the few affairs she admitted to.

As further evidence that Maud's Salome had captivated the public's imagination, the Alhambra Theatre presented a burlesque entitled "Sal Oh Mee," and Lady Constance Stewart Richardson, a rebellious young lady of the British aristocracy, even appeared at a house party for the king dressed as Salome. Throwing herself at His Majesty's feet, she declared, "Sire, I claim the head of Sir Ernest Cassell."[26] Cassell was one of England's wealthiest men and a close friend of the king. The king was not amused and the bridge tables were immediately erected without comment.

Two books published in 1910 were inspired by Maud's fame. *Salome and the Head* involved men competing for Maud's favors, a real dripping dead head delivered in the mail, and an evening devoted to Maud and her entourage gleefully counting the day's intake of jewels. The other tome, *Maudie*, was an undisguised pornographic tale, brimming with details of "Maudie's" erotic life: nude modeling sessions and sexual favors granted to the fortunate.

Always eager to counteract any hint of salacious publicity, Maud was ever present at charity fund-raisers for worthy public causes. She continued to walk the precarious line between the vulgar and the acceptable. The Edwardian sensibility needed someone to embody sex, and Maud received in return for this service what she most needed, fame and fortune.

There were, of course, surrounding her sensational rise to public recognition, the requisite clerical protests usually targeting John's head. Archdeacon Sinclair proffered the opinion that her dance should be given without the head, "an unwise and unnecessary accessory."[27] In Manchester, Maud's appearance was banned by the local Watch Committee, to the ridicule of sophisticated Londoners. There were rumblings from another faction, the Isadora Duncan camp. During Maud's sold-out run at the Palace Theatre, Isadora was playing to sparse houses at the Duke of York's Theatre, and some bitter accusations in the press declared that Maud was nothing but a cheap imitation of Duncan. But Maud's Salome dance separated her forever from mere Duncan imitators. "At least," scoffed Isadora in her memoirs, "I was not Salome. I wanted the head of no one."[28]

Maud's head-hunting, however, made her rich. Earning two hundred and fifty pounds a week at the Palace and as much again for private performances, she moved into sumptuous quarters in the West Wing of the palatial Holford House off Regent's Park — and into high social circles. Salome had conquered London and was welcomed into her most sacrosanct drawing rooms. What's more, she was invited by the wives of powerful men.

Ten years earlier, in America, women led the campaign against Little Egypt at the Chicago World's Fair, and now, in London, Maud was receiving her greatest acclaim and interest from women, who not only invited her into their homes, but even imitated her dance. Maud had hypnotized her public. For them she was an artist expressing lofty emotions of a spiritual nature, and so her apparent nudity was appraised, not as flagrantly sexual, but as daringly artistic. Maud gave these women, who were used to endless layers of undergarments, license to admire and even exhibit their own bodies. Maud was making exhibitionism socially acceptable, and the speed with which women embraced her was indicative of just how very ready they were. Given to garden parties, they now threw "Maud Allan" parties. In August 1908 the *New York Times* reported on the phenomenon:

> It seems that Miss Maud Allan's Salome dance has so fired the imagination of London society women that one of the great hostesses of the metropolis . . . issued invitations to twenty or thirty ladies whose names figure in Court and other fashionable lists, to attend a "Maud Allan" dinner dance, which would be undesecrated by the presence of any man. . . . Dinner was

served to an accompaniment of Salome music tinkled by an orchestra hidden discreetly behind a fortification of palms and flowers, and when the coffee and cigarette stage had been reached, some of the most graceful members of the party demonstrated that they not only succeeded in matching Miss Allan's costume, but had learned some of her most captivating steps in movements.[29]

By now, Maudie Gwendolyn Durrant of San Francisco, sister of the city's most notorious murderer, was doing quite well for herself. She had not only received the favorable attention of the king of England and been welcomed into the aristocracy, but she was also embraced by the most important figure in the British Government, the prime minister himself. Appointed to the highest civil office in the land one month after Maud's debut at the Palace, Herbert Asquith and his wife, Margot, befriended Maud, inviting her to numerous official gatherings of the rich and powerful. On one occasion she was seated between the prime minister and the Austrian ambassador, and on another, beside a young Winston Churchill.

The prime minister's enemies looked on this association with a critical eye. Margot Asquith had a well-earned reputation for outrageous behavior with hints of lesbian leanings. Her association with Maud added fuel to the fire. Margot and her coterie of female friends, it was rumored, visited Maud in her dressing room at the Palace, where they were allowed to fondle her bare back. Margot, in fact, paid for the lease on Maud's Regent's Park abode from 1910 until her husband's death in 1928 and, in a symbolic gesture of female complicity, even paid for the enormous floor-to-ceiling drawing-room mirrors — measuring eight feet by twenty-four. Before this vast lake of reflection Maud engineered her dances.

Purveyors of public morality in America were also horrified to see that a lowly theatrical entertainer, especially a half-naked one, was being treated with such respect. In a lengthy Sunday magazine piece on 16 August 1908, the *New York Times* issued a warning about the current threat and where this virus could lead — to North America.

> At the present rate it is probable that Salome dances will invade the fashionable drawing rooms of New York during the coming Winter, as they have of the London Great World during the season which has just come to an end. . . . From the presentation of the Salome dance in English homes,

and the lionization of the performer as an honored and gushed-over guest, to the appearance of some of these feminine enthusiasts of rank and lineage in the same role, is but a step. It is bound to come unless a halt is called.

Things were strangely backward; while women were celebrating Maud's corsetless display, men were calling for a cover-up. But wasn't it men who were supposed to indulge the "male gaze" at female flesh? When women embraced their own sexuality, the power receded from the male arena, and male protest became about their imminent loss of control. Maud's Salome hit London just as women were launching their campaign for the vote, and Maud provided a curious link between the newborn feminists and the conservatives, as a political satire entitled "Salome and the Suffragettes" suggested.

The play told the story of a Maud/Salome character being kidnapped and held hostage by the Suffragettes. The ransom for her return was the vote for women. The satire acknowledged that in the hands of her own sex the femme fatale possesses enough power to effect political change. And there was Maud at the pinnacle of her fame representing a female sexual icon.

To commemorate Maud's two hundred and fiftieth performance at the Palace Theatre in October 1908 a small hard-covered souvenir book was produced called *My Life and Dancing* in which Maud told her story. In a self-congratulatory tone, Maud dropped names and reprinted flattering reviews and letters, but there was no brother in Maud's autobiography, only "sorrows too great and deep to mention." She discussed her nudity as evoking the beauty of ancient cultures and Italian Renaissance masters, elevating it from any association with overt sexual exhibitionism. In a chapter entitled "A Word About Women," she walked a politically fine line, stating that "the rightful destiny of every woman is to be the wife and mother, to make that inner sanctuary known by the sweet name of 'Home.'" She is not "convinced" that the vote for women "is at present necessary."[30] While supporting the right of every woman to a complete education, she confessed that she would still prefer a male surgeon for any anatomical probings.

Again, Maud says one thing but does another, for she remained an unmarried, childless woman who earned her own living, baring body and soul onstage for public consumption. Had she not capitulated to the status quo, however, she would not have been allowed onstage. Maud Allan did a brilliant job of appearing conservative while rebelling like hell. She thus earned her freedom, and for Maud, freedom was the ability to parade her demons, disguised in Salome's story. The formality of a staged event was the refining element to her radical, cathartic act, and she proceeded without censorship.

Maud's success as the Salome dancer resided in her ability to embody contradictions: her own, and those of the time and place in which she performed. She was the Victorian lady portraying a femme fatale. The household nun by day who, come dusk, dons a diaphanous gown and searches out the man she will devour. But the madonna who plays the whore inevitably leaves the imagination working and wondering. Who is she really? Maud's erotic appeal was founded in this conflict.

Women praised and admired her exhibitionism, her narcissism, and her courage, all cloaked in the language of spiritual transcendence. Voyeurism paraded easily as the appreciation of "classical" beauty. Maud could both display and deny her sexuality without apparent hypocrisy; her body itself held the contradiction without confusion. With Salome as saint, her sexual voraciousness stood alone on the stage, seen by all, acknowledged by none. She proclaimed subservient femininity, while performing an anarchic act of emancipation.

Maud's eighteen months of success in England's capital gave her relief from her terrible burden. As her public fame increased, the private shame receded. The more apparent her flesh, the less apparent her wound. She attained both notoriety and respectability. Maud Allan got what Maud Durrant needed. It would prove a brief furlough.

By late 1909 a newly confident Maud was ready to take Salome on the road. London had had its fill, and Maud headed to Russia, where Isadora Duncan had been received as the goddess of a new dance language. But Russia had little tolerance for what critics dismissed as a "caricature" of Isadora, and Maud's tour was all empty houses and snickering reviews. This disaster beyond the safety of Edwardian England set the tone for the next eight years, as Maud dragged Salome and her other classical dances to every habitable continent. Her British fame got her bookings, but, with a few exceptions, her receptions were lukewarm.

On 10 January 1910, Maud boarded the *Lusitania* to cross the Atlantic, her first trip to America since her departure fifteen years earlier.

This would be a true test of her new identity as someone apart from Theodore Durrant's sister. Commencing in Boston, the tour landed Maud at Carnegie Hall in a much anticipated matinee. Miscalculating expectations, Maud elected to perform her repertoire of classic pieces and not "The Vision of Salome." The fashionable standing-room only crowd was disappointed.

In an attempt to counteract this reserved reaction, Maud performed "Salome" nine days later, even though John the Baptist's head had been confiscated by U.S. immigration officers. Carl Van Vechten, the critic for the *New York Times,* reported: "Yesterday the head itself was left to the imagination but none of the caressing was. However, New York has seen so many dances of this sort by now that there were no exclamations of shocked surprise, no one fainted, and at the end there was no very definite applause."[31]

Salomania had already had its sensational run in New York. Maud found herself in the exasperating position of looking like a weak reproduction of herself, her originality lost on a public already satiated by numerous Salomes performing in every theatrical venue. Gertrude Hoffmann, whose career had soared as a result of her imitation of Maud two years earlier, sent a huge bucket of orchids to Carnegie Hall. Was it gratitude or gloating?

After six dismal weeks on the East Coast, Maud moved west for her homecoming. Her San Francisco debut provided the one bright spot in her American tour. Her old hometown embraced her as a star, with warm ovations and glowing reviews. "Take me to your hearts," pleaded a sentimental Maud to her audience during a curtain call, "and keep me there."[32] Applause and bouquets aside, the greatest personal triumph lay elsewhere: during three months in America and eighty-five performances, not one review mentioned Theo.

Back in London, searching for something to revive her sagging career, she commissioned music from Claude Debussy for a new dance. The collaboration was a disaster: Maud disliked the music, and the composer called her "the detestable Maud Allan."[33] The next few years found Maud, ever in quest for a new audience, globetrotting with the musical trio of the Cherniavsky brothers to India, Hong Kong, Australia, Tasmania, and New Zealand. Despite her lead billing, the trio consistently received the acclaim. Maud became increasingly demanding and difficult, as evidenced by a tempestuous affair with one of the musical brothers who was fifteen years her junior.

Defeated by touring, Maud returned to San Francisco to live with her parents while she acted in a now lost silent movie entitled *The Rugmaker's Daughter*. The film was a long five-reeler and opened in Chicago on 3 July 1915. Maud's dances were termed "wiggly, writhy, squirmy" — rendering them more reptilian than artistic in tone.[34] After one more attempt at touring North America and Canada, desperation began seeping into her demeanor. Her star was fading, the "Vision" receding.

She returned to London and her sumptuous lodgings at Holford House to stage a comeback. It arrived in the form of an invitation by J. T. Grein, the distinguished drama critic of the *Sunday Times* and founder, in 1891, of the Independent Theatre Society, which attempted to circumvent censorship with "noncommercial" productions. Having been a fan of Maud's "Vision of Salome" at the Palace ten years earlier, and observing her capacity for tragedy, Grein offered Maud the lead in Oscar Wilde's play *Salome* at several "private" performances. She grabbed the opportunity, but Maud, in her desperation, misjudged. Alliance with Salome had, ten years earlier, brought Maud Allan her dream. Now, with similar speed, the princess dropped her last veil and became her downfall. This was not to be the glorious resurrection of Maud Allan, Salome, or Oscar Wilde. It was their execution.

Chapter Six

The Trial

THE trouble began innocuously enough, with a small-print item in *The Times* on 10 February 1918 announcing two consecutive Sunday performances of Wilde's *Salome* to take place on 7 and 14 April at London's Prince of Wales's Theatre. Though Maud at age forty-five seemed rather old to play the young seductress, she was still two years younger than Sarah Bernhardt had been when cast twenty-six years earlier. It must have been of some satisfaction to Maud that she would now play the same role, in the same city, in which her heroine had been banned. "She was the one woman in the world I wanted to rival," wrote Allan in 1908, and now she would play the role Bernhardt never did.[35] There would not even be a chance for cruel comparison.

Jack Thomas Grein, in choosing Maud for the lead in his production, was relying not only on her fame as the Salome dancer but also on her previous good fortune in outsmarting the censors on the subject. *Salome* had not had an easy time in England. The Strauss opera had been banned for three years in London and was performed in 1910 only after Thomas Beecham altered the libretto, while the play itself did not have a public premiere until 1931. Maud, however, with her royal endorsement, had silenced the censors for her own Salome dance, and Grein no doubt hoped his production, by association, would receive the same approval. Indeed, the Lord Chamberlain never got the chance to register a moral complaint against this production; others with a more pressing political agenda got there first.

The Great War was raging, and in the early months of 1918 things were looking very bad for the British. Their losses were huge and in late March the Germans, after concluding a peace treaty with Russia, focused their attack on the Western Front. Someone was surely to blame for Britain's bad showing; it was time for a scapegoat and some mudslinging. In fact, according to one political publication, the *Imperialist*, "more than 47,000" British men and women were to blame.

Two weeks prior to *The Times* announcement about *Salome*, this right-wing weekly broadsheet alleged that a German prince had compiled a "Black Book" that detailed in its thousand pages the depraved and lecherous behavior of 47,000 British men and women. The list included "the names of Privy Councillors, youths of the chorus, wives of Cabinet Ministers, dancing girls, even Cabinet Ministers themselves," as well as the houses and bars of ill-repute where their debaucheries took place.[36] With the threat of exposure and blackmail, the *Imperialist* theorized, these forty-seven thousand corrupted souls were under complete German influence and were thus responsible for British losses in the trenches.

Behind this outrageous story was Noel Pemberton-Billing, the Independent M.P. who ran the *Imperialist*. He was inviting a libel suit, but no one was foolish enough to take this incredible story to task. Except, in her ignorance, Maud Allan.

Pemberton-Billing had been elected to Parliament in 1916 on a platform encouraging a vigorous air campaign against the Germans. He was thirty-eight years old in 1918 and already had a resumé of diverse talents and passions. An actor and singer for four years, he had, along the way, developed an obsession about the possibilities of aerial offensive in war. He was also an inventor, and one of his curious patents, despite his evident misogyny — or perhaps in light of it — was for a tidy little feminine item, a powder puff attached to a handkerchief. A handsome, charismatic man, Pemberton-Billing liked fast planes, fast cars, and fast women. And he had a German wife.

To buttress his conspiracy theory, Pemberton-Billing resorted to every conceivable prejudice in his allegations, from anti-Semitism and misogyny to any kind of sexual preference that was not strictly straight. Even heterosexual relations, he suggested, were undermining the war: "Germany has found that diseased women cause more casualties than bullets." For those soldiers not devoured by the syphilis-carrying femme fatale, there was the dreaded degenerate homosexual pull, the "Kultur of Urnings," and the "systematic seduction of young British soldiers by the German urnings."[37]

The English, according to Pemberton-Billing, were also under attack by climaxing British lesbians. "In lesbian ecstasy the most sacred secrets of State were betrayed," reported the *Imperialist*.[38] From this implication of lesbian treachery it was but a short step to the sensational headline that would bring Maud Allan face to face with Pemberton-Billing in a courtroom.

The popular British novelist and Pemberton-Billing supporter Marie Corelli provided the link between the Independent M.P. and the Salome dancer. In a personal note to Pemberton-Billing, Corelli suggested that the subscribers to the upcoming Maud Allan *Salome* production were surely among the degenerate "47,000." This was the catalyst Pemberton-Billing had been waiting for, an event to which he could tie his whole smear campaign.

On 16 February under the captivating headline "The Cult of the Clitoris," the *Imperialist*, now renamed the *Vigilante,* threw down the gauntlet, suggesting that Maud was heading a group of perverts in her *Salome* production. The witch-hunt was on.

The five-word headline begged for a denial, and Maud walked into the trap. By 5 March, Grein and Maud were talking to solicitors, and on

8 March they sued Pemberton-Billing for obscene and defamatory libel. The M.P. could not have asked for an easier target. Unmarried, female, childless, and foreign, Maud had the reputation of being a lesbian — her lovers were in fact both men and women — and was closely linked with Margot Asquith, who was accused of having German sympathies. Maud was also the model for a book of erotic tales, a dancer who performed questionable material in a half-naked manner, and a woman who had studied and had her first successes in Germany and Austria, the enemy countries. There were even insinuations that Maud might be Jewish. She was meat for Pemberton-Billing's grinder.

While simply attempting to clear her good name, Maud unknowingly became the pawn in a high-stakes political chess game that involved Liberal Prime Minister Lloyd George and the proceedings of the war itself. If this weren't enough, it also drew poor, dead Oscar Wilde into another sensational trial. For the first time in history Salome emerged from her place in art, poetry, and sexual fantasy to face a jury in a legitimate courtroom. Maud was in way over her head, but, caught in the myopia of her own outrage, her fatal pride drove her blindly forward.

Under pressure from the Lord Chamberlain, the public censor, the performances of *Salome* were twice delayed. When it finally opened on 9 April at the Kennington Theatre, the reviews were unfavorable both for Wilde's nasty little drama and for Maud as its heroine. But Maud had other concerns on her mind as her libel suit against Pemberton-Billing was about to go to court.

The trial took place at the Old Bailey, London's Central Criminal Court, where Oscar Wilde had been convicted twenty-three years earlier for sodomy. Given that the charges against Pemberton-Billing were deemed criminal, the Crown was to prosecute him. If found guilty, he would go to jail for nine years. The trial was set for 23 April, but Pemberton-Billing managed to have it delayed until 29 May by filing a Plea of Justification. In a reversal of his initial denial of the charges, he now claimed that he would substantiate the libel. If he could prove that this information was published for the public good, then he would win his case.

Pemberton-Billing's bid for a trial delay was, of course, a cover to buy time to fry a much larger fish than Maud Allan. He had joined a political conspiracy to overthrow Prime Minister Lloyd George who, according to the conspirators, was bungling the war effort and engaging in secret peace talks with the German Foreign Minister. In turn, Lloyd

George and his advisers hired a young woman, with some experience in political subterfuge, as an agent-provocateur. She was to offer Pemberton-Billing her support, information, and sexual favors if necessary, and then lure him to a male brothel to be secretly photographed for blackmail.

Eileen Villiers-Stewart was a political adventuress primed for the job. She was an attractive, twenty-five-year-old bigamist, and her lunch with the Independent M.P. was all too successful. By the end of the afternoon, mesmerized by him, she flipped her allegiance, slept with him, and divulged the Liberals' conspiracy to blackmail him. She even agreed to testify as a star witness in her new lover's libel case, asserting that, through her previous political associations, she had actually seen the notorious "Black Book."

There was one last piece of business for Pemberton-Billing to fulfill prior to the opening of his trial, further evidence of the extreme beliefs held by this dangerous man. As the appointed Savior for the Christian Science movement, he needed to produce an heir, just in case he was convicted and put out of circulation for nine years. Committed as he was when it came to his own self-importance, he dutifully bedded a suitably selfless Christian Scientist lady, and nine months later a son was indeed produced. Secure in his pious perpetuity, he entered Justice Darling's courtroom on 29 May for the showdown.

Along with Maud, the blaspheming, naked, lesbian Salome dancer, and Eileen, the bigamist double-agent, Pemberton-Billing had recruited three other equally bizarre misfits as his witnesses. Captain Harold Spencer was an American who had been dismissed from his employment by the British Secret Service eight months earlier for "delusional insanity." This was the man who actually penned the headline "The Cult of the Clitoris."

Dr. Serrell Cooke, who was in charge of lunatics at Paddington Hospital, was to give his medical opinion that *Salome* was in fact a propagandist sado-masochistic tract based on the work of the notorious German, Polish, and Austrian sexologists Richard von Krafft-Ebing, Leopold von Sacher-Masoch, Ivan Bloch, and Otto Weininger. Lord Alfred Douglas, no stranger to libel cases as Oscar Wilde's former lover, was to receive a very public forum for his vicious campaign against Wilde's memory, exacerbated by a personal feud with Wilde's literary executor, Robert Ross.

Maud's two lawyers, Travers Humphreys and Ellis Hume-Williams, were both highly qualified barristers, yet they were entirely unprepared for the guerrilla tactics and lawless antics that would prevail during the six-day trial. Humphreys, as the son of C. O. Humphreys, one of Oscar Wilde's lawyers during his 1895 trial, was continuing the noble, though unsuccessful, family tradition of defending Wilde in life, and now posthumously, against his numerous enemies.

Presiding over the trial was Acting Chief Justice "Little" Darling, a former Tory M.P. and a Victorian prude, who not only permitted the circus-like atmosphere in court but even encouraged it with his own eccentric asides. In the course of the trial he described a sadist as one who "bites and wishes to draw blood from the loved one" (263) and spoke of the "dreadful form of vice called 'fetishism'" (262), using Jack the Ripper as a good example.[39] As for Oscar Wilde, Darling referred to his "filthy works" and "filthy practices" and showed considerable satisfaction that he was "convicted in this court, and suffered imprisonment, and social extinction, and death in due course" (261).

Virtually everyone appearing at the Old Bailey on 29 May had a mission to conceal their own dirty secrets while exposing those of others. Maud had her criminal brother, Pemberton-Billing had his German wife and his liaison with his star witness, and Eileen had her bigamy and her affair with the defendant. Dr. Cooke was attempting to camouflage his personal prejudices behind his medical credentials, Captain Spencer had merely to hide his medically certified insanity, while Lord Alfred Douglas needed to conceal incriminating love letters from Wilde and his own double standard about sodomy and other literary matters.

The prosecution had to hide the blackmail conspiracy of the prime minister's government, evident in a letter Eileen could produce, while Justice Darling made no attempt to conceal his ripe vanity. The case itself, however, was studiously omitted from his memoirs. Everyone involved was at risk for perjury, as their pride, paranoia, and hypocrisy raged in a very public forum. Under front-page headlines right alongside the ongoing devastating war casualties, the press reported all but the detailed clitoral discussions, definitions, and dimensions.

Maud was Pemberton-Billing's first witness. In his Plea of Justification, he had referred to her as "a lewd, unchaste and immoral woman, [who] was about to give private performances of an obscene and indecent character, so designed as to foster and encourage obscene unnatural practices among women; and that the said Maud Allan associated herself with persons addicted to obscene and unnatural practices" (313). This was not to be a friendly encounter.

After shocking Maud by exposing her relationship to Theo and then incriminating her sexually with the clitoral questions, Pemberton-Billing went on to ask if she found the title "The Cult of the Clitoris" to be an "unveiled" reference. "I think," responded Maud, continuing the analogy, "it is draped from the shoulder" (78).

Indicating that her scantily clad dancing was "a German art" previously unknown in England (69), Pemberton-Billing then added a few lesbian implications when he asked if Margot Asquith had not visited Maud in her dressing room at the Palace Theatre. Maud denied everything, to little effect.

Pemberton-Billing then began one of the endless themes of the next few days, the sexual analysis of the play itself. While many lines were read aloud, Maud became Wilde's pathetic apologist, denying repeatedly that she found any incest, sadism, or sexual desire in the text. "Do you wish the jury to understand," queried Pemberton-Billing, "that any pureminded woman would demand for her own sensual satisfaction the head of a man she loved, and would toy with it?" Maud, reaching for innocence, suggested that in Salome's own time and place to witness a decapitated head was "nothing" (74).

In attempting to save her own dignity from perverted associations, Maud denied Wilde's play its undeniable lustiness. She continually asserted that she heard only loving and spiritual yearnings emanate from Salome's mouth. Pemberton-Billing persisted, claiming that Salome's desire to "bite the lips" of John the Baptist was an act of pure sadism (74). "I cannot be responsible," replied Maud, "for what other persons read into it" (76). There was a moment of silence as Judge Darling agreed, forcing the courtroom to silently consider Pemberton-Billing's own lewd frame of mind. It was Maud's only moment of victory.

The following morning Eileen was on the stand claiming to have been shown the infamous "Black Book," and the long diversionary tactics of the trial began. When Eileen mentioned the Asquiths, Lord Haldane, Asquith's Lord Chancellor, the British ambassador to Italy, and Justice Darling himself as being listed in the book, the courtroom was stunned.

Captain Spencer then took the stand and added considerably to the commotion by accusing Mrs. George Keppel, mistress to King Edward VII, of conveying German messages to England. Now the royal family was implicated and the case was no longer about Maud, but about the "Black Book," royal mistresses, and spies at Buckingham Palace. Justice Darling let the hysteria and slander proceed unchecked.

Returning briefly to the libel in question, Spencer ended his testimony by explaining that he had acquired the term *clitoris* from a local village doctor, who suggested that the anatomical term would cover Spencer's various concerns. Elaborating on his newfound expertise, he claimed that the clitoris "when unduly excited or overdeveloped, possessed the most dreadful influence on any woman . . . [and] might even drive a woman to an elephant." Or a saint. Salome's final kiss to John the Baptist, Spencer continued, would have "produced an orgasm" (144). This information was received with some confusion by both the judge and Maud's lawyer. "Is that some unnatural vice?" inquired Counsel, and to their ensuing embarrassment the term was duly explained (119).

This buffoonery continued with Spencer saying that he viewed Maud Allan "as a very unfortunate hereditary degenerate" (145). This from a man dismissed from public service for insanity. Maud, secretly afraid that he was right, suffered the humiliation of her family shame being alluded to before a British courtroom.

The next day Dr. Cooke took the stand and explained that Wilde's play was a virtual compendium of German-identified perversions — sadism, masochism, vampirism, incest, homosexuality, fetishism, and necrophilia — and that "a person performing the part of Salome must be a Sadist" (164). These women, he opined, "cannot get any sexual excitement unless they bite with violence enough to draw blood, even suck it, taste it, and then they have a violent sexual orgasm" (151). The jury regarded Maud with increasing skepticism.

Cooke's expertise, however, was tested under cross-examination. When asked if, by his reasoning, Strauss's opera *Salome* should also be titled "The Cult of the Clitoris," he replied, without hesitation, in the affirmative. The courtroom laughed and his quackery was exposed.

The insanity intensified the following day when Lord Alfred Douglas took the stand. He confirmed for Pemberton-Billing that Wilde "intended the play to be an exhibition of perverted sexual passion excited in a young girl." He called Wilde "the great force for evil that has appeared in Europe during the last 350 years . . . the agent of the devil in every possible way" (172–173).

Two days later the antics continued when Lord Douglas began raving uncontrollably after it was suggested that his role as translator of *Salome* rendered him complicit in its filthy contents. Judge Darling had him removed, bodily, from court. In an attempt to rectify this embarrassment Pemberton-Billing called the clergy to the stand. Having garnered the medical opinion on *Salome*, he arranged for God's. Father Vaughan, an old Jesuit priest, declared that Salome was nothing other than "a hideously impure woman" and that any woman who consented to play her on the stage "*must* be a perverted creature" (193–194). Once again all eyes turned suspiciously to Maud.

On the fifth day of the trial, Pemberton-Billing gave his closing remarks, a tour de force of righteous rhetoric. "Do you think that I am going to keep quiet," he stated dramatically, "in my position as a public man while nine men die a minute to make a sodomite's holiday?" (222). He led the jury to believe that the morality of Wilde's *Salome* itself was on trial and that it was their patriotic duty to render him innocent of libel. He attempted to minimize his attack on Maud's character, saying, "Miss Allan may be a pervert, or she may not be" (230). He finished his diatribe to stupendous applause from the courtroom. Maud wept quietly in her seat.

Maud's lawyer proceeded with his own summation, but his reiteration of the actual facts had little impact beside Pemberton-Billing's charismatic performance. The jury evidenced little interest and Maud wept on.

After an hour and twenty-five minutes of deliberation, the jury returned to find Pemberton-Billing innocent of all charges. The courtroom exploded in cheers. Maud left the Old Bailey quietly through a side door, her reputation ruined, her psyche shattered, and her alliance with Salome an embarrassment. The princess of Judea had lost her veils of illusion and of glory, and Maud was again, thirty years after his execution, merely the miserable sister of Theodore Durrant, a murderer.

While Maud and Grein were left smeared by the trial's accusations of lesbianism, homosexuality, and general perversion, Eileen's bigamy, Pemberton-Billing's adulterous affair with her, and Captain Spencer's clinical insanity had all remained hidden. But not for long. The very next day the press began the backlash. "No one has ever thrown so much dirt on people more respected than himself," wrote the *Manchester Guardian* of Pemberton-Billing, "and yet come so near to being a popular hero" (270).

Within a month Pemberton-Billing and Eileen were exposed. She was arrested for bigamy and, after giving a sworn statement condemning both Spencer and Pemberton-Billing for perjury, served a reduced sentence of nine months in prison. On 1 July, Pemberton-Billing himself was removed bodily from the House of Commons while yelling uncontrollably, "Intern the aliens!" (296).

Grein, financially and emotionally destroyed, resigned from the *Sunday Times* and had a nervous breakdown. Lord Alfred Douglas continued in his paranoid attacks, one of which — criminal libel against Winston Churchill — landed him in jail for six months. Pemberton-Billing recovered in time and continued his eclectic career, running a casino in Mexico with Jack Dempsey during the 1930s and publishing, in 1941, *The Aeroplane of Tomorrow*, an influential book that predicted space travel.

Under the headline "A Scandalous Trial," the *Times* had the final word. "Every well-proven canon of British fair play was frankly disregarded," it stated in its condemnation. "Whatever the qualities of the play *Salome* . . . it is surely intolerable that it should ever have been adopted for a moment as an instrument of British propaganda. It is itself a complete explanation of the jury's verdict, which we take to represent an honest British repugnance for the whole Salome business" (272).

By mid-September 1918, with victory over the Germans imminent, the witch-hunt of Maud's libel trial was quickly forgotten. Even so, her reputation was in tatters, and she could not find a theater manager willing to book her act. Salome was dead, and with her went Maud's career. Ten years earlier London had made her a star, and now, in an equally sensational manner, it destroyed her. Maud carried the wretched humiliation for the remainder of her long life.

Over the next several decades Maud tried numerous times, with little success, to revive her career. There were scattered performances on several continents. In August 1926 she became the first non-instrumentalist to appear at the Hollywood Bowl, dancing to Tchaikovsky's *Pathétique* and the *Blue Danube* with an orchestra of 120 musicians. In 1932 she took on two minor acting roles in England, one in Max Reinhardt's production of *The Miracle* with Lady Diana Cooper, Léonide Massine, and Tilly Losch, and then in Manchester in *The Barker* with Claudette Colbert and her husband, Norman Foster. Maud was featured as a "Hawaiian Dancer." She was sixty years old, and it was her last appearance on a British stage. Four years later, she made her last public appearance in a recital in Los Angeles.

During the long periods of time between these various appearances, Maud's private life became increasingly unstable and obsessive. In 1921, the *San Francisco Call and Post* published her life story in twenty-four installments, a tale full of evasions, alterations, and titillating suggestions about her love life with Indian princes and King Leopold I of Belgium. Avoidance of the truth became, more than ever, Maud's means of survival. As her finances dried up, she became dependent on her rich friends for support, and her means of manipulation and deceit grew. On one occasion she rented Ginger Rogers's ranch outside of Los Angeles and coerced a sympathetic friend into paying the rent.

Her grandiosity flourished in proportion to her poverty. When her mother died in the early 1930s, she employed the Cherniavsky Trio to play for her funeral, held at Holford House in London. Maud appeared draped in voluminous black veils. She danced Chopin's *Marche funèbre*, ending the macabre event by flinging herself dramatically upon her mother's open coffin. The body was then taken for burial in a carriage drawn by five magnificent black horses also draped in black veils. None of this extravaganza was paid for.

When Herbert Asquith died in 1928 and Margot stopped paying the lease on Holford House, Maud began an affair with her secretary. This ten-year relationship, the longest Maud would ever have, manifested curious echoes from the Pemberton-Billing trial, where Maud was engaged in not only a lesbian liaison, but one with definite sadistic overtones.

Verna Aldrich was twenty years Maud's junior, and their affair was punctuated by Maud's demanding and deceitful paranoia. When Verna received a proposal of marriage from a wealthy widower, Maud threw a tantrum and threatened to expose their coupling and then commit suicide. Verna ended the engagement and became ever more entrenched in Maud's selfishness, even using her own limited funds to pay the lease on Holford House. When that money was gone, Maud embarked on devious stratagems to filch money from Verna's rich relatives. Symbolic of her glory days, Maud refused to give up the spacious quarters on Regent's Park, and only when it was bombed by the Germans in 1940 did she leave. Maud finally went too far when she accused her lover of being a thief and threatened to sue her. Verna moved out of her life, leaving Maud to her ever-increasing misery.

During World War II Maud volunteered as an ambulance driver and chauffeur until a friend paid her debts and bought her a one-way ticket to America. Making her way to California, she took a job for the remainder of the war as a drafter at the Douglas Aircraft Company, where Ruth St. Denis, another Salome past, also spent the war years as a riveter.

By 1949, Maud was seventy-six years old and three months in arrears on her shabby one-room rental. But she was still telling acquaintances that she had money in England that would soon arrive. She was moved to a convalescent home, where she dwindled to 114 pounds, a sad and forgotten old woman with memories of once charming the king of England. Haunted by Theo, her thoughts became rambling and vague. She died on 7 October 1956 at the age of eighty-four.

There were a few brief obituaries all reporting her age as seventy-three, among other incorrect facts. After living in ever-increasing obscurity and poverty for almost fifty years after the height of her fame in 1908, she was virtually forgotten by the time of her death. Maud Allan, the Salome dancer, had been long dead, and Maud had done little to keep her own story straight. Her death certificate listed her birth date as 1880, reducing her age by seven years, and listed her parents as William and Isabella Allan. Maud even attempted to carry the shame of the Durrant name to the grave with her.

Salome had offered Maud escape — from her blighted name, from the horror of anonymity, from inherited pain — and in doing so she gave Maud fame, money, and a veil for her past. As Salome, she loved John the Baptist, but as Maud Allan it was Theodore Durrant.

Maud's success in Edwardian London was founded in her ability to balance Salome's obvious sexuality with the requisite decency. She was the British Salome during the Salome Craze, and the public happily colluded with her to their mutual benefit: Maud gave them sex and they gave her class.

Her libel trial of 1918 dismantled this relationship and found Maud trapped in Salome's image attempting to renounce her sexual essence. Without the carapace of a living woman to embody her, Salome, too, ended her nineteenth-century incarnation. After her complex resurrection at the turn of the twentieth century, Maud Allan had catapulted her into the centerfold of world politics, not to be blamed just for one man's death, but for thousands. Her embodiment in Maud, the unmarried woman in the beaded bikini and transparent veils, was declared guilty.

Never had Salome been allotted such power; never had she had so little.

PART III

Mata Hari:
The Horizontal Agent

I never could dance well. People came to see me because I was
the first who dared to show myself naked to the public.

— Mata Hari

Chapter Seven

Intoxication

HE last year of World War I was not a good one for Salome. Across the English Channel in France another of her sisters had gone on trial, less than a year before Maud Allan. Her name was Mata Hari, and she, too, had been found guilty of treason. Though Maud lost her case, her image, and her respectability, she walked out of the courtroom a free woman, but Mata Hari, the most famous female spy of the twentieth century, did not. She was condemned to a death by firing squad and thus achieved the immortality that Maud Allan coveted. But at the time, all Mata Hari had wanted was to be with the man she loved. He was the first she had ever loved, despite the hundreds she had bedded. Her story, like so many women's and like Salome's, traces the tragedy of surrendering to one beautiful young man.

On 13 December 1916 French military officers working at the top of the Eiffel Tower picked up the signal of a coded radiogram sent from German intelligence in Madrid to its headquarters in Berlin. The intercepted message was quickly dispatched to Captain Georges Ladoux, head of French intelligence. This was good news indeed for Ladoux. The Great War across Europe was in its third year, and the Allies were losing—there was chaos in the government, mutiny in the ranks, and slaughter at the front. The Americans had not yet entered the war, and the French were desperate. But they had deciphered the German code, and this radiogram reported the findings of the German agent "H-21."

Ladoux was already hot on the trail of "H-21," a woman most of Europe knew as Mata Hari. Alerted months earlier by British intelligence that the courtesan was "To Be Watched," Ladoux had been doing just that — and more. Hopeful of a misstep, he had her followed, her every move accounted for, but even here his efforts resulted in no evidence of her ties to the German spy network, only of her multitudes of lovers and her penchant for fortune tellers. Until now.

Over the next several months, thirteen additional messages between Madrid and Berlin were intercepted on the subject of German agent H-21. On 13 February 1917 Mata Hari was arrested in a Parisian hotel room by five French police officers. She was taken to Saint-Lazare prison and during the next few months was interrogated fourteen times by Pierre Bouchardon, the examining magistrate. Catching a German spy was a powerful coup for the French.

But after interviews with most of the fifty-three gentlemen whose cards were found in her hotel room and a detailed examination of her toiletries, couturiers, bank accounts, and correspondence, a frustrated Bouchardon confessed to Ladoux on 20 April that his excavations had turned up no convincing evidence that Mata Hari was a German spy. The following day, Ladoux presented Bouchardon with the Madrid–Berlin telegrams concerning H-21, and Mata Hari's fate was sealed. But why had Ladoux waited so long before giving his prosecutor this incontrovertible evidence?

The truth is alarming. These intercepted telegrams contained "intoxication" — false evidence. The Germans knew the French had deciphered their code, and the telegrams about H-21 were intended to be intercepted by the French. Furthermore, Ladoux had been informed that the messages were intoxication, but, desperate for evidence in a case in which he had none, he kept this fact to himself, without any apparent show of conscience.

In a fatal game of implicit collusion, Mata Hari was framed by both the French and German intelligence services, with some help from the British, who initiated the suspicion. The French were losing thousands of soldiers on the battlefield in the early months of 1917, and delivering up one foreign courtesan who danced without her clothes as a gesture of victory seemed small sacrifice indeed. Mata Hari was worth more dead than alive and so, with icy calculation, it was arranged.

In plotting her murder, Ladoux gave Mata Hari something money could not buy: immortality. Prosecutor André Mornet was writing history with fallacy when he proclaimed during her trial, "The evil that this woman has done is unbelievable. This is perhaps the greatest woman spy of the century."[1] Her execution before a firing squad was the final drama that confirmed her legendary status. In her overwhelming lust for attention it is hard to imagine that Mata Hari would not, now, be pleased.

The great irony of her fame, based on her role as a beautiful, seductive, and powerful double agent, responsible for hundreds of thousands of wartime deaths, is that it is a fabulous tale that will not die despite its divergence from the truth. Mata Hari was, however, beautiful and seductive, and, when her life was held in the balance, brave, but she retains only the posthumous power that legend has given her. While still breathing, she could not even save her own neck with the pathetic truth of her ineffectual political dalliances. By the time Mata Hari entered the courtroom in July 1917, it was too late; she had already assumed for her accusers a face of evil against which mere facts, or lack thereof, were simple inconveniences easily overlooked.

For decades after her demise, the mystery of Mata Hari was debated in movies, books, plays, and musicals, confirming her legend while propagating the confusion. Was she guilty of spying? Everyone had an opinion but no one had the facts. Those were located in a confidential dossier in the archives of the Historical Service of the Armies at the Château de Vincennes in Paris, sealed until 2017, one hundred years from the date of her death.

In 1985 biographer Russell Warren Howe persuaded Charles Hernu, the French minister of National Defense, to break that seal, thirty-two years early, and from those voluminous pages tumbled the indisputable truth about Mata Hari. She was innocent of espionage. Far from ending the mystery, this revelation only gives birth to a greater one. If innocent, what then did this mediocre Oriental dancer, citizen of a neutral country, actually do to merit a hatred that drove the leaders of British, French, and German intelligence to spend a great deal of time, money, and effort in the middle of a raging world war in the attempt to exterminate her? War had been declared on Salome.

Chapter Eight

The Little Dutch Girl

OU ask me if I would like to do silly things? Rather ten times than once! Just do whatever you want, for in a few weeks I'll be your wife anyhow."[2] Margaretha Geertruida Zelle was only eighteen when she wrote these flirtatious words to a man she had known only a few months. They suggested highly inappropriate activity for a well-brought-up nineteenth-century young lady. Her sexually adventurous spirit was already apparent, the embryo of the courtesan evident.

Born on 7 August 1876, in a small rural town in the province of Friesland in northern Holland, to Adam Zelle and his wife, Atje van der Meulan, Margaretha was the eldest child and had three younger brothers. Zelle owned a chic and successful hat store in the humble town of Leeuwarden, and he was considered both wealthy and respectable. He spoiled his little dark-haired daughter with clothes of velvet and silk that rendered the other girls at Miss Buys's academy for young ladies envious. Little Margaretha added to the fantasy, telling her peers that her father was a baron and that she had been born in a castle. When for her sixth birthday her father went so far as to buy Margaretha a four-seater carriage drawn by two horned goats in which she rode proudly down the main street in her red velvet dress, the envy was tempered by ridicule.

When Zelle's business went bankrupt in 1889, young Margaretha learned about the horrors of losing one's social status, especially humiliating to those like Zelle and his daughter for whom impressing others was a lifelong obsession. Within a year her parents separated and nine months later her mother was dead. Margaretha was fifteen, and in three short years her world of ease, comfort, and love had been destroyed.

The family disintegrated and Margaretha was sent to live with a godfather. Her nomadic existence had begun. She began to train as a kindergarten teacher, but that effort was promptly aborted when her teacher fell in love and Margaretha's response was inappropriately welcoming. Shipped off to an uncle in The Hague, Margaretha received her first taste of city life and the men who populate it. Left to her own devices, she answered a personal advertisement in the newspaper: "Officer on home leave from Dutch East Indies would like to meet girl of pleasant character — object matrimony."[3]

Rudolph Macleod was home on sick leave for two years after serving in the Dutch Indies for seventeen tough years. At thirty-nine years of age, he was old enough to be Margaretha's father, more of an attraction than a repellent to a girl who adored her generous, now absent, father. Bald, with a sturdy body and a mustache of impressive length and width, Macleod was of Scottish descent, his ancestors having served in the Dutch army since the late seventeenth century. His arduous years in Sumatra, Java, and Borneo had left him with diabetes, rheumatism, and a dangerous propensity for alcohol. He had never married, and one of his friends, as a joke, had placed the ad in the newspaper. Macleod, with great disinterest, received sixteen responses from eligible young ladies. He responded two weeks later to only one letter, the one that contained a photograph of a dark-haired, sensual, slightly mischievous eighteen-year-old beauty.

Margaretha met her future husband for the first time on 30 March 1895 at a museum and was impressed with his military uniform. This marked the beginning of a lifelong passion for officers that would end, ironically, when she was shot dead by twelve of them. Margaretha cut an equally striking figure, standing a majestic five foot ten inches, with a svelte hourglass figure despite her small breasts. Macleod proposed two months later, and they were married at City Hall a few weeks prior to her nineteenth birthday. The bride wore yellow (fig. 12).

Despite his young wife's apparent eagerness in the bedroom, evident in her letters to him, Macleod saw no reason to give up old habits, and within weeks he was depositing his new bride with friends for the evening while he went out drinking and whoring with his officer buddies. This was not what Adam Zelle's princess had in mind for her marriage. But it was only the beginning of the nightmare. Like most women of the late nineteenth century, Margaretha had virtually no recourse, financial or familial, but to accept her boorish husband. A son, Norman John, was born on 30 January 1897, and within three months the family departed for Java. Macleod's leave was over and his wife looked on the new adventure with optimism.

The East Indies, today Indonesia, had been under staunch Dutch rule since 1799, and the inhabitants were treated by the Dutch military as

FIG. 12. Margaretha Geertruida Zelle and Captain Rudolph Macleod
on their wedding day, The Hague, 1895
(Collection Viollet)

virtual slaves. This small inequity aside, the Indies offered a tropical paradise to the visiting European. Rich in fauna, birds, and fish, the landscape teemed with lush vegetation and cascading waterfalls that provided fertile ground for the valuable tea, coffee, tobacco, indigo, sugar,
and rubber crops. Bustling markets brimmed with nuts, spices, brightly
hued fabrics, local art and craftware, ripe exotic fruits, and magnificent
flowers never seen in Europe. Far from the constraints of her European
upbringing, Margaretha could explore her own sensuality in this exotic
atmosphere unobserved.

But there was a dark side to this colorful world that provided the setting in which the Macleod marriage would founder. Tropical illnesses — cholera, malaria, typhoid — abounded and were accompanied by the threat of poisonous scorpions, lethal snakes, and large flying insects. Maintaining good hygiene was an almost impossible task, and the frequent rains and monsoons often threatened to wipe out houses and whole towns. At the center of this land of impending danger stood the sacred Hindu temples; their ancient rituals would be Margaretha's solace and inspiration.

Living the first year in Java, Margaretha gave birth to a daughter, Jeanne Louise (called Non), in May 1898, before the family transferred to Sumatra. There, with his military career stalled, Macleod's drinking escalated. He began raging and swearing at every encounter and blamed Margaretha for his misery. "You are too narrow-minded, too stupid," he wrote to her, "and too superficial to ever write an interesting letter and you are no longer allowed to speak of beautiful dresses, of hairstyles, of other banalities. Do you understand now that I am constantly in a bad temper because of you?" He even blamed his infant son's need for affection on his wife — "That perpetual urge for kissing he certainly has from you!"[4]

He humiliated her publicly, yelling, "Go to hell, bitch!" in front of his fellow officers, who were paying far too much attention to his pretty young wife. Margaretha had also noticed her effect on them, and she would not forget it. "The young lieutenants pursue me and are in love with me," she wrote to a friend. "It's difficult for me to behave in a way which will give my husband no cause for reproaches."[5]

To his sister in Holland, Macleod sent an endless stream of invectives, calling his wife a "beast" and a "bloodsucker," and said he wished he "could get rid of her."[6] The inequity of the power structure in the marriage paralleled that of the Indonesians and their Dutch rulers. When verbal abuse was not enough, Macleod resorted to physical brutality, hitting and even whipping his wife.

Then real tragedy struck. Late one night in June 1899, the two children began violently vomiting black bile. Norman John died. Non survived the attack. They had been poisoned by their nurse in an act of revenge against Macleod for some transgression against either a lover or a fellow officer. The case remained unsolved. Perhaps Macleod's only redeeming characteristic, which proved a lifelong commitment, was his love for his children. The death of his son devastated him, and the marriage suffered all the more.

Margaretha, unlike her husband, appeared to withdraw in her grief, a vulnerability died in her, and never again did she exhibit much maternal interest in her surviving child. Her dreams of happiness in love, marriage, and children were destroyed, and her heart closed in the face of broken illusions. An attack of typhoid fever the following March left her even more removed from reality. As the new century began, Margaretha had lost the only life she knew.

By October 1900, Macleod, in a rage over his lack of promotion to lieutenant-colonel after twenty-four years of service, resigned from the army. He was forty-four years old, his career a shameful blight on the family legacy of military honors. On 27 May 1901 Margaretha wrote to Amsterdam asking for a divorce on the grounds of cruelty and maltreatment, but nothing came of her request. By August she reported to her father that her husband had spat in her face and threatened to kill her with a gun.

The following year, Macleod gave in to Margaretha's pleas to return to Holland, and so after five years of tropical exile, the miserable couple returned with their daughter to civilization. Within months, Margaretha filed for a legal separation. Macleod requested custody of four-year-old Non, and Margaretha, with no means of taking care of her, agreed. She would never see her daughter again, except in passing glimpses. She returned to an uncle in Amsterdam but found herself unwelcome. In the final irony of this disastrous marriage, which began with a personal ad in the newspaper, Macleod filed another such announcement in the press. He warned all salesmen to avoid his estranged wife — with her love of the luxurious, he would not be responsible for her debts.

Margaretha was now twenty-six years old and perched on the edge of complete ruin. She had been married for seven years to a brute, her son had been murdered, she had no family to house or support her, no means by which to earn a living, and the ill will of a society toward a woman who has deserted her husband. Love became not a haven but a hell, children produced more pain than pleasure, and men were not to be trusted with heart, body, or soul.

Despite her state of total destitution, Margaretha still had choices. She could easily have succumbed to the misery and lived out her life in poverty, prostitution, or maybe washing laundry for the more fortunate. But she was still Adam Zelle's little princess, and she found in her loss the opportunity for complete self-reinvention. Now that her standing in society as daughter, wife, and mother was destroyed, she had lost any pretense of social decency and could now do, or be, anything she desired with impunity. And, having not lost her insatiable desire for attention, she remembered the two things she had learned in Indonesia: the power of her beauty over men . . . and, one Saturday night at the officers' club, she had done a dance.

Chapter Nine

The Hindu Hoax

PEOPLE were dancing in prewar Paris. The Belle Epoque was the age of risqué theater in dark alleys, legitimate cabarets-concerts, equestrian circuses, and packed houses at the Folies-Bergère and the Moulin Rouge, where gaiety reigned and the can-can had altered the perspective on pantaloons forever. Nightlife was real life, where entertainment and luxury were the key to the good life, whereas work was only for those whose circumstances were unfortunate enough to require it. Electricity was a novelty that forever altered the length of waking hours, and the American Loie Fuller, with her dances of colored veils, was crowned the "Fairy of Light."

Art Nouveau lilies, Oriental palms, and tasseled cushions decorated the languid, low-lit salon gatherings, opium dens, and attendant cross-gender sexual experiments. The popular bedroom farces of Georges Feydeau at the Palais Royale conveyed an easy conscience concerning sexual peccadilloes, depicting clerics squirming under bouncing beds, men greeting their wives without trousers, and various other indiscretions associated with the cacophony of men and women engaged in libidinous adventures. It was to this city of sexual freedom that Margaretha fled after her marriage to find herself — and her fortune.

The art of twentieth-century voyeurism, something Margaretha would thrive on, was born in Belle Epoque Paris. Life was theater, with everyone a witness and everyone a character, everyone an audience and everyone an actor. Defining masks were essential. From the aristocratic classes there were the salonières, boulevardiers, flâneurs, dandies, Sapphic sisters, homosexuals, aesthetes, and nocturnals, not to mention the demimondaine performers who were actually paid for their talents. Documenting this endless stream of personalities were the journalists, the men of letters who, in the age before television and film, informed society of everyone else's business. The line between fact and fiction became blurred as fanciful and serialized tales of romance and intrigue were printed right alongside hard news in the numerous daily papers.

Bourgeois women were sealed off in their marital abodes from all this frenetic activity. From the time of the French Revolution, when it was even declared a crime for a woman to appear in public (this legislation was understandably short-lived), to the Napoleonic Code of 1804 that left the burden of all guilt for sexual misconduct on women, a decent woman had a long road to travel to equality. In Belle Epoque Paris, women could not dine alone in a restaurant, and *Le Figaro* declared that "a woman who reads a novel is no longer entirely respectable."[7] But some women were beginning to read, not to mention publish, their own literature, and while feminist periodicals and international conferences multiplied, divorce became legal, and the slow progress of women's rights was under way.

But there existed another world of women—the one into which Margaretha would slip—the women of the demimonde, the working women, the theatrical women, singers, actresses, dancers, and prostitutes who had traded in their "decency" for freedom over their own lives. This was a freedom that was unknown to the middle-class wife and mother and even the newborn feminist. For many in this rebellious class of females, marriage was a social prison that offered little in the way of fun. Men had wives and children at home and mistresses in the afternoon or evening; barring scandal or public exposure, the situation was ideal.

Prostitutes and mistresses fell into numerous categories, and, as Mata Hari, Margaretha would rapidly traverse the hierarchial lines. There were the sad street whores, often carriers of sexually transmitted disease and illegitimate children, and the "demi-castors," educated and sophisticated women kept by a single wealthy man in a modest but comfortable house. At the summit of the sex-for-sale pyramid sat the most colorful and outsized characters of the Belle Epoque, the Grand Horizontals, the courtesans who had survived the competitive climb to the peak of their arduous profession and who became the stars of the demimonde. They were the celebrities of the time as movie stars are today. Their private lives, loves, extravagances, fashions, and vast wealth were documented in considerable detail by the dueling journalists. This was the heyday of the Grand Cocotte, and the handful of beauties who achieved this enviable status were regarded as national treasures. In her glamorous trade of sex for power, the courtesan was the most successful, ambitious, and astute career woman of her time.

Each had her gimmick, and their rivalries over beauty, diamonds, and lovers were legendary. Liane de Pougy insisted that one favorite lover refer to his wife and child, if he must, as the "monster" and the "little monster" and, after suffering tears over an unfaithful man, made a vow to take only lovers she didn't like. The Spanish Caroline Otero was dubbed "the Suicide Siren" in honor of the men who had killed themselves for her, while Emilienne d'Alençon traveled everywhere with her performing pink bunnies. Mata Hari would be a Hindu temple dancer. Many of these connoisseurs of love were bisexual, and their busy lives often traced an ironic arc that began with removing their clothes and ended by taking refuge behind the veil of chastity.

But long before becoming a bride of Christ was a consideration, there was the magnificent attire, as described by Jean Cocteau, where more-will-reveal-more was the password to seduction: "It was no small affair. Armour, escutcheons, carcans, corsets, whalebones, braids, epaulieres, greaves, thighpieces, gauntlets, corselets, pearl baldricks, feather bucklers, satin, velvet and bejeweled halters, coats of mail. . . . The idea of undressing one of these ladies was an expensive undertaking which was better arranged in advance, like moving house."[8]

Paul Poiret, the greatest fashion designer of the day, would soon unleash women from the corset, liberating their bodies from whalebone prisons into public life. They could now walk with intent, sway their hips, and the world began to look. It was to this city of courtesans, dancers, and women on the verge that Margaretha Zelle-Macleod fled in the spring of 1903. There was no better place for a woman to lose her identity and emerge with another. "I thought," she explained later, "that all women who ran away from their husbands went to Paris."[9]

Arriving in the French capital with no money, friends or connections, Margaretha tried her luck at modeling. At first shocked when asked to disrobe by a painter, she quietly acquiesced rather than lose the job. But modeling for a pittance in some artist's garret was not Margaretha's idea of stardom, and she returned, penniless, to Amsterdam within a few months, only to be greeted by Macleod suing her for desertion of Non. With little to recommend her as a viable mother, she lost the plea and her estranged husband became the sole custodian of her daughter. Her last attachment in Holland broken, she gathered her courage for another assault on Paris.

This time failure was not an option. "I had a gun ready and my decision was taken," she later told a journalist in her self-dramatizing style.[10] Since her first visit to Paris a year earlier, Margaretha's attitude toward her own possibilities had altered radically, and she now, through the dark passage of desperation, had the necessary resolve.

Without a franc to her name she checked into the Grand Hotel, one of the most expensive hotels in the city. It was her first gutsy move—and it worked. She quickly got a job at the Cirque Molier, an unusual and very popular circus founded in 1880 by Ernest Molier for an annual benefit performance in which his aristocratic friends would perform fencing, trapeze, and gymnastic tricks for a cheering audience of their peers. Margaretha, using the equestrian skills she had learned in the Dutch Indies, rode horses in such an alluring style that Monsieur Molier suggested that dancing might be her metier.

She had by this time taken her first lover, Henri de Marguérie, a kindly man who would become her lifelong friend. The right kind of lover, Margaretha found, unlike a husband, could really enhance one's situation. Marguérie paid her hotel bills, introduced her to society, and encouraged her pursuits. Margaretha had never taken a dancing lesson in her life, but this proved no deterrent. As "Lady Macleod" she made her debut in a dance of suggestive Oriental tones at the salon of Madame Kiréevksy, a singer.

In the audience that evening was Emile Guimet, a wealthy industrialist whose amateur passion was all things Eastern. His collection was so vast and valuable that he had built a museum in 1885 on the place d'Iéna on the Right Bank of the Seine to house it. Captivated by Lady Macleod, Guimet invited her to perform at his museum, giving her public debut the ultimate stamp of authenticity. It was Margaretha Zelle's first magnificent deceit—though not her last.

Three hundred men and women of the Parisian aristocracy, including the German and Japanese ambassadors, gathered at 9 P.M. on 13 March

FIG. 13. Mata Hari in her debut as an Eastern temple dancer
at the Musée Guimet, Paris, 13 March 1905
(Réunion des Musées Nationaux/Art Resource, New York)

1905 at the Musée Guimet to witness "Les Danses Brahmaniques." The
small second-floor library was converted to a sacred Hindu temple, with
an eleventh-century statue of Siva on the altar. The eight ridged columns
topped with classic nude beauties that encircled the rotunda were draped
with garlands of white flowers. Jasmine and sandlewood incense wafted
through the air while flickering candles lit a floor strewn with rose petals.
The musicians began the first sad tones of an Eastern rite . . . and Mata
Hari was born (fig. 13).

Guimet had suggested to Margaretha that the name Lady Macleod
would not sufficiently suggest her ancestral Eastern roots. So she became
Mata Hari, Malay for Eye of Day, the Sun. Even the effusive prose of
Belle Epoque journalism rose to new heights in describing this exotic
creature. "If it were possible for a sinuous reptile to enter the body of a
woman," wrote H. Ashton-Wolfe, "then the miracle was accomplished
before my dilated eyes. Writhing, twisting, coiling, shivering with serpentine grace, Mata Hari glided over the oval stage."[11]

The scantiness of Margaretha's costume did not escape notice.

"With veils, bejewelled brassières, and that is about all," reported *La Presse,* "no one before her has dared to remain like this with trembling ecstasy and without any veils in front of the god."

> Mata Hari does not only act with her feet, her arms, eyes, mouth and crimson fingernails. Mata Hari, unhampered by any clothes, plays with her whole body. And then, when the gods remained unmoved by the offer of her beauty and youth, she offers them her love, her chastity — and one by one her veils, symbols of feminine honour, fall at the feet of the god. But Siva wants even more . . . one more veil, a mere nothing — and erect in her proud and victorious nudity, she offers the god the passion which burns in her.[12]

Margaretha's beauty transfixed her admirers, who saw in her the allure, the danger, the personification of a femme fatale. Other witnesses emphasized less the flesh and more the spirit. "Majestically tragic, the thousand curves and movements of her body trembling in a thousand rhythms," *Le Gaulois* observed, "one finds oneself far from the conventional *entrechats* of our classic dancers . . . like David before the Holy of Holies, like Salambo before Tanit, like Salome before Herod!"[13] Marcel Lami writing in the *Courrier Français* reveals racist undertones along with his lusty thoughts. The theme would reemerge at her criminal trial. "Strong, brown, hot-blooded, her swarthy complexion, full lips and liquid eyes speak of distant lands, burning sun and tropical rain. . . . It is like nothing we have ever seen before . . . an eternal desire for we-know-not-what offered to we-know-not-whom . . . like desire dissolving in desire."[14]

Margaretha had captured the imaginations of the willing Parisians in their restless search for erotic entertainment, and within days she was flooded with invitations to dance at some of the most elegant salons in the city. Toting along her veils, potted palms, candles, and incense, she performed at soirées of the Baron Henri de Rothschild, Cécile Sorel, the great actress of the Comédie-Française, Emma Calvé, the French soprano, and the Italian singer Lina Cavalieri. She received enormous sums of gold francs for each appearance, and within the year she had performed thirty times, including six times at the Trocadero music hall. At the Salle Mors, performing for an audience of more than three hundred people, she shared the stage with some of Monsieur Gaumont's earliest motion picture projections.

Margaretha was mingling with the theatrical royalty of Europe as one of their own and felt perfectly at ease. Her grandiosity was no longer a silent, internal belief but an external reality being applauded. Adam Zelle's daughter was indeed a princess, it was the Dutch part that had been ill-fitting. She had become Javanese and lost no time in leading the already hypnotized press astray — she reveled in revealing her body while concealing the truth of her origins. "My mother was a glorious temple dancer who died on the day I was born," she elaborated. "When I reached the threshold of womanhood, my foster mother saw in me a pre-destined soul and resolved to dedicate me to Shiva. . . . It was on the purple granite alter of Kanda Swany that, at the age of thirteen, I danced for the first time, completely nude."[15]

Her imagination knew few boundaries and her story changed daily, though it was always appropriately tragic, exotic, and strangely suggestive. And the Parisians, only too eager to suspend belief, loved it. It was a prerequisite for a star performer to have a dramatic past to fulfill the projected fantasies of her audience, and Mata Hari gave Paris its first genuinely fake Oriental temple dancer. Just as Maud Allan had provided the British with a sexy dancer with spiritual intentions, so too Mata Hari obliged the French. The irresistible combination of the sacred and the profane satisfied intellectual pretensions while legitimizing the prurient (fig. 14).

Several other ladies of the day who dared to show too much flesh and too little piety in their entertainments were arrested for indecency. But Mata Hari, in her spiritual disguise, received only ever more prestigious invitations, performing on one occasion for the recipients of the Legion of Honor, and on another for a benefit in aid of the Russians in the midst of the Russo-Japanese war.

In her strip act, Mata Hari provided Belle Epoque Paris with a delightful blend of mysterious, high-brow art and racy, low-brow sex. That she was in truth European, not Eastern, an abused wife who had deserted her daughter, and a complete amateur with no training in dance whose "sacred dances" were little more than a series of vague poses and discarded veils was all happily overlooked. Erté, the Russian designer who created his first theatrical costume for Mata Hari in 1913, wrote that "her talent was not much, in fact it was not enough, so she fabricated this aura of mystery around her to conceal any lack of it."[16] Authenticity held little allure in the face of an erotic novelty.

There was the inevitable comparison to Isadora. While Duncan in

FIG. 14. Mata Hari, ca. 1907
(Jerome Robbins Dance Division, The New York Public Library
for the Performing Arts, Astor, Lenox and Tilden Foundations)

her loose and flowing robes portrayed classical Greece, Mata Hari had a
monopoly on the Hindu, the Indian, and the naked. A British magazine
reported that Duncan had "delighted Paris with her classical dances, until the heavy German atmosphere left its imprint upon her. . . . It is impossible to see two manifestations of art so totally different. Miss Duncan
is the Vestal, Lady MacLeod is Venus."[17]

    To implement her sensationalized "nudity," Mata Hari had at her
disposal, depending on the occasion, two forms of exposition. For her
Guimet debut she wore a one-piece body stocking underneath her jew-

eled breastplates and veiled skirt, a cover-up that produced the curious apparition of a naked woman without a belly button. For more intimate soirées, however, the body stocking was left at home and the titillation of her flesh was apparent as the veils were removed. For one such appearance, for women only, at the Neuilly residence of Natalie Barney, the American heiress, Mata Hari demanded an elephant for her entrance. "No, you'll get in the way of Berthe [the maid]," protested Barney. "There are cookies and tea, and we can't have an elephant stamping around in my garden!"[18] A horse would have to do.

The young Colette, who was soon to bare her own bosom to the public, was also performing that afternoon. She was not, however, convinced by Mata Hari's talents.

> Her dancing and the naive legends surrounding her were of no better quality than the ordinary claptrap of the current "Indian turns" in the music hall. The only pleasant certainties on which her drawing-room audience could count were a slender waist below breasts that she prudently kept hidden, a fine, supple moving back, muscular loins, long thighs, and slim knees. . . . In the May sunshine . . . the color of her skin was disconcerting, no longer brown and luscious as it had been by artificial light, but a dubious, uneven purple.[19]

Mata Hari's breasts have come under considerable scrutiny: one writer claimed to have seen them and voted them objects of "envy," while Colette assumes them best hidden. The irony of Mata Hari's nudity is, in fact, that while she exposed herself from the waist down, no one ever did see her breasts, an unusual feat for a nude dancer. There are several photographs of her in nothing but the famous breastplates. One biographer hypothesized that her husband had bitten off her nipples in a fit of jealousy, an idea she herself might have forwarded to her lovers to explain her unusual modesty in that area. Léon Bizard, the prison doctor at Saint-Lazare during her final days, uncovered the mystery: "Mata Hari had small breasts with highly discolored, overdeveloped nipples, and she was not interested at all to show them."[20] It is testament to Mata Hari's ingenuity that she managed to become so famously desired for her body and her exquisite beauty. All her life, even under her costumes, she wore a "cache-sein" (literally, hide-breast), a kind of bra of her own devising, stuffed with feathers.

The concealment of her breasts was clearly no deterrent to her lovers, and Mata Hari had many. Along with the numerous invitations to dance came even more to make love, and she took on men as fast as the francs flowed. There were bankers, diplomats, politicians, composers, impresarios, industrialists, and the rich and aristocratic. They paid her bills, bought her jewels, gowns, furs, horses, and carriages, and enabled her to set up house on the rue de Balzac in distinguished comfort. And then there were the uniforms, the soldiers of all ranks and nationalities who were her favorites and from whom she required little in return, except their passion. She would later speak respectfully of how they would fold their uniforms with care before coming to bed, whereas the wealthy bankers would drop their clothes impatiently on the floor.

Mata Hari enjoyed a meteoric rise into the land of the Grand Horizontals, dining at Maxim's, touring the Bois de Boulogne in her carriage, and holding court at Longchamps in her chinchilla. A new Turkish cigarette called the "Mata Hari" was issued, and her symbolism as a seductive female was recalled one drag at a time. While the queens of the demimonde generally had little love for each other, a special disdain was reserved for this interloper. "I deny that I was ever a friend of hers," claimed Liane de Pougy in her memoirs. "Though her eyes are beautiful her look is glowering, her expression is shifty, her countenance is hard and vulgar. . . . She had a loud voice and a heavy manner, she lied, she dressed badly, she had no notion of shape or colour, and she walked like a man."[21]

One of Mata Hari's lovers was the distinguished lawyer Maître Edouard Clunet, who would remain her friend throughout her ordeals and defend her in court in 1917. Shortly after her debut at the Guimet, Clunet introduced her to the man who would become her manager for the next ten years. Gabriel Astruc was the leading impresario in prewar Europe, handling the careers of Fyodor Chaliapin, Artur Rubinstein, and Wanda Landowska. Astruc, ironically, had refused to handle Isadora Duncan, finding her too subtle for the large audiences he cherished, but he took on Mata Hari with her vast popular appeal and booked her into the Olympia Theater on the boulevard des Capucines in August 1905 for the stunning fee of ten thousand francs.

Having conquered Paris, it was time to exploit her growing fame. And so by the end of the year, under Astruc's direction, Mata Hari packed her breastplates, body stockings, and jeweled sarongs and set out, just as her British rival Maud Allan was doing, to seduce Europe.

In January 1906, for her first foreign foray in Madrid, Mata Hari chose the conservative approach, wearing her flesh-colored bodysuit underneath her costume, and the audience registered its disappointment. By mid-February she was in Monte Carlo for an auspicious debut, fully clothed, in Jules Massenet's opera *Le Roi de Lahore*. She shared the stage in act III with a Paris Opera ballerina, Carlotta Zambelli, and American soprano Geraldine Farrar, lending legitimacy to her pretensions as a serious artist. She survived the test with grace, receiving admiring notes from both Giacomo Puccini and Massenet himself. She quickly added the sixty-four-year-old French composer to her growing list of illustrious lovers. Despite her acclaim in one of Europe's most prestigious opera houses, Mata Hari was not snobbish about her source of attention, and she was to be seen shortly thereafter at the annual Nice carnival, posing in a state of undress as Venus.

Her husband used this exhibitionism, in the form of nude photos of his estranged wife, to force a divorce. Margaretha made it clear that legal separation was enough for her. She had her dancing and her lovers and didn't want the extra stigma allocated to a divorced woman. But when Macleod produced the photos as blackmail, she acquiesced, and the warring couple was granted a divorce after four years of separation. Margaretha's adultery was the grounds; Macleod's abuse remained unmentioned.

Adam Zelle had his own opportunistic designs on his now-famous daughter, and within months published a book with a turgid title. *The Life of Mata Hari: The Biography of My Daughter and My Grievances Against Her Former Husband* was a self-serving fabrication about her close relations to dukes, kings, and sundry noblemen. When Macleod and his lawyer retaliated with an equally ridiculous pamphlet entitled "The Naked Truth About Mata Hari," the public quickly lost interest in the whole debate. No one, not even the Dutch, were interested in the "truth" about Margaretha Macleod's past; they just wanted to see her, and the more of her the better. Her flesh was the only truth that mattered.

Mata Hari traveled to Berlin for her next engagement, but, after acquiring the wealthy landowner Herr Alfred Kiepert, a lieutenant in the German army, as a lover, proceeded to cancel her appearances. Not wishing his mistress to perform in the same city in which he conducted his business, Kiepert installed Mata Hari in an apartment and visited her when he was not living with his beautiful Hungarian wife on his estate outside Berlin. Margaretha had had quite a year since her debut in Paris and welcomed six months as a kept woman to recharge herself and learn

German. Later, at her trial, her time in Berlin supported by a man in the German military and her attendance at the Imperial Army maneuvers were viewed as evidence of her German sympathies. They were, in fact, evidence only of her sympathy for any man with a bank account.

Rested and rejuvenated, she parted ways with Kiepert and traveled south for her debut in Vienna in December 1906. She was to share the city with both Isadora Duncan and Maud Allan, and she triumphed. She danced at Secession Art Hall without the body stocking and at the Apollo Theater with it, setting off great discussion and deliberation in the city of Freud among intellectuals on the fascinating subject of nudity — to be or not to be. The "war of the tights" generated much press for Mata Hari, to which she added her own sly assessment. "In my dancing one forgets the woman in me," she told the correspondent for the *Deutsches Volksblatt*. "I offer everything and finally myself to the god — which is symbolized by the slow loosening of my loincloth, the last piece of clothing I have on, and stand there . . . entirely naked." While her reviews were mixed, the *Neues Wiener Journal* had the final word. "Isadora Duncan is dead, long live Mata Hari!"[22]

When she learned that Strauss's controversial production of *Salome* was to have its Paris premiere in May 1907, Mata Hari pounced on the part. "I would like to create 'The Dance,'" she wrote to Astruc, "and above all I would like to dance it in Paris, where I am well known and only I will be able to interpret the real thoughts of Salome."[23] She asked her agent to forward the letter to Strauss, but Astruc did not oblige and, to her lasting resentment, the "Dance of the Seven Veils" was performed by a dancer from the Paris Opera.

There were other signs that her celebrity was uninsured. Back in Paris she discovered that every stage of every music hall now featured a Mata Hari imitator, and it became apparent that many young French women could evoke Eastern mysticism as seductively and inaccurately as their model. This trespassing on her territory left Mata Hari in the bizarre position of defending her own inauthenticity against that of other impostors. "There are real precious stones," she claimed, "and there are also imitation ones."[24]

While Salome remained for the moment out of reach, Mata Hari was hired to play Cleopatra by director André Antoine in a play entitled *Antar*, to premiere in Monte Carlo in January 1910. Despite the success of the production, Antoine did not appreciate Mata Hari's prima donna attitude — in addition to her predictable lateness, she was offended at being asked to rehearse in front of another dancer — and he hired someone else for the Paris run. Unconvinced by her exotic guise, Antoine later claimed that Mata Hari "was just a big, decorative savage."[25]

The thinness of her material and abilities was becoming evident; her talent could not support the attitude her pride dictated. She retreated. Her latest lover, Félix Rousseau, a married Parisian banker, set her up in style at the Château de la Dorée in Esvres, southwest of Paris, where she lived a quiet and private life for a year and a half, riding horses and awaiting her lover's weekend visits. By 1911, after she became tired of the slow country life, Rousseau set her up in a lovely house with a garden in a chic suburb of Paris, Neuilly-sur-Seine, where Isadora Duncan also had a studio. She rode in the Bois de Boulogne in her horse-drawn carriage and hired the authentic Indian musician Inayat Khan — who went on to found Britain's first Sufi order — to play for her private garden dances, which were featured in a series of photographs in *Vogue*. It was in Neuilly that Misia Sert, the great hostess and patron of Diaghilev, first met Mata Hari. She was not impressed: "At last, dressed in three triangles of jewel paste, the expected wonder appeared. . . . Alas! . . . she was a trite nightclub dancer, whose art consisted in showing her body. . . . The whole thing was grim, miserable and rather nauseating."[26]

Behind Mata Hari's brave public face, there was trouble. Rousseau had gone bankrupt in the service of his mistress, and with engagements few and far between, Mata Hari soon resorted to outright prostitution. She frequented hotel lobbies and the "maisons de rendez-vous" on the streets just around the corner from the Musée Guimet, the site of her fabulous debut only six years earlier.

Just when things were grimmest and her debts were mounting beyond all hope, Astruc managed to arrange an appearance at La Scala, one of the leading opera houses in all of Europe. In a performance conducted by the young Tullio Serafin, Mata Hari played Venus in the ballet *Bacchus and Gambrinus* as well as making a cameo appearance in act V of Gluck's opera *Armide*. The prestige of La Scala temporarily revived her spirits, and she proceeded to Rome to perform the role once denied her, Salome. In a private performance at the Palazzo Barberini, the palace of Prince di San Faustino, she used the Strauss music for the "Dance of the Seven

Veils" and in the intimacy of the setting chose to get very naked. The prince was so pleased with the display that he commissioned a painting of Mata Hari as a topless and laughing Salome.

If she could dance at La Scala, Mata Hari reasoned, then she could dance for Diaghilev. In 1909 Diaghilev's Ballets Russes had come to Paris and changed the face of both dance and fashion with its fabulous Oriental ballet *Cléopâtre,* followed in 1910 by *Schéhérezade.* Dance had never looked like this before, with gorgeous, superbly trained dancers like Anna Pavlova and Vaslav Nijinsky, designs by such artists as Georges Braque and Pablo Picasso, choreography by Michel Fokine, and music by Claude Debussy and the young Igor Stravinsky. The Ballets Russes set a new standard in theatrical production, and Paris was in love. Mata Hari, in her insatiable ambition — and naïveté — wanted to join the ranks.

Astruc, being Diaghilev's European agent, arranged for a contract to be drawn up, and Mata Hari quickly announced to all who would listen that she was to be Diaghilev's newest star. But the impresario wanted to examine his new dancer. Traveling to Monte Carlo, Mata Hari was snubbed when the great man failed to appear at the appointed time and it was left to the designer Léon Bakst to view, literally, the potential employee. "I undressed *completely* before Bakst in my room," she claimed in outrage to Astruc, and that was the full extent of her affiliation with the Ballets Russes.[27] Humiliated, she returned to Paris, to dance, fully clothed, in a Spanish number at the Folies Bergère in June 1913.

The following year saw only mounting debts and fewer lovers: Paris had already had its fill of Mata Hari. By May 1914 she decided to make a fresh start in another city where she had never danced. She closed her house in Neuilly, sold her beloved horses, and signed a contract to appear at the Metropole Theater in Berlin starting in September. She would conquer the German public with a new dance that depicted, in a bow to Salome, the dream of a young priest whose celibacy is threatened by the vision of a goddess. This was to be called "Chimère ou Vision Profane," but this profane vision was to remain a chimera in Mata Hari's imagination. She moved to Berlin, and on 4 August, when she attempted to retrieve her furs from safe keeping in the wardrobe of the Metropole, she was stunned when told that they had been confiscated.

Two days later she wrote in her scrapbook, "War — left Berlin — theatre closed."[28] Her greatest act was about to begin.

Chapter Ten

The Scapegoat

O NLY three short years after this abrupt departure from Berlin, Mata Hari, convicted of espionage against France, was to be found on death row in cell 12 of the notorious Paris prison of Saint-Lazare. Guarded against suicide by Sister Marie and Sister Léonide, Mata Hari spent her last days dressed in filthy prison frocks, furiously writing letters of appeal to the various officials who had condemned her and those who might save her. Like any self-respecting lady she also arranged with her maid, Anna Lintjens, for payment of her debts to her couturier. She hoped, to the very end, that one day she would again be fitted for a gown.

How did Mata Hari end up in a rat-infested prison, scribbling pathetic letters in the attempt to save her own neck when exotic dancing, divorce, and relentless ambition were her only crimes?

After hustling out of Berlin with some difficulty owing to the lack of newly required identification papers, Mata Hari arrived in Amsterdam without her furs, jewels, or luggage. Holland, like Belgium, which had been invaded by the Germans in the first days of the war, was in a strategically vulnerable position and maintained a strict policy of neutrality to avoid the Belgian fate. Checking into the elegant Victoria Hotel, Mata Hari, as was her habit, soon found a kindly Dutchman to pay the bill. This was the first time she had lived in Holland since leaving as the estranged wife of Rudolph Macleod ten years earlier.

Within a few months she had acquired a more lasting protector in the form of moody, autocratic Baron Edouard van der Capellen, a fifty-two-year-old colonel in the Dutch cavalry. He had, ironically, the rank that her husband had so coveted and the aristocratic roots that her father had aspired to. The baron set her up in a comfortable house in The Hague within one month of their meeting and paid all her expenses. While in attendance he was a demanding lover, but he was frequently away on duty, leaving Mata Hari plenty of time for herself. She tried one last time to see her daughter, who was now sixteen years old, but again Macleod, several times remarried, prevented it. She never saw Non again.

Mata Hari arranged her Dutch debut on 14 December 1914 in a ballet entitled *Les Folies Françaises* at the Royal Theatre in The Hague. The theater was packed, and four days later she danced again at Arnhem, in what was to be her last stage performance. She was fully clothed on both occasions.

By December of the following year she had grown impatient with the quiet Dutch life and longed for the gaiety of Paris. With the intention of retrieving her belongings from storage in her house in Neuilly, she set off by sea. But she had not been in Paris for two years and, much to Mata Hari's inconvenience, Europe was at war and border crossings were risky affairs. Her ship was stopped at Folkestone on the English Channel on 3 December for inspection, and, unknown to her, Mata Hari's troubles began.

The British immigration officer took down the particulars of her life, mixing up dates and people along the way, and compiled his findings in a file marked "Secret." He added to his uncertain facts these statements: "Handsome, bold type of woman. Well and fashionably dressed in brown costume with racoon fur trimming and hat to match. . . . She appeared most unsatisfactory and should be refused permission to return to the U.K."[29] The chain of suspicion and paranoia about Mata Hari had begun with the unsubstantiated intuition of a single British immigration officer under pressure to protect his country from foreign infiltration. Copies of this file were sent to nine official British offices as well as Scotland Yard.

The French were in an equally vigilant mood. When Mata Hari finally arrived in Paris, a private group calling itself La Ligue pour la Guerre d'Appui (League in Support of the War), started by Léon Daudet, also made a memo — "To Be Watched" — about this divorced foreign woman with a grand manner and expensive clothes. Mata Hari had not learned that during a war involving much death, hunger, and suffering a certain dignified discretion in her appearance might have been more appropriate. But she had made a career out of her desire to be inappropriate, and it was too late now for revisions. Unaware of either the British or French memos about her, Mata Hari went about her business, which included the usual array of lovers. Her every move was watched by the Ligue, and as the men in uniform came and went from her suite at the Grand Hotel, suspicions grew. Her shameless audacity, so applauded during the Belle Epoque, was now a liability. After yet another failed attempt to be hired by Diaghilev, Mata Hari returned without incident to The Hague and Baron Capellen. She had been gone for one month.

Growing bored yet again with a life involving no performances and only one very absent lover, Mata Hari was intrigued when she met Karl Cramer, the German consul in Amsterdam and a member of the German intelligence service. When Cramer paid her an unannounced visit late one evening in May 1916, she thought, understandably, that love was on his mind. But he had a different agenda. He offered her twenty thousand francs to, in her summation, "undertake some small commissions in Paris that would be much appreciated by the people of Germany."[30] Flattered that her international reputation was still intact, and enticed by both the money and the prospect of another visit to Paris, Mata Hari agreed to the mission. In addition to the money, Cramer gave her three bottles of invisible ink to use for conveying her findings.

This offer to be a low-level informer was one made to many civilians during wartime. Contrary to legend, the Germans did not ask Mata Hari to use her sexuality to seduce the enemy, only to keep her eyes and ears open. This was the first real contact Mata Hari had with the prospect of spying, despite the already rampant British and French suspicions of her. Accepting the money from Cramer was her first bad move — particularly as she had no intention of doing any spying for Germany. In her mind the twenty thousand francs were compensation for her furs confiscated in Berlin at the start of the war. As she parted on the *Zeelandia* for Paris a few weeks later, she celebrated her underhand machination by pouring the invisible ink into the ocean. Having lived for so long in her own fantasies, she was ill-equipped to adjust to the serious realities of war. She was no longer deceiving a jealous lover; she was deceiving German intelligence.

When she applied for a new passport for this trip to Paris, the British refused to grant her a visa. On 22 February 1916 they had issued to all their ports and permit offices yet another memo of warning about the Dutch dancer. "This woman is now in Holland," it read. "If she comes to this country she should be arrested and sent to Scotland Yard."[31] She was now also under surveillance by Dutch agents in The Hague. Oblivious to all danger, she proceeded with her travel plans.

Because of the German occupation of Belgium, the route to France from Holland was complex. Traveling by sea via an English Channel port to Vigo in northern Spain, she then took a train, via Madrid, to the Spanish-French border at Hendaye and finally to Paris. During the ocean voyage, Henry Hoedemaker, an inefficient Dutch agent, had ransacked her cabin, resulting in an on-deck confrontation in which Mata Hari slapped him "so violently," she later told interrogators proudly, "that blood spurted from his mouth. The other passengers cheered my action."[32]

At Hendaye, Hoedemaker raised doubts to French immigration and she was temporarily refused entry into France. Enraged, she threatened to enlist the aid of her friend and former lover Jules Cambon, now the secretary general of the French Ministry for Foreign Affairs. The immigration officer relented and she was allowed to proceed to Paris. Not only was Mata Hari still unaware of the danger surrounding her, but her forthright actions in this episode indicate that she was acting with a clear conscience and not as a German agent.

She checked into the Grand Hotel on 16 June and within two days she was under twenty-four-hour surveillance by two officers from the Deuxième Bureau, the French intelligence center. They followed her to couturiers, fortunetellers, and restaurants and noted that between 12 July and 31 August no less than eleven different lovers visited her. All military men, they hailed from France, England, Ireland, Scotland, Italy, and Russia — Mata Hari liked uniforms of any nationality. "I like to compare nations," she explained, like any woman interested in her own profession.[33] "Ever since my childhood," she later confessed to interrogators at her trial, "nothing seemed more seductive to me than an officer. . . . I love men whose profession is dying. They have other needs than those who vegetate until they reach the grave. I am a woman who gets paid for her favors, but I have never hesitated between a rich banker and a poor officer. It was the latter I always chose. Always. My greatest pleasure was to sleep with them."[34]

While Mata Hari's favors could be viewed as her own form of offering solace during the war, to the Deuxième Bureau her activities proved not only her highly immoral nature but her indiscriminate allegiance: the actions of a German spy. She was already on trial.

Her next mistake, the fatal one, was to fall in love for the first time in her life — it would prove her undoing. The vulnerability that accompanies love dictated a loss of rational perspective that proved her greatest liability and led her to her death. Vadime de Masloff, a Russian officer in the First Russian Special Imperial Regiment, was twenty-one years old, almost the age her dead son would have been — and he was a blue-eyed beauty. Mata Hari was almost forty and fell for this young man quickly and deeply. He was the only lover she ever admitted to loving, and when she was arrested she was carrying a photo of Vadime inscribed, "Vittel 1916, In memory of the most beautiful days of my life, spent with my Vadime whom I love above everything."[35]

Vadime was wounded in the face, blinded in one eye by poison gas, shortly after meeting Mata Hari, and she was determined to visit him in hospital at Vittel. Being in the Zone des Armées, she needed a special permit and thus was directed straight into the hands of her nemesis. Captain Georges Ladoux had been appointed to head the Deuxième Bureau by General Joffre in 1915. Described by Mata Hari as "a fat man with a very black beard and very black hair and spectacles,"[36] Ladoux had been awaiting their meeting, having already amassed a sizable file on her activities. Since receiving the British warnings in December 1915, he had decided that she was a German spy and was simply waiting to gather enough evidence to capture her. After the shame of the Dreyfus affair, French intelligence was under pressure to rectify its sullied reputation and the capture of a German spy would be just such a move. It was all the more ironic that with Mata Hari they would again, as with Captain Alfred Dreyfus, be framing an innocent person as a scapegoat.

Mata Hari was now before Ladoux requesting a permit for Vittel, further evidence to him of her enemy complicity, as the town was near an airfield being used to bomb German factories. Ladoux played his trump card. He asked if she would be willing to spy for France. This was her second such offer, this time from the Allies, and her self-importance was again engaged. Now in love and with a desire for the financial freedom to give up her professions — both of them — she considered a third and stated that she would require the astonishing sum of one million francs. Ladoux hesitated at the amount but said he would give it full consideration, and gave her the permit for Vittel.

After two weeks visiting her beloved Vadime and accepting his proposal of marriage, she returned to Ladoux's office in Paris in mid-September and agreed to spy for France. Her plan, ambitious as usual, was to seduce General Moritz von Bissing, who commanded the German occupation of Belgium, and to reseduce none other than her old lover, the German crown prince. Ladoux said she must prove herself before receiving any money, any ink, or even a code name and instructed her to return home to Holland and await further orders. He was now "convinced,"[37] he wrote at this time, that she worked for the Germans.

Following Ladoux's orders, Mata Hari departed France on the *Hollandia* on 5 November en route to Holland. The ship was diverted to Falmouth for inspection, and, after suffragettes volunteered to search her cabin, she was promptly arrested. But, just to confuse matters, she was not even accused of being herself, but of being another German spy called Clara Benedix. Taken to London for interrogation, she was interviewed by Sir Basil Thomson, the Assistant Police Commissioner in charge of counterespionage for Scotland Yard. Her true identity was finally established by officers in Spain familiar with Benedix, but the British nevertheless maintained against her "a grave suspicion of un-neutral acts."[38]

Desperate to prove her innocence, Mata Hari confessed to Thomson that she was, in fact, a spy, but for France, working for Captain Georges Ladoux. He was quite surprised to hear this, as it was his office that had originally warned Ladoux of her possible German allegiance. He cabled Ladoux to clarify the situation and Ladoux, embarrassed that he had indeed engaged Mata Hari as a French agent, evaded the truth and replied, "Understand nothing. Send Mata Hari back to Spain."[39] Mata Hari had now made Ladoux a fool in front of British intelligence, and his resolve against this woman became a personal vendetta.

Thomson released Mata Hari with a warning and sent her on to Spain as Ladoux had suggested. Finally, she now knew that she was suspected of being a German spy. Rather than withdrawing from the whole espionage game while she still could, she became more determined than ever to win her million francs and prove her Allied sympathies.

Arriving in Madrid in early December, she checked into the Palace Hotel. Not bothering to wait for instructions from Ladoux, she made yet another disastrous move by taking matters into her own hands, something a trained spy would never do. She located the name Arnold Kalle, military attaché to the German Embassy in Madrid, in the diplomatic register and sent him a note. Kalle agreed to an appointment, perhaps curious to meet the famous courtesan. They met several times, had sex in his office, and he paid for her services. Mata Hari extracted some old and insignificant information from him about submarine fuelings at Spanish ports and the planned infiltration of Morocco by German and Turkish officers. Mata Hari was proud of her spy work and was sure it would prove to Ladoux her French allegiance. Mata Hari delivered her information to the French Embassy for transmission to Ladoux. Her million francs was now within reach.

Mata Hari's naïveté in thinking that spying was such a simple profession, with such easy access to vital information, says much about her ignorance of the gravity of war and her unshakable faith in the powers of her own sexual allure. This was, after all, the power that had given her a sumptuous life for ten years. In reality, Kalle was manipulating her, and on 13 December sent off the first H-21 intoxication cable to Berlin, feeding the French with the information that would convict her as a German spy. The Germans, like Ladoux, had a vendetta against Mata Hari. She had accepted the twenty thousand francs from Karl Cramer six months earlier and had done nothing for the money but agree to spy for France, their enemy. As with Ladoux, she had rendered them fools. While she thought she was in control of events, she had, in truth, become the victim of humiliated men who had no mercy, least of all for a courtesan's life.

Indignant at Ladoux's silence about her findings, she decided to confront him directly. This impulsive move led her back to Paris, the city of her greatest triumph, and, now, her greatest enemy. She arrived in early January and checked into the elegant Plaza Athénée Hotel, but while the surveillance on her continued as before, Ladoux studiously avoided her. On 13 January she had an emotional reunion with Vadime, the same day Ladoux ceased the surveillance, having learned that the German cables about Mata Hari contained false information. But Ladoux wanted to capture her, and lack of evidence would not deter him.

At the end of January, low on funds, Mata Hari moved to the more modest Elysée-Palace Hotel, and two weeks later Ladoux ordered her arrest. "The woman Zelle, Marguerite, known as Mata Hari," read the statement, "living at the Palace Hotel, of Protestant religion, foreigner, born in Holland on August 7, 1876, one metre 75 centimeters tall [five feet ten], being able to read and write, is accused of espionage, complicity and intelligence with the enemy, in an effort to assist them in their operations."[40] She was taken directly to prison.

Police Chief Priolet, the arresting officer, examined the accused spy's toiletry bag for evidence and reported his findings. "Five face powders, three pomades, a bar of soap, a stick of lip-rouge, a stick of mascara, two brushes for applying these products, seven liquids (perfumes and toilet waters), a small bottle of benzine and six therapeutic products."[41] These were indeed the weapons of a horizontal agent — or any woman. Two of the bottles were sent to a lab to be tested as invisible ink.

Mata Hari was taken immediately to her first interrogation by Captain Pierre Bouchardon, the Chief Investigating Officer of the Military Tribunal. A small man in his mid-forties with a large sweeping mustache that hid a bitterness about his mouth, Bouchardon had failed at his first two professions. His inability at math had prevented his dream of being a doctor, and his terror of horses had prevented his being a commander in the army. Now he was reduced to the desk job of examining magistrate for the military courts. Like Ladoux, he had something to prove in the area of his manhood, and what better foil than a courtesan and exotic dancer suspected of espionage? He recorded his impressions of Mata Hari at their first meeting.

> I saw a large, thick lipped woman with skin like leather and false pearl earrings. Was she, had she ever been beautiful? . . . The woman brought to me that day had suffered badly from the ravages of time. Eyes as large as eggs, bulging, tinged with yellow and threaded with livid red veins, flattened nose, huge mouth reaching almost to her ears, teeth like tombstones, hair greying at the temples where the dye had worn off . . . she still moved with something of the grace of a tiger in the jungle.[42]

This brutal description of Mata Hari was a portent of the misogyny, bestial references, and racism that would conveniently convert the beautiful seductress into the demon spy.

Life in Saint-Lazare, also known as "The Slaughterhouse," was rough. As prisoner #721–44625 Mata Hari was first incarcerated in a damp, padded cell in case of suicide, but within a few days she was moved to the Ménagerie, another prison on the rue du Faubourg St. Denis. Kept in complete isolation, she had little or no exercise, paid for her own two meager meals a day, had no heat during an especially cold winter, encountered the occasional rat, and was allowed no visitors. This once glamorous courtesan endured the ultimate humiliation of living in filth. She would never sleep outside prison walls again.

"You have made me suffer too much," she wrote to Bouchardon after several weeks in prison. "I am completely mad. I beg of you, put an end to this."[43] Despite these hardships, the prison doctor, Léon Bizard, recorded that Mata Hari was a well-behaved inmate.

Her letters to her maid in Holland, as well as to the Dutch legation, for help were all opened, read, and put in her file unsent — there are twenty-one undelivered letters in her trial dossier. Even her faithful lawyer, Maître Clunet, was forbidden access to his client, writing to Bouchardon twice a week for four months requesting to see her. Each letter elicited a chilly "No." No one even knew that she was in prison, including her lover. Despite warnings against his mistress, Vadime initially remained faithful, writing several notes to her addressed to the Elysée-Palace Hotel, the first arriving the day of her arrest, the second two days later.

> Querida Marguerita, you can't believe how awful this hospital is. I only wish I had you beside me so I could murmur words of love into your ear. Alas the distance between us allows me only to dream of this. I see you in my dreams and sometimes it is so strong I forget it is only a dream. I love you. Your photograph which I hold to my heart, is a constant consolation. I send you my love and long to cover your wonderful body with crazy kisses. Your Vadime.[44]

Mata Hari never saw the note. It was merely added to the ever-growing file Bouchardon was building. He decided very quickly that Mata Hari's treason was "an open and shut case,"[45] but still he had to find some evidence to present at trial. During his endless hours with her during fourteen interrogations, her every word was recorded while Bouchardon waited patiently for the truth to emerge.

Mata Hari defended herself with a clarity and impressive rationale. Despite her own confusion about dates, certain events, and the fantasies of her exotic origins, her story as she told it was consistent and logical. But this was only, to Bouchardon, further evidence of her cunning spy's mind. He saw her numerous German lovers, many of them in the military or police force, as well as her visits to Berlin, as damning. "Maintaining such contacts with the enemy," he reasoned conveniently, "is equivalent to the actual transmitting of information."[46] Several money orders from Baron Capellen in Holland were construed as payments from the Germans for her work, as were the thirty-five hundred pesetas from Kalle. Every consummation with a Frenchman was viewed as an opportunity for pillow talk that could betray France. Her visit to Vadime in Vittel rendered her responsible, in part, for the nearby battle of Verdun, where 350,000 French soldiers lost their lives. An "open and shut" case.

Bouchardon saw her motives clearly. "She spoke of her divorce," he wrote, "and I had the impression that the suffering she had endured at the hands of her husband left her with a burning desire to avenge herself on all men." He expanded on his theory of the dangerous seductress: "She was a born spy. She had all the qualifications. Feline, supple and deceitful, accustomed to amusing herself at the expense of anyone and everyone, without scruples, attracting men with her body, devouring their fortunes, and then breaking their hearts."[47]

The prisoner's own version of her motives was regarded as a simplistic ploy. "I have it all worked out," she told Bouchardon of her grand plan. "I am going to ask Ladoux for enough money so as to not have to deceive Vadime with other men. . . . Captain Ladoux is going to pay me, I'll marry my lover and I'll be the happiest woman in the world." Now that Mata Hari, for once in her life, was telling the truth, it appeared ridiculous. She continued her pleas, writing to Bouchardon daily from her prison cell. "I am not coward enough to invent names under the threat of death,"[48] she declared with considerable integrity in one note.

On 10 April the liquid tested for invisible ink proved a false alarm. Oxycyanide of mercury, a well-known disinfectant, was the suspicious potion and was, in fact, a form of birth control at the time, something with which a courtesan like Mata Hari had understandable concern. Bouchardon, despite his numerous theories, was running short on hard facts — until Ladoux presented him with the intoxication telegrams. Confronted with them, Mata Hari was baffled, and stumbled upon the truth herself. "Might it be possible that the Germans themselves threw French intelligence on a false track," she wrote to Bouchardon, "to permit some true woman agent to be left unbothered?"[49] But the truth was of little concern to Bouchardon or Ladoux. Mata Hari continued to plead: "With all my sincerity I swear that I haven't made the least attempt at espionage and I have always been sincere towards France. Captain Ladoux didn't understand me — he treated me like a complicated Parisienne but he was only dealing with a Hollander from the north, from Friesland where one deals with things in a straightforward manner without all these complicated detours. I repeat that I am not a traitor to France."[50]

It was too late in her notorious life of complicated detours to claim simplicity of action or motive. She had lied far too often to be believed now, and the declaration of her innocence appeared to be another subterfuge. Under the relentless pressure of prison and interrogation, she finally confessed on 21 May to her encounter in Holland with Cramer, his offer to spy for Germany, and the payment of twenty thousand francs. Now Bouchardon had his evidence, and the case went to trial in late July.

Moved to the Conciergerie beside the Palais de Justice, Mata Hari was now in the prison that had housed Marie Antoinette and Robespierre. She was allowed some of her own clothes for the trial, and on 19 July ankle-boots, pantaloons, corsets, blouses, and a tailored suit arrived at the prison. The trial took place in the Cour d'Assises, a spectacular wood-paneled courtroom with a gilded ceiling overseen by the image of balanced weights — a place of justice. Madame Henriette Caillaux, who shot her husband's enemy in cold blood, had been tried three years earlier in this very courtroom. Though guilty, she was acquitted as a respectable bourgeois woman whose hormonal fluctuations rendered her innocent. But for the woman, like Mata Hari, whose sexuality had roamed beyond the marital moat, such sympathies were abandoned and, though innocent, she was found guilty.

Attitudes toward both war and women following the Belle Epoque were the guiding factors in Mata Hari's trial and its outcome. The truth of the particular accusations as related to this particular woman was of little import with these much larger issues at stake, and this inconvenience was swiftly surmounted with a brief, behind-closed-doors trial.

At 1 P.M. on 24 July, Mata Hari, in a tricorne hat and low-cut blue blouse, took her seat before the seven judges of the military tribunal that would hear her case. "I only hope that I shall have the strength not to cry," she wrote. She did not. "From time to time she wielded mirror and lipstick," wrote one biographer of her courtroom weaponry.[51]

Initially open to the public, the courtroom both inside and out was packed with civilians and press eager to catch a glimpse of the courtesan who had betrayed France. It was, however, immediately agreed that the trial should be conducted "huis clos" — behind closed doors — "because the publicity might endanger the safety of the State."[52] Furthermore, any publication of the proceedings was forbidden, and the public and press were escorted out of the courtroom. Mata Hari was left alone with her accusers and her seventy-four-year-old lawyer who, despite his long and illustrious career, had never tried a criminal case, much less one involving espionage.

Lieutenant André Mornet, a brilliant and experienced lawyer, prosecuted with the aid of the six-inch-thick dossier compiled by Bouchardon. Determined as were Ladoux and Bouchardon to convict Mata Hari, the two-day trial was a sham, and as it was presented could produce only a conviction. Mornet pontificated at length, demonstrating various paranoias about women, uncontested suppositions about motives, and unsubstantiated judgments about character. Calling her "this sinister Salome who plays games with the heads of French soldiers," Mornet had only to say a fact was "known" for it to be assumed to be the truth.[53] Besides, she would be easy to convict, as a dancer and a courtesan. Mata Hari was already draped in guilt — any woman capable of sleeping with men for money must be equally heartless about shedding their blood, he reasoned.

> The Zelle lady appeared to us as one of those international women — the word is her own — who have become so dangerous since the hostilities. . . . Her aplomb, her remarkable intelligence, her immorality, congenital or acquired, all contributed to make her suspect.[54]

In summation he called her "a sort of Messalina, dragging a horde of admirers behind her chariot. . . . The evil that this woman has done is unbelievable." Another observer commented, "She was really German in form and in heart," echoing the evil Germanic association that would be made at Maud Allan's trial the following year.[55]

Because of the confidentiality of the trial, Clunet was not allowed to call any civilian witnesses for his client, and thus Anna Lintjens and Baron Capellen — both of whom could have told the court that the money she had received was from the baron, her lover, not from German intelligence — were not allowed to give evidence. They did not even know Mata Hari had been arrested, much less that she was on trial for her life. Ladoux and several of her French lovers in the military, married and not, were all mysteriously unable to attend the trial and give testimony. Reputations had to be protected. General Adolphe Messimy, a former lover who had been Minister of War, sent a note via his wife saying he did not even know the accused. Mata Hari laughed, "That's a good one! He hasn't known me! He's got some cheek!"[56]

The second and final day of the trial began at 8:30 A.M. with a written statement from Vadime. He denied his plan to marry her, claiming he went to Paris only to break off the affair. He also denied, as did a few other of her military lovers, that she ever extracted information from him. Upon hearing her beloved's denial of their union, Mata Hari bowed her head and murmured quietly, "I have nothing to say."[57] Only her old friend and lover Henri de Marguérie testified on her behalf, but to little avail. She took the stand herself as her own witness and answered all questions in a calm and dignified manner, but her credibility was long gone.

After thirty minutes of deliberation the military jury found Mata Hari guilty of espionage against France and sentenced her to die before a firing squad. She sat in silence. The European press reported that she had confessed.

Taken back to Saint-Lazare, she spent almost three months on death row. Conditions in the prison were miserable. "I need some air and exercise," she pleaded to her jailers. "This will not prevent them killing me if they absolutely want to, but it is useless to make me suffer, closed in the way I am."[58] Appeals of all sorts were lodged by both Mata Hari and Clunet to the Dutch government and French President Poincaré, but all came to nothing.

Given her months of isolation and decreasing hope, Mata Hari, at age forty, became self-reflective, perhaps for the first time. With no one left to impress, to dazzle, or to love, she took stock of herself, sending her personal confessions to her captors. These letters were added to her criminal file.

She admitted to selfishness and greed, and though inconsiderate, she denied ever being intentionally cruel. She longed all her life, she wrote, for the admiration and acceptance of those whose birth, money, or talent was above her own humble origins. She had so wanted to join their ranks and be one of them, only to discover that those she admired were no better than herself, even worse; they were willing to betray her. She was aware that her fate was the result of "half vengeance and half fatality of appearances," but she accepted it with considerable dignity.[59] "As for myself, I have been sincere. My love and my self-interest are guarantees

FIG. 15. Mata Hari in prison before her execution on 15 October 1917. Despite
impending death, she poses, poignantly, with her purse.
(Collection Harlingue-Viollet)

of that. Today, around me, everything is collapsing, everyone turns his
back, even he [Vadime] for whom I would have gone through fire. Never
would I have believed in so much human cowardice. Well, so be it. I am
alone. I will defend myself and if I must fall it will be with a smile of profound contempt."[60]

At 4 A.M. on Monday, 15 October, Mata Hari was awakened in her
cell by a group of men at the door. It was time. Sister Léonide, who had
spent thirty-seven years in the jail watching prisoners come and go, began weeping. "Don't be afraid, sister," Mata Hari consoled her. "I'll know

how to die."[61] She dressed quietly, asking Dr. Bizard if she could wear a corset. He consented; it would not stop the bullets. She put on her silk stockings, a pearl-gray dress, hat, and veil, and Pastor Jules Arboux baptized her with water from a prison mug. With a dark coat about her shoulders, she left her cell (fig. 15).

Maître Clunet attempted a last-minute stay of execution by declaring that Mata Hari was pregnant. There was a law that stated that a pregnant woman could not be executed until she gave birth. Since she had been in prison for eight months there was considerable surprise, and Clunet claimed, in his desperation, that he was the father, despite his seventy-four years. Mata Hari was equally surprised when asked if she was carrying a child, and denied it with a glance of gratitude to her lawyer. She was given ten minutes to write three short letters, to her daughter Non, to Vadime, and to Henri de Marguérie. They were not forwarded.

Refusing the grip of a guard, declaring she was neither thief nor criminal, she was ushered into a military car as a crowd looked on. Word had gotten out that the notorious spy would be executed on this day. The weather outside underscored the chilly scene: it was cold, thirty-five degrees, gray, and drizzling. After a long ride across Paris to the Château de Vincennes, she was led to a clearing in the polygon where a stake marked the spot. She walked with Sister Léonide to the pole and hugged her goodbye. She refused to be tied to the stake and she refused a blindfold. She looked straight ahead at the twelve soldiers from the Fourth Regiment of Zouaves, positioned in two rows of six.

The official order had been to have four privates, four corporals, and four sergeants shoot her, to give the various ranks the pleasure and experience of shooting a German spy. The commanding officer, however, was afraid of the less experienced men's reactions to shooting a woman and only sergeants were in the lineup. He raised his sword and shots rang out.

One officer fainted, but eleven other bullets hit their mark. Legend has it that she flung open her coat to reveal a nude body, causing many bullets to be diverted from their mark. But this was not true: the men in uniform, whom she had so loved, killed her. At 6:15 A.M. Mata Hari fell to her knees, then backward, face to the sky.

No one claimed her body. In a final, ironic exposition for the woman who had in life so loved to show her flesh, her corpse was delivered to a municipal hospital for dissection. This "sinister Salome" became a human anatomical Venus for young men with medicine in mind. Her blood, her heart, her bones, and her orifices were examined and analyzed, but the mystery of the seductress remained unrevealed. Mata Hari has no grave, but her incinerated ashes dispersed into legend.

Chapter Eleven

The Legendary Backlash

ATA Hari's usefulness to the war cause only increased with her execution. Her death was a victory for both French and German intelligence — the French had caught a German spy, and the Germans used her death as anti-French propaganda. Claiming her innocence, German intelligence called her "a Victim of War Madness" and, hypocritically, pounced upon her death as Allied hypocrisy. In 1930 an authorized German book on German spies during World War I stated that Mata Hari was "absolutely innocent. She was only a great paramour."[62] There was no reason in 1930 to lie. Thus Mata Hari, in yet another twist of fate, was declared innocent as a German spy, though her demise in the guise of a German spy was, in part, engineered by Germany.

And, of course, her death served the French not only in giving the appearance of efficiency in the war effort but in sending the Germans a powerful message. Like Winston Churchill's decision to let Coventry be bombed during World War II in order not to reveal to the Germans that their secret code had been broken, Mata Hari's death reinforced, erroneously, the belief that their current code had not been broken. The sacrifice of Mata Hari in this context carries a kind of horrible validity.

The three French officers responsible for Mata Hari's execution continued their careers of ethical mishaps and questionable loyalties. Captain Georges Ladoux was arrested for collaboration with the Germans a mere four days after Mata Hari's execution. He was dismissed from the Deuxième Bureau and kept under house arrest until the end of the war. His arrest caused no one to question his handling of Mata Hari's case. Both Pierre Bouchardon and André Mornet swore allegiance to Vichy during World

War II, extricating themselves in time to secure immunity. Both were soon involved in prosecuting Marshal Philippe Pétain on charges of collaboration with the Germans. "In the Mata Hari trial," admitted Mornet with little remorse years later, "there wasn't enough evidence to whip a cat."[63]

Mata Hari's life falls into alternating phases of reality, which she abhorred, and fantasy, which she adored. The losses and abuses of her childhood and marriage gave way to the achieved fantasy of the Oriental dancer and wealthy courtesan, only to succumb again to the bitter drama of a victim of war, the bullets giving birth to the ultimate fantasy as a mythological creature. The question of Mata Hari's innocence or guilt has been of little concern to history. Her posthumous life as the ultimate femme fatale spy has not only been more glamorous than her real life ever was but of far more use to the public's imagination. She represents the romance of the spy who uses silk stockings, furs, and invisible ink as her weapons. In death she achieved a fame far beyond her prosecutors, and far beyond the ten other women and three hundred men executed by the French for treason during the war. Just as Mornet announced at her trial, she has become "the greatest woman spy of the century," not because she was, but because the idea was too good to not make it so.[64]

The particulars of Mata Hari's life and death provided the skeletal structure upon which history — and Hollywood — could hang its fantasies. The voluminous dossier on her trial, the only source of the truth, was to be sealed for one hundred years after her execution, and under military law the seven judges involved in the trial were forbidden to ever speak of the events. This total concealment of the facts gave license to her biographers for the ensuing decades, to invent and embellish her tale without possibility of contradiction. The truth would not get in the way of a good story, and the story would be even better in being called the truth. Thus began a fifty-year campaign of fallacies.

The first full-scale biography of Mata Hari was published in 1930 by the British Major Thomas Coulson. Calling her "Delilah in the garments of Magdalene," Coulson gives her "periwinkle-blue eyes, the eyes that were physically beautiful but morally terrible," and calls her bosom "pendulous and ugly." He has Mata Hari strangling the man who poisoned her son, attending a spy academy in Bavaria, and reclining in the nude upon her arrest. He also revealed that she had inherited her "amber-

tinted body . . . not from her Hindu parents, but from Jewish progeni-
tors."[65] Like Salome, the evil woman must have been Jewish, and the
ugly head of anti-Semitism arose in Mata Hari's story, just as it was doing
all over Europe in the years preceding World War II.

In early 1932 Metro-Goldwyn-Mayer produced *Mata Hari,* starring
Greta Garbo as the exotic, chain-smoking spy who manipulates her powerful lovers, one of them a crotchety Lionel Barrymore, to aid her cause
until handsome Ramon Novarro enters as a humble Russian fighter pilot.
She loses her heart to him just in time to be led, repentant, to her execution. Draped in turbans and shimmering gold lamé tunics, Garbo's
dancer is portrayed as guilty of espionage but redeemed by love. Thus
Mata Hari was given her largest audience yet in the aloof and glamorous,
though erroneous, image of Greta Garbo. A year earlier Paramount had
produced Marlene Dietrich as a seductive Austrian spy in the Mata Hari
mold in Joseph von Sternberg's *Dishonored.* "You bring something into
war that doesn't belong in it," observes a soldier. "You trick men into
death with your body." With Garbo and Dietrich, Mata Hari's posthumous career as a Hollywood screen goddess was well under way.

By 1951 Kurt Singer updated her resumé by finding her to be a com-
munist, the "Red Dancer of the Hundred Veils," who enlisted her daughter as a double agent for the Japanese and Indonesian underground.
Mata Hari's real daughter Non had died in 1919 of a cerebral hem-
morhage at the age of twenty-one. A few years later Bernard Newman
connected Mata Hari and Maud Allan, the two Salomes of World War I,
as virtual coauthors of the "Black Book of 47,000," the document that revealed the degenerate behaviors of Allies who were subject to German
blackmail. He claims that Mata Hari's "entries were the most important."[66]

Other biographers blamed Mata Hari for various World War I dis-
asters — the success of Ludendorff's submarine campaign against Allied
shipping, the battle of Verdun in which 350,000 Frenchmen died, and, in
general, for the devastating problem of mutiny in the French army. As
late as 1966 Charles Wighton stated that she was "almost certainly" a German agent, as well as a nymphomaniac and a whore who deserved the
beatings her husband gave her.[67]

The first rumblings of the truth about Mata Hari began to emerge in
1964 with the publication of a book by Sam Waagenaar entitled *The Murder of Mata Hari.* Her innocence was not, however, confirmed until the

sealed dossier was opened for author Russell Warren Howe in 1985. Almost seventy years after her death, his findings brought little interest.[68] Just like her sister, Salome, Mata Hari's incarnation as an evil sexual predator has remained a more seductive and entrenched idea than the revelation that she was framed by French, German, and British intelligence.

Innocent as she was of espionage, Mata Hari was, however, guilty of the self-importance that had initially made her a noticed woman — and a condemned one. At every turn she might have saved herself, but she was acting consistently with the same traits that had previously given her a life when she had none, and given her the attention, money, lovers, and fame she wanted more than anything in the world. "Little things never interested me," she had claimed. "When I conceive great things, I go right at them."[69] But she could not have imagined how great would be her immortality. In death the real woman was quickly forgotten, and Mata Hari became the object of mythical projections. The romantic link between espionage and sexuality was confirmed by her example.

After a long reign it was time for the nineteenth-century femme fatale to die, and Mata Hari received the harshest punishment of all Salomes. Venus in Furs was dead; Mistress Wanda was whipped to death with her own cane. In executing Mata Hari the culture was disposing of the Belle Epoque courtesan, the seductress of Wilde, Moreau, and Flaubert, the woman who threatened patriarchy with her overt sexuality. Mata Hari was the scapegoat, an unmarried woman who danced naked, acted independently of a man's approval, took lovers of all and any nationality, and was a citizen of a neutral country that didn't want the trouble of defending her. Ladoux, Bouchardon, and Mornet performed the dirty deed and no one protested. There was too much to gain by capturing and executing a German spy. Mata Hari was perfect.

World War I saw the death of Salome, and in her spy incarnation as Mata Hari she was held responsible not just for one man's death but for thousands. Her execution marked the backlash of all those years of pleasure and sensual indulgence. Everything Eastern, exotic, primitive, and sexual that had been so adored and encouraged during the fin-de-siècle could, with Mata Hari, be destroyed with eleven bullets in a single moment. The intoxication of her Eastern legacy turned to bestial terror. "Like her favorite reptile, the serpent," wrote Major Thomas Coulson, "the slime of her writhing body, coiled from one city to another, leaving its track of debauchery and treacherous betrayal."[70] All this vilification about a middle-class Dutch woman. Was it the savage that was being demonized, or was it the independent woman who dared to show herself naked and take lovers for money in an attempt to be master of her own fate?

During peacetime, the adoration of a powerful sexual woman gave rise to an enjoyable passivity and loss of sexual anxiety, but now that war was achieving this emasculation for the whole world to witness, the femme fatale had become a liability. It was no longer safe to admit to the pleasure of controlled domination, and her role quickly switched from treasured mistress to fatal enemy capable of inciting the ultimate horror — humiliation before other men.

It was fiction not fact that convicted Margaretha Zelle-Macleod. Never was a murder more symbolic or less personal. Herod's final edict at the end of Wilde's *Salome* — "Kill That Woman!" — became manifest in the murder of Mata Hari.

PART IV

Ida Rubinstein: The Phallic Female

She has only two idols, her art and her body.
—Gabriele D'Annunzio

□ □

Chapter Twelve
──────────

The Queen of the Nile

*T*HE year was 1909. A very distinguished member of the Salome sorority was about to make her Parisian stage debut. It was four years since Mata Hari had revealed her Javanese temple dancer at the Musée Guimet, and two since Maud Allan had performed her "Vision" at the Théâtre des Variétés. The vast Théâtre du Châtelet at the center of the Right Bank near the Seine was the site chosen for this particular unveiling. A sumptuous renovation revived this old theater to grand splendor with plush new seats, glimmering chandeliers, and an expanded orchestra pit. Diaghilev's Ballets Russes, with dancers from the Imperial Russian Ballet, was about to make its debut in the Western world. This was the season that first introduced such legends as Michel Fokine, Vaslav Nijinsky, Anna Pavlova, and Tamara Karsavina into dance history.

On the other side of the curtain, the audience for this much anticipated season comprised many of the great artists of the day, who mingled alongside nobility and bejeweled patrons of the fashionable and the beautiful while the aesthete Comte Robert de Montesquiou, the ultimate arbiter of good taste, surveyed the proceedings from behind his monocle. He found much to please his eye.

Late in the evening of 2 June the curtain was raised on *Cléopâtre*, the third ballet of the evening, and Diaghilev's final star was revealed to a public riveted to their velvet seats. Ida Rubinstein, an exotic, wealthy Russian Jew with hardly a ballet lesson to her name, was Cleopatra. Salome's seven veils were increased to twelve to denote her graduation from princess to queen of all Egypt (fig. 16).

FIG. 16. Ida Rubinstein in the title role of *Cléopâtre*, Paris, 1909

After a long, ritualized procession of musicians, fauns, and beautiful maidens, the prize was presented. Held aloft by six slaves, a gold and ebony chest was carried to the center of a temple, where its doors were unsealed to expose an immobile mummy swathed in silk. Four slaves proceeded to unwind the veils, one by one, each of a brilliant hue and sacred meaning. Jean Cocteau, a nineteen-year-old boy smitten with the "red-and-gold disease" of theatrical intoxication, wrote that "the unforgettable entrance of Mme. Rubinstein must be recorded for all time," and he did so.

The twelfth veil of deep blue released Madame Rubinstein, who let it fall herself with a sweeping circular gesture, and stood before us, perched unsteadily on her pattens, slightly bent forward with something of the movement of the Ibis's wings, and sick with waiting, for within her dark retreat she had felt, as we had, the effect of the sublimely enervating music of her retinue. On her head she wore a little blue wig with short golden braids on either side of her face, and so she stood, with vacant eyes, pallid cheeks, and open mouth, before the spell-bound audience, penetratingly beautiful, like the pungent perfume of some exotic essence.[1]

After this magnificent revelation the ballet recounts the tale of Amoun, danced by Michel Fokine. Despite his betrothal to Ta-hor, danced by Anna Pavlova, Amoun is mesmerized at the sight of Cleopatra. "I love you and offer my life in exchange for one night of love," he declares, and his fate is sealed as love and death become one. Two years after Strauss's *Salome* premiered in Paris, the Judean princess was reappearing as the queen of Egypt, with men now volunteering — instead of protesting as did John the Baptist — to surrender their very lives to her sexual allure.

Ida Rubinstein as Cleopatra was the apotheosis of the nineteenth-century femme fatale, a fantasy crystallized in the icy eroticism of Ida's languid ibis image. Never before had she been framed in such opulent grandeur nor undressed with such royal servitude. But she was not only the ultimate incarnation of Flaubert's Herodias, Moreau's Salome, and Wilde's perverse princess. As she perched on her pattens surveying the scene, she was a princess become a queen whose power far exceeded young Salome's. "Here was not a pretty artiste appearing in frank *deshabillé*," explained the Russian stage designer Alexandre Benois, "but a real, fatal enchantress, in the tradition of the cruel and grasping Astarte."[2] Not only could this queen request the death of any man she pleased; she could rule armies and change the course of history.

Ida's Cleopatra, with her great height, small breasts, slim boyish hips, and long legs, heralded the entrance into the twentieth century of the phallic female who towered over the feminized, magnetized male. She presented a startling modern image, an early metaphor for the athletic, demanding woman ruling her fearful, emasculated man.

As Diaghilev's Cleopatra, Salome had arrived barefoot in the land of the toe shoe. Ida's performance embodied the integration of the music hall Salome of Maud Allan and Mata Hari, and the improvisational sensibility of the new "modern dance" as presented by Loie Fuller, Ruth St. Denis, and Isadora Duncan, with ballet, the most classical of dance forms. For a ballet company with a centuries-old tradition, *Cléopâtre* presented a modern novelty — there were no tutus, no pointe shoes, more turn-in than turn-out, and bare midriffs glowing with body paint.

Most radically, the ballet, based on a story, *Une Nuit d'Egypte,* by Théophile Gautier, told a tale of unbridled sexuality. Cleopatra's harem from the Arabian Nights was a distant place indeed from the fairy-tale castle where Sleeping Beauty waited a hundred years for her Prince Charming. This was not the waiflike Giselle pleading to save the life of her lover, but a statuesque woman demanding the death of her lover. This was a ballet no longer about spiritualized romantic love; it was a fin de siècle version of sex, drugs, and rock 'n' roll.

Salome was infiltrating the shores of *Swan Lake,* the land where promises of eternal love dominate the aesthetic, with her own version of romance: the one-night stand. This infusion of veils into the world of tiaras represented the sexualizing of the virgin ballerina. The dusty sylph of the Romantic ballet was replaced by the queen of hedonism. This transition was illustrated within the ballet itself where Pavlova, the Dying Swan incarnate, danced the role of the faithful woman who loses her fiancé to Cleopatra's insatiable sexual appetite. The public was enthralled by this display, and, underscoring the point, Ida's success eclipsed even that of Pavlova.

As an untrained dancer performing with a ballet company, Ida Rubinstein personified the enlivening influence of modern dance on a classical tradition, which, prior to Diaghilev, had fallen into a period of decadence, repetition, and dullness. Ida carried the mantle of this extraordinary transition, bridging the gap not only between modern dance and classical ballet, but also between burlesque and ballet. Indeed, only six years earlier, F. Berkeley Smith, an American visiting in Paris, wrote this account of a sumptuous music hall number that had graced the very same stage of the Châtelet. The style, structure, and story are strikingly similar to *Cléopâtre's.*

> A veil midway down the vast stage lifts, disclosing an oriental city. A cortege of slaves advances. . . . Behind this barrier of grace and color, come the retinue of a barbaric court, gorgeously costumed, and headed by white Arabian horses, caparisoned in turquoise and gold. The favorite of the Sultan is borne past, reclining on a crimson velvet litter. . . . Upon the topmost pinnacle of this apotheosis of color stands a woman, nude, her hair glittering with jewels. . . . Such is the Châtelet.[3]

It was as if Diaghilev, in his eclectic genius, had borrowed liberally from this glitzy music hall number, condensed its script, replaced its pageantry with dancing, its French flourishes with Russian bravado, the showgirls with highly trained dancers, and produced the ultimate burlesque ballet squeezed into a brief and tumultuous twenty minutes. And at its center stood Ida in her jewels and pale blue hair, the ultimate showgirl, surveying the scene first from her sarcophagus and then from her satin divan with the ambiguous and proud demeanor of a mummified Mona Lisa. Paris adored *Cléopâtre,* and it was hailed as a revelation, the greatest theatrical event in twenty-five years. Ida, with her vacant eyes and pallid cheeks, became an overnight sensation.

Where had Diaghilev found his extraordinary Cleopatra? Not at the Imperial Ballet School executing pliés and tendus, but on the stage where she had performed the princess of Judea in the first Russian version of Oscar Wilde's *Salome.* This committed young woman had fought her family, the police, and even the Holy Synod of the Russian Orthodox Church in order to portray Salome because, as she stated unequivocally, "I so love her."[4]

Chapter Thirteen

The Russian Salome

THE young Lydiia Lvovna Rubinstein, who called herself Ida, was a romantic idealist, an appropriate response to her very privileged though sad start in life. She was born in the Ukrainian city of Kharkov on 21 September 1883 (old style),[5] though some sources list the year variously as 1885 or 1888. Her father, Lvov Rubinstein, was from an old Ashkinazim family that had amassed huge wealth from various commercial ventures and grain trade in the Ukraine. In marrying Ida's mother, Ernestine, he linked himself to yet another fortune that derived from international financial interests as well as the lucrative railway construction in nineteenth-century Russia.

At the age of five, shortly after the family had moved to St. Petersburg, Ida lost her mother, probably to a cholera epidemic, and within four years her father was also dead. Orphaned, Ida was sent with one of her sisters to live with Madame Horwitz, a cousin of their father's, in her magnificent house on the Angliskaya Boulevard overlooking the Neva River. Surrounded by numerous cousins, they grew up in an atmosphere saturated in artistic considerations.

St. Petersburg was, in the late nineteenth century prior to the Bolshevik Revolution, the cultural center of Russia, where art, poetry, music, ballet, and theater thrived. Madame Horwitz's home was filled with gatherings and concerts by the most esteemed artists of the time. Ida's education was impeccable in the European tradition — English, French, German, and Italian, Greek from a Hellenistic scholar, and Goethe and Nietzsche recited by heart. There were also lessons in the fine arts — painting, dancing, and dramatic gesture. Ida took her lessons seriously and began her lifelong identification with great dramatic heroines when she decided to present herself onstage as the protagonist in Sophocles' *Antigone*.

Ida began her preparations by arriving unannounced, governess in tow, at the studio of Lev Rosenberg, a thirty-eight-year-old artist whose theatrical commissions and artwork had been receiving considerable acclaim. Ida's choice of collaborator was propitious. As Léon Bakst, Rosenberg would become a cornerstone influence on Diaghilev's Ballets Russes, a renowned painter, and one of the visionary men who would help Ida shape her image.

Bakst was instantly attracted to the stunning young woman who stood in his doorway. With her thick dark hair, gray-green eyes, and aquiline nose, she looked like an Egyptian bas-relief come to life. Her tall, angular body with trailing limbs completed the image of an Eastern goddess. Surrounding this face and figure of exotic extremes was an enigmatic aura, a mysterious reserve. "This is a fabulous being. We are blessed to have her among us," Bakst said of her. "She I adore like a beautiful tulip, insolent and dazzling, proud of herself and shedding pride around her."[6]

Ida had just returned from Greece, bubbling with visions of the Acropolis, and wanted the artist to spare no expense in designing sets and costumes for an *Antigone* that would stun the world. Bakst convinced her to produce only one act and to present the piece privately. Under the stage name "L'vovskaia" Ida made her debut on 16 April 1904 in the long Greek robes of Bakst's voluminous imagination.[7]

Ida spent the following several years at the Moscow Theatre School, where she studied French, drama, diction, singing, makeup, mime, and even fencing. In 1905 she met Isadora Duncan, who had taken Russia by storm with her radical free-flowing improvisations, classical music, and Grecian robes. Duncan made a deep impression on young Ida, who soon declared, "All of me must be flexible: my voice, my face and plastique."[8]

By September 1906 she had transferred to the Drama Department of the St. Petersburg Theatre School where she performed in several Shakespeare plays. Ida was obsessed by the theater with the enthusiasm of an adolescent dreamer, although she was already twenty-three. Writing to a friend, she declared her intentions: "To absorb all feelings, all thoughts, to experience everything, then to come to people with a full heart and exalted mind, to be mad for truth, then to sing this truth and light the whole world with my song."[9] These early jottings reveal a passion that her life would sturdily bear out, though rarely again would she share herself so intimately on a page. "I love and believe in that theater of the future," she continued. "It will burn with a fire ever bright, so fearfully bright that it must kindle all the world."[10] Ida planned to be one of its brightest lights — although she was to choose for her next production a character of dark intentions.

Ida had discovered Oscar Wilde's *Salome* and immediately identified with this daughter of ancient iniquities like a long-lost sister. The subversive drama, the decadent sexuality, and the Dance of the Seven Veils appealed to the fantasies of this rich, young Jewish woman. She had to be the princess. There had been an astonishing six editions of Oscar Wilde's *Salome* published in Russia since 1904, but there had yet to be a stage rendition. Though state censorship was abolished in 1905, an attempt to mount the play in 1907 at the Moscow Art Theatre was blocked, as it was in England, on religious grounds: the Russian Orthodox Church forbade the representation of biblical figures on the stage.

One planned production, by Vera Komissarzhevskaya's private theater in St. Petersburg, attempted to skirt the censors by sanitizing the text and transposing the characters to a generic king, prophet, and dancing girl and retitling the whole affair *The King's Daughter*. Ida wrote to Komissarzhevskaya requesting the lead role, but was denied the part in favor of a more established actress. Undeterred, Ida, already the iconoclastic princess, simply decided to mount her own production. Remarkably for a young actress, she had the financial means to do so.

In her headstrong pursuit of Salome, Ida would be brought face to face not only with the censors and the Church, but also with her own extended family. One by one she overcame each, breaking all ties that prevented her from embodying her heroine.

In early 1908, with *Salome* tucked under her arm, Ida traveled to Paris to visit one of her sisters who had become a generous patron in elite artistic circles. But despite this appreciation, when Ida declared her intention to be an actress herself, the family was appalled. It was one thing to applaud artists, but to appear on a stage for all to see was an unseemly display tantamount to being a courtesan or prostitute. Severe measures were taken to prevent this family shame from going any further. Ida's brother-in-law, a well-respected doctor, diagnosed her as mentally unstable and she was shipped off to a clinic just outside of Paris.

Sent back to St. Petersburg at the request of her family there, Ida took prompt and decisive action to secure freedom from her family in order to pursue Salome: she married. Her terms to Vladimir Horwitz, a smitten and compliant cousin, were clear: it was to be a marriage in name only, no sex, and she would be left free to pursue her stage career. After setting up house in a lavish apartment on the Neva, Ida left Vladimir to his own devices and soon departed on a research trip to Palestine.

Crossing the Syrian desert to immerse herself in the landscape of her heroine, Ida was not planning to just act the role of Salome; she wanted to become her. With an elderly Russian as her chaperon, she traveled with servants and her hairdresser, who brushed out the knots in her windswept hair each evening. A Syrian prince, the story goes, became smitten with the gangly Russian girl and offered her chaperon caravans, several local women, and a gold watch in exchange for Ida.[11] But, as boss of her unusual entourage, Ida declined to sell herself into sexual slavery; she had other ideas for her future.

Back in St. Petersburg, she went to work with a vengeance, hiring a bevy of talent for her production: Alexander Glazunov, pupil of Rimsky-Korsakov, to compose the music; Bakst to design the sets and costumes; the young Fokine, who was just beginning to make his mark at the Imperial Ballet, to give her private dance lessons for the Dance of the Seven Veils; and Vsevolod Meyerhold, a leader of the new avant-garde theater and collaborator with Stanislavsky, to direct the whole thing. Thus did Ida initiate her lifelong pattern of amassing artists of the very highest caliber to collaborate on her productions — and though a combination of her personal presence and conviction attracted them, it was her money, in liberal doses, that glued it all together.

While Ida worked hard in her acting and voice lessons, her dance lessons with Fokine demanded most of her attention. It was highly unusual for a choreographer from the insular world of classical ballet to agree to take on a twenty-four-year-old neophyte who had no previous training — ballet lessons must begin in childhood while the body is still pliable enough to absorb a whole new language of movement. But Fokine, like Bakst, was transfixed by Ida's beauty and determination and agreed to teach her. Ida even followed Fokine and his wife to Switzerland during the summer of 1908 in order to continue her daily lessons. She was an amateur of inordinate stature in the making.

The rival Komissarzhevskaya's production was conveniently removed on 28 October when the Church banned the premiere. Within days, however, Ida's own premiere, booked for the Mikhailovsky Theatre on 3 November, was similarly banned. But Ida would not so easily be dismissed and, pulling some strings among her influential friends, was granted permission to perform the play in mime. The censors assumed that without Wilde's text, the production would be effectively silenced. Ida had another idea. Rescheduling the performance for the Grand Hall at the St. Petersburg Conservatory on 20 December, Ida simply had the text quietly distributed to the invited audience several days beforehand. But the authorities continued to watch her, and John the Baptist's head was the next obstacle.

Two hours before the curtain was to rise, the prefect of police arrived at the stage door and demanded of Bakst, "Where is the head of John the Baptist?" It was sacrilege to produce a three-dimensional representation of a holy figure on the stage. Bakst assured him that the head would not appear. Assurances aside, the prefect insisted, like Salome herself, on seeing the head in the flesh, as it were, and left the theater with the papier-mâché prophet under his arm. Without text or head, the play went on, with Ida miming to an empty platter. The silent poseur was born, and, as Bakst would later comment, "*Salome* became a ballet by the grace of the Holy Synod."[12]

Despite their vigilance, the censors could not remove Salome's veils — Ida would do that herself. Never before had a young society woman of such impeccable upbringing been seen dancing so voluptuously to oriental music, while dropping each of her seven veils with a

grace that soothed and a deliberateness that shocked. At the end she was
covered, barely, by only a wisp of green gauze and a few strings of beads.
"One feels that in her veins flows the blood of the Edomite who seduced
old Herod," wrote the critic Valerian Svetlov. "She has the suppleness of
a serpent in the physical form of a woman; her dance presents the stereo-
typical, voluptuous charm of oriental grace full of the indolence and reserve of an impulsive passion."[13] The curtain fell to tumultuous applause.

Chapter Fourteen

Diaghilev's Dilettante

N the select audience for Ida's high-class striptease was Serge Diaghilev. With his trademark streak of white hair, this dynamic man,
heavyset, homosexual, highly intelligent, cultured, and of noble birth,
embodied and defined for the twentieth century the term *impresario.*
His genius was to recognize genius in artists of all persuasions —
painters, designers, dancers, choreographers, composers — and com-
bine these talents into a single, unified vision. His was a difficult, jealous
temperament, full of insecurity, enormous persuasion, magnetic charm,
and massive ambition. In the early years of the century, he was the man
who virtually single-handedly brought the beauty, innovation, and com-
plexity of Russian culture to Europe.

Beginning this potent cultural onslaught in 1906, Diaghilev arranged
an exhibition of Russian paintings in Paris that took the art world by
storm. The following year he presented a series of concerts of Russian
music, and in 1908 staged Mussorgsky's *Boris Godunov* with Fyodor Chaliapin at the Paris Opéra. For the summer 1909 season he contracted to
bring to Paris a company comprising the greatest Russian dancers from
the Imperial Russian Ballet, in addition to the Imperial Opera.

Michel Fokine was Diaghilev's choreographer, and when one of the
ballets scheduled for the first Paris season ran into casting problems,
both Bakst and Fokine, having just worked with her on *Salome,* suggested Ida for the role of Cleopatra. Despite protests from management
because Ida was neither a classical dancer nor a member of the elite com-

pany, Diaghilev agreed that this striking amazon, under Fokine's careful tutelage, could indeed be the queen of the Nile resurrected from the pyramids. She would head a cast that included Fokine, Vaslav Nijinsky, Tamara Karsavina, and Anna Pavlova. Ida would be Diaghilev's least-trained dancer but most-talked-about star. Her unveiling as Cleopatra was, in fact, her most magnificent moment.

With his designs and costumes for *Cléopâtre*, Léon Bakst had replaced the pale, pastel world of nineteenth-century classic ballet with the violent, sexual hues of an imagined Orient — sapphire blue, oceanic turquoise, blazing yellow, burning orange, and shocking pink filled the stage and spilled over onto the boulevards of Paris. "The lady is nude, under bejeweled veils," wrote Montesquiou of Ida's costume, "just like these scarfs by Fortuny with which our Parisian women have fallen in love. . . . Some have come up to me to say, 'This is the most beautiful thing that I have ever seen.'" These women now arrived at their couturiers demanding gowns à la Cleopatra. "The thin woman," commented Sir Osbert Sitwell, "had hardly aspired to be a femme fatale until Léon Bakst introduced her as a paragon into Western Europe."[14]

Ida's persona quickly became a focus of great interest to society, and she provided just enough information to encourage the infatuation. She had herself painted by the great Russian painter Valentin Serov, in the nude, on a blue divan, with red lips and a long, green, snakelike scarf. She posed for this portrait, aware of certain scandal, in the chapel of a former monastery on the boulevard des Invalides. It was said that she never wore the same gown twice and maintained her skeletal physique dining on biscuits and champagne drunk from Madonna lilies. "Among the frivolous actresses of Paris," observed Gabriele D'Annunzio, the Italian poet, "Ida creates the effect of a Russian icon among the trinkets of the Rue de la Paix."[15]

Diaghilev presented his newest star at the home of the young Diana Vreeland, future editor of *Vogue*, who was mightily impressed with the stylish Russian woman.

> She was all in black — a straight black coat to the ground. . . . At the bottom
> of the coat was a wide band of black fox to *here;* at the collar and cuffs were
> wide bands of black fox to *here* and *here;* and she carried an *enormous* black
> fox muff. . . . Under the coat she wore high black suede Russian boots. And
> her *hair* was like Medusa's — these great big black curls, draped in black

tulle. . . . Then her *eyes,* through the veil . . . I'd never seen kohl before. If you've never seen kohl before, brother, was that a time to see it! These long, slow eyes — black, black, *black* — and she *moved* like a serpent. . . . It was all line, line, *line* . . . a sexy Jewish girl with quite a lot of money.[16]

After the Ballets Russes season ended, Ida performed in a gala that featured Nijinsky, Pavlova, Sacha Guitry, and Sarah Bernhardt. She then moved to the Olympia music hall, where Mata Hari had danced four years earlier, and reprised, seventeen times, Salome's Dance of the Seven Veils in a variety program that included dog acts. Some of her admirers protested that their "beautiful idol" should not appear in a music hall, but Ida, never one to listen to her critics, proceeded across the Channel to perform at a London theater under similar circumstances.

After spending the winter in St. Petersburg, Ida returned the following spring to Paris to star in another Diaghilev ballet, *Schéhérazade,* where she again played the voracious female. With choreography by Fokine and music by Rimsky-Korsakov, this ballet detailed the dangers of the sultan who leaves his seraglio for war. His favorite wife, Zobeida, played by Ida, now left alone, bribes the eunuchs to open the doors of the slave quarters, and she and her fellow concubines indulge their every desire in fabulous harem fashion. The last door releases the Golden Slave, played by Nijinsky, naked to the waist, painted gold, teeth gleaming, and he and Zobeida indulge in a sexual orgy of mistress and slave.

The sultan returns to witness the debauchery, and slaves, eunuchs, and wives are all promptly slaughtered. Fokine, once again, used Ida'a talents as a statuesque mime to great advantage, and she remained the great silent center in the midst of the bloodshed around her. Finally, full of remorse, Zobeida stabs a dagger into her own heart, dragging herself to die at the feet of her master.

Schéhérazade introduced yet another variation in the genesis of the nineteenth-century femme fatale. Here, in a symbolic gesture, she dies from a self-inflicted wound as atonement for her unleashed sexuality. This fatal woman feels remorse, a sentiment previously alien to her, and becomes fatal to none other than her own self. The femme fatale, in Ida's Zobeida, was now a suicide.

The ballet's success exceeded even that of *Cléopâtre* the previous year, and in the attempt to look like Ida, Parisian hostesses fought over Bakst's services, employing him to design both their clothes and their salons in the style of the Arabian Nights. The effect of *Schéhérazade,* as the

British critic Harold Acton explained, reached far beyond the stage into the whole world of art: "For many a young artist *Schéhérazade* was an inspiration equivalent to Gothic architecture for the Romantics or Quattrocento frescoes for the Pre-Raphaelites."[17]

While *le tout Paris* clamored around Diaghilev and his Ballets Russes, one gentleman assigned himself to worshipping Ida exclusively. It was through this alliance that Ida began to look beyond the world of Diaghilev and the fatal woman she had incarnated for him. Comte Robert de Montesquiou-Fezensac was the French Oscar Wilde, a dandy, a man of impeccable taste with a sharp tongue and a fondness for spiritualism and the supernatural. The heir of an aristocratic French family, Montesquiou traced his bloodline back to the tenth century, and he grew up in a chateau with no less than twenty-eight staircases.

His own essays and poetry have not withstood the test of time, but he is immortalized in the literature of others as the model for Huysmans's Des Esseintes in *Against Nature,* and for Baron Charlus, "The Professor of Beauty," in his friend Marcel Proust's epic, *Remembrance of Things Past.* His acquaintances included some of the greatest artists of his time — Whistler, Debussy, Degas, Verlaine, and Mallarmé — but notable women were his specialty. A brief romp with his friend Sarah Bernhardt that left him feeling nauseous for twenty-four hours confirmed his supressed homosexuality. "He is not dangerous," commented one husband, [18] and as a result Montesquiou enjoyed full access to the wives and lovers of others, cultivating complex friendships with numerous women of great beauty, intelligence, and talent.

After seeing Ida in *Cléopâtre,* Montesquiou had visited her backstage, knelt and kissed her hand, and, overcome with awe, promptly lost his ever-ready tongue. In her amazon androgyny, Montesquiou found his ideal woman. "Was she not the flat cruel hermaphrodite of whom he had dreamed when he was twenty?" asked his biographer Philippe Jullian.[19] Assigning himself to her education, he escorted her to the museum that housed Gustave Moreau's fantastical visions of fatal women, to the Maison Worth, where she ordered her gowns and furs, and to the salons and galas where she displayed them. Ida became his protégé, and their mutual narcissism combined to form an elite friendship of adoration and appreciation that would last until his death in 1921.

Montesquiou, a man in search of heroes, had recently also be-

friended Italy's king of decadent literature, Gabriele D'Annunzio, and
with Ida in tow, they became a curious trio. A Renaissance man of the
sadomasochistic school in fin-de-siècle Europe, D'Annunzio is best remembered not so much for his flowering prose but as a great lover of
women, despite his short, balding appearance, rounded shoulders and
hips, and sallow skin. After he fled to Paris in 1910 to escape his Italian
creditors, women flocked to his bed like bees to the hive. He had a seductive voice, a poetic mind, and his gods were the female body and the exal-
tation, and perversions, to be found therein. "The women who had not
slept with him," commented one observer, "became a laughing-stock."
Isadora Duncan and Eleanora Duse featured among his numerous con-
quests of rich beauties and married mistresses. After her affair with him,
one lesbian woman wrote, "Even in heaven, dear poet, there will be reserved for you an enormous octopus with a thousand women's legs (and
no head) which will renew themselves to infinity. There will be no more
sadness, cher Maître."[20]

Montesquiou lured his Italian idol with women — and Ida was his
most prized offering. After attending one of her performances, D'Annunzio was smitten. A platonic threesome of sublimated desire formed
among these artistic rebels, each garnering inspiration, encouragement,
and power from the adoration of the others. That D'Annunzio never con-
summated his relationship with Ida is most unusual and can only point to
Ida's sexual disinterest. Ida "did not, or rather could not, return D'Annunzio's affection," wrote Romaine Brooks in her unpublished memoir.
The hungry American press, however, still managed to print a racy story
entitled "The Only Girl Who Ever Broke D'Annunzio's Heart."[21] These
three focused their poetic aspirations not around the bedroom but
around the stage.

"Now that I've seen Cleopatra I cannot master my emotions," wrote
D'Annunzio to Montesquiou breathlessly one evening. "What am I to
do?" Montesquiou suggested he write something for Ida, and a long-
lived obsession of the poet's suddenly came to life. "Here are the legs of St.
Sebastian," he declared, "for which I have been searching for years!"[22]

Encouraged by her two passionate advocates, Ida chose to leave the
fold where Diaghilev's fatal enchantresses had given her fame. Tired of
playing a suicide queen, she wanted to play a murdered saint, and as
D'Annunzio's St. Sebastian she would be pierced by Christian sacrifice
not pagan debauchery. It was as if this particular Salome wanted to re-

verse roles and play John the Baptist. As a former seductress now stabbed with the phallic arrows of martyrdom, Ida would embody the transition from the curvaceous nineteenth-century femme fatale into the slim-hipped androgyny of the twentieth century's independent woman. Salome would no longer do a striptease to possess the head of a holy man; she would be the holy man herself.

Chapter Fifteen

The Male Martyr

WHILE Ida was preparing to embark on a mammoth stage production that would publicly illustrate this remarkable reversal of both faith and gender, she was mirroring this ambiguous sexuality in her own bedroom. During her Parisian seasons with the Ballets Russes, she met the two people with whom she would initiate concurrent sexual affairs.

Walter Guinness, an Englishman, was only three years older than Ida and fulfilled the role of consort to a Russian heiress. Handsome, dashing, and intelligent, Guinness was married with children, and, as heir to the British beer fortune, immensely rich. They began an affair so discreet that no one, including Ida's husband (who, at one point, employed a private detective to follow them in an attempt to get a divorce), could ascertain the exact nature of the union — but it was one that lasted more than three decades. Their liaison has left no letters, no stories, no traces. They never cohabited, even when living in the same city, and the longevity of their alliance may indeed suggest one more of friendship than of heated sexual passion. African safaris, trips down the Nile, and expeditions to the Galápagos marked their yearly sojourns together. Most crucial to Ida's story is the fact that Guinness was to spend his money on her and her career as freely as the dark stout poured from the vat. "Dear, there will always be, in a black bank of that black City," he told her, "what it takes to satisfy all of your aspirations."[23] And Ida's "aspirations" did not come cheap.

Within the same year of meeting Guinness and forming the triumvirate with her two male admirers, D'Annunzio and Montesquiou, Ida also embarked on an affair with an American woman. Romaine Brooks, an heiress like Ida, had married but remained estranged from her spouse, paying him a yearly allowance from her vast inheritance to stay away from her. Living in Paris and keeping things incestuously connected, Romaine was D'Annunzio's most recent lover — a notable coupling considering Brooks's predominantly lesbian disposition. Despite her varied experiments, she referred to the sexual act itself distastefully as "a commotion, rather than an emotion."[24]

Romaine Brooks was a painter of extraordinary vision, and D'Annunzio worshipped her talent, an aphrodisiac for Romaine that clearly transcended gender preference. She lived with him in 1910, loaning him money, paying off his debts, and painting his portrait, but when a former lover of his began stalking them, Brooks ended the affair. Fueled by lover's loss — "I was for you only another female to destroy," she wrote — she began an affair with his new muse, Ida, a particularly sweet form of retaliation only a bisexual could enjoy.[25]

Revenge aside, Romaine saw in Ida something far more vital and lasting. She found a model for her ideal of the female body — and this image delineated Ida's transition from Salome's lively hedonist to a modern, pale, even anorexic woman. *Le Trajet* (The Crossing), painted in 1911, depicts Ida naked and suspended on a great wing of darkness, skeletal, androgynous, elongated — and dead. One critic referred, understandably, to the "unhealthy nudes" that emerged from the brush of Brooks's tortured imagination. These paintings were based on an extraordinary series of photographs taken by Brooks at the time (fig. 17). In subsequent years she painted several penetrating portraits of Ida clothed, images that are an eloquent reminder of Ida's grave and exotic beauty (fig. 18). Years later, Brooks described what she had seen: "She seemed even more beautiful when off stage; like some heraldic bird delicately knit together by the finest of bone structures giving flexibility to curveless lines. . . . Hers was a mask whose outward glow emanated from a disturbed inner depth."[26]

The liaison between Romaine and Ida, though enduring for several years, was not of equal passion. Ida was smitten and declared on one occasion that she would give up the stage to live quietly with Romaine in a rural farmhouse. The idea horrified Romaine, who claimed, "Hell is other people."[27]

This affair seems to have had little effect upon Ida's more enduring one with Guinness and remains the only documented lesbian affair

FIG. 17. Ida Rubinstein photographed by Romaine Brooks, ca. 1911–12
(Courtesy of Joe Lucchesi)

she had. Her dual sexual life suggests an interesting balance between bi-
sexuality and asexuality. She practiced both, and her relationships provide a clear picture of this ambivalence, or an unconventional desire for
variety: an unconsummated marriage that she insisted on maintaining,
platonic friendships with a homosexual aesthete and a notorious womanizer, a long-term affair of limited contact with a married man, and an intense lesbian affair with a woman who immortalized her in oils. This was
a woman who tried both sexes but appeared, ultimately, dispassionate
about both.

Never living with anyone but servants, Ida cherished her privacy
and avoided domesticity. She needed time and space to construct her
dreams. Her energies were devoted to her career, her own image, and the
theatrical productions in which it could flourish. Safely removed from
real life, she embraced creatures of wayward extremities, obsessions, and
inversions. Her next role would in fact find her cross-dressing as a man in

FIG. 18. Romaine Brooks, *Ida Rubinstein,* oil on canvas, 1917
(Smithsonian American Art Museum, gift of the artist)

a tale that eerily echoes Wilde's *Salome* in its battle between the sacred
and the profane.

D'Annunzio's lyric play *The Martyrdom of St. Sebastian,* which he
wrote for Ida, tells the story of a beautiful young Lebanese officer named
Sebastian who is adored by the Emperor Diocletian. Sebastian converts
to Christianity after shooting an arrow to heaven that does not return; it
has been received by God. But Diocletian is in love, and lust, with Sebastian and, fearing the loss of his object of affection, protests that the boy
cannot renounce Apollo for Christ without proof, without a miracle. Sebastian obliges by dancing on hot coals that turn to lilies and healing a
sick woman. Distraught at the mounting evidence, Diocletian attempts
to force Sebastian to renounce his faith on threat of death. Unswayed

from his belief, Sebastian performs the Passion of Christ and faces his destiny with peace. Tied to a laurel tree, he is shot through with arrows — like Mata Hari riddled with bullets. His soul ascends to heaven and he is canonized.

D'Annunzio had been haunted by the mystical link between eroticism and spirituality since 1885, when he had an assignation with a lady lover, an oleander tree, and the love bites that marked their passion. The image of an androgynous Adonis shot through with arrows mesmerized his sadomasochistic imagination. To have this icon of sexual ambiguity, this boy "more beautiful than pain and purer than blood," the patron saint of homosexual tradition, be portrayed by a woman, the androgynous Ida Rubinstein, was the ultimate perversion.[28]

Ida and her collaborators worked intensely, day and night, for eleven months to produce D'Annunzio's verse play, announced in the press in July 1910, only a month after her debut in *Schéhérazade*. Ida immediately embarked on extensive acting lessons under the supervision of an actress from the Comédie-Française, French lessons to overcome her Russian accent, as well as continuing dance classes. Claude Debussy was commissioned to write the music (he was at the time also writing *Khamma* for another Salome, Maud Allan), Bakst to design the decor and costumes, and Fokine to choreograph the two dance sequences — Sebastian negotiating hot coals in act I and miming the passion of Christ in act III. Gabriel Astruc, Mata Hari's agent, was engaged to produce the event, booking the Théâtre du Châtelet for the 22 May 1911 premiere.

Ida paid for the vast project herself — with the aid of Guinness — and it proceeded with the Comte de Montesquiou advising everyone from the wings. The intimacy among Ida, the comte, and the Italian poet was hailed as a platonic "brotherhood," each writing to the other as "Cher Frère" and Ida signing herself "the Saint." Her identification with St. Sebastian was transforming her. Seduced by the Italian poet's effusive style, she spoke about her role to the press: "I am Saint Sebastian the moment I step on the stage. I live his life and I know his innermost feelings . . . every movement and every word come from me spontaneously. I am, as it were, impregnated with the soul of Saint Sebastian. . . . I experience the most sublime ecstasy, although I remain quite lucid."[29]

Astruc, the son of a rabbi, feared repercussions from having not only a woman, but a Jewish one play a Christian saint. "They will try to make a sacrilegious person of you," he wrote to D'Annunzio, "and soon they will have proved that for the second time I have crucified God!"[30] (In 1907 Astruc had produced the Paris premiere of Strauss's scandalous *Salome*.) The concern was not misplaced, and on 8 May, two weeks prior to the premiere, the archbishop of Paris condemned *St. Sebastian* as offensive to Christian conscience and forbade all French Catholics to attend under the threat of excommunication. As with the Russian Holy Synod in 1908, Ida was at the center of a theatrical production that was testing religious boundaries and causing trouble.

The public, however, was more interested in scandal and sexually irreverent art than in their immortal souls and, defying the archbishop, showed up in droves. Opening night brought out, as had Diaghilev's premieres, an illustrious audience that included Isadora Duncan, Marcel Proust, and Jean Cocteau. What they witnessed was astonishing — all six hours of it.

There were an extraordinary six hundred costumes worn by 150 actors and 350 extras, including Ida in the armor of Joan of Arc and the bare ropes and rags of Sebastian's final martyrdom. In five acts, Bakst covered the stage in the emerald greens, lapis lazuli blues, and brilliant crimsons of third-century Rome. The sets included a vast, columned throne room and an elliptical vault with clouds of light representing Paradise. At the center of all this grandeur was Ida, miming, dancing, acting, and declaiming the purple verses of D'Annunzio in a stifled Russian accent. The play was scheduled for twelve performances, alternating at the Châtelet with the third Paris season of the Ballets Russes.

Bakst's stupendous designs increased his reputation as a designer of theatrical brilliance tenfold. Other collaborators were less successful — Debussy thought that his music was sacrificed to the elaborate staging, and D'Annunzio received little praise for his interminable, complex verse. A succès de scandale without question, *The Martyrdom of St. Sebastian* was received with critical reservation.

Although Ida claimed proudly, "it was D'Annunzio who gave me my voice," that voice came in for particular derision. "Mme. Ida Rubinstein," wrote the critic for *Comoedia*, "has a deplorable voice for the stage: her diction is poor; her accent distorts the words; between her shrieks and sighs, one can hardly distinguish the author's text." Marcel Proust "found the piece very boring. . . . It is a flop for both poet and composer." But, he continued, "I find the legs of Madame Rubinstein (which are like those of both Closmenil and Maurice de Rothschild) sublime."[31]

FIG. 19. Ida Rubinstein in Gabriele D'Annunzio's *Martyrdom of St. Sebastian,*
by Léon Bakst, ca. 1911. On the lower left is a quote from D'Annunzio:
"Each must kill his love for it to return seven times more ardently."

Jean Cocteau, however, found in Ida images of beauty between the
cracking voice, the overstated prose, and the 2 A.M. finale: "She hangs,
pierced by the arrows, against the tree, like the wreck of some gallant ship
entangled in its rigging. . . . Her armour aglow, her legs scorched, her toes
seared, she treads the red embers as lightly as though they were, in fact, a
magic carpet fashioned of the miraculous lilies in the blue arcades beyond. . . . From the beginning where she suggests a tall stately torch, to
the end . . . she is but a great flame dying in a pool of wax" (fig. 19).[32]

Ida created in the beautiful St. Sebastian Salome's spiritual brother,
transforming the fatal woman of *Schéhérazade* into her newest incarna-

tion: a fatal man . . . who is a woman. As written by D'Annunzio, St. Sebastian is clearly related to Wilde's Salome, with his beauty that tempts a
king with illegitimate lusts and provokes a battle between desire and
faith. "He is fair! He is fair!" cries Diocletian of Ida as the young officer,
in words reminiscent of Herod's passion for Salome. He even offers Sebastian, as did Herod to Salome, his kingdom — "All I will give you,
all. . . . The whole world will you hold."[33]

As each drama proceeds, both Salome and St. Sebastian dance, one
in veils, one on burning coals, and each is murdered by the autocrat they
have tempted, Salome for choosing lust, Sebastian for choosing God. But
in both roles Ida remained an object of beauty eliciting destructive passions in those about her. Playing St. Sebastian gave Ida a rite of passage
from the Eastern femmes fatales of Diaghilev's productions into her own
idiosyncratic vision of herself as saint and sinner, man and woman. This
cross-gender experiment, however, reached beyond Ida's personal explorations to symbolize the modern woman propelled by her "male"
energy.

Despite the decidedly mixed reception of *The Martyrdom of St. Sebastian,* Diaghilev felt betrayed by the woman he had plucked from obscurity, brought to Paris, and placed in the center of his most lavish productions. Ida was now not only performing in the same theater with her own
pricey production while he was constantly short of money, but she had
hired his own collaborators — Debussy, Fokine, Astruc, and Bakst. Ida's
decision to venture out on her own resulted in several inconveniences for
Diaghilev: two new ballets, *La Peri* and *Le Dieu Bleu,* with designs by
Bakst were delayed owing to the designer's work with Ida, and replacing
Ida herself in *Cléopâtre* and *Schéhérazade* proved difficult. Complaining to
Astruc, Diaghilev declared dramatically, "we have been completely sac-
rificed to the work of Rubinstein and d'Annunzio."[34]

Ida exacerbated the impresario's resentment in early 1912 when she
agreed to perform the lead Nymph in Nijinsky's new ballet *L'Après-midi
d'un Faune* and then promptly withdrew from rehearsals. She declared
Nijinsky's innovative choreography to be "topsy-turvy. . . . If I had sub-
mitted to his direction I would have been transformed into a maimed
marionette!"[35] The ballet proved to be a milestone in the history of the
Ballets Russes, and Ida's refusal to be in it illustrates the first of many

questionable decisions she would make, driven by her obsessive self-image.

But Ida's heroine was not, at this time, a ballerina, and her separation from the Ballets Russes was a conscious choice. Her idol was an actress of all-consuming fame, Sarah Bernhardt. Having seen Ida perform in *Schéhérazade*, Bernhardt was impressed and wrote to Montesquiou offering to guide the young Russian woman in her stage career: "Ask her to put her trust in me. I shall make her work and I alone can succeed in making of this admirable artist a complete artist. . . . It goes without saying that I refuse all recompense. I am doing this out of love of beauty and because the young woman loves beauty as I do."[36]

Ida was thrilled with the attention and complied with every suggestion her mentor offered. When Bernhardt was made a Chevalier of the Legion of Honor in 1914, Ida demonstrated her gratitude by giving her a party in her suite at the Hotel Bristol.

While continuing to live in hotels, Ida rented a large studio on the rue Vaneau, and there she received her guests and conducted all her rehearsals. The walls of the Bakst-designed studio were a soft blue, lit by skylights, and a piano, a sofa piled high with cushions, and a bookcase were the only furniture. Oriental incense burned in one corner. At the end of the vast room was a raised platform with red carpet and railing, Ida's private stage used to prepare for her public one. "It was all very cold and systematic," commented one American journalist granted the honor of an interview. Ida made an entrance that disarmed him: "She wore a veil, well over her face. It was a curious riddle of a face. She was livid — almost green. The whiteness of her skin gleamed strangely. Her lips, scarlet, like a wound, gave one an odd sensation of mingled fascination and repulsion. Two dark eyes pierced the veil. Mlle. Rubinstein looked pensive, *distraite*, and exceedingly sad. . . . The sight of her oppressed me vaguely."[37]

Although French society welcomed the Russian star as an icon of fashion — one admirer named her the *"arbiter elegantiarum* of the period"[38] — and kept note of her every move, every gown and fur, and every painted portrait, Ida kept a dignified distance from its parties and its sapphic circles, preferring her solitude or the company of her artistic collaborators. She retained a brooding Russian disdain for the vanity of Parisian society, her own vanity taking form in the mournful tones of assumed gravity. "Paris is so frivolous," she told one interviewer. "Paris wants to laugh all the time. Then Paris must dine, and Paris must sup and the theatres must not interfere with that. . . . My nature is serious, I cannot laugh at the Boulevard Theatres in Paris. They oppress me."[39]

If frivolity oppressed her, she was far from immune to cultivating an image, and, like Sarah Bernhardt, Ida aligned herself with large, wild felines. Her pet panther caused considerable trouble climbing the curtains and devouring the keys, hats, and gloves of visitors. His tenure came to an abrupt end when, scared by Diaghilev's black frock coat, he lunged at the visiting impresario, who sought refuge on a tabletop while the confused animal howled in a corner. Ida, laughing, dragged her pet by the scruff of the neck out of the room, and Diaghilev descended from his perch, unamused. Three days later the authorities confiscated the panther. Ida was not pleased with the loss of her exotic beast, and the differences between Diaghilev and Ida took on a more personal tone. For the ensuing eighteen years until his death in 1929, he continued his public diatribes against his wayward Cleopatra, who dared to venture beyond his jurisdiction and compete with him.

Chapter Sixteen

La Folie d'Ida

UNDAUNTED by the mixed reception of *St. Sebastian* and unrestricted by financial concerns, Ida proceeded for the next three decades to search out one forum after another in which to frame her image. She chose her roles from a distinguished pantheon of women — goddesses from mythology, queens from ancient history, nuns from medieval romance, courtesans from great literature — but none surpassed the magnificence of *Cléopâtre* and *Schéhérazade*.

There was Helen of Troy in *Hélène de Sparte*, and two more versions of Salome's story: Wilde's play with the text and head intact, and a danced version, where Ida appeared, precariously, on pointe. In 1913 there was another five-hour D'Annunzian extravaganza, *La Pisanelle, ou*

La Mort Parfumée, which found Ida as courtesan turned nun, pelted to death by a storm of red roses. The public stayed away.

Ida spent the war years in Paris and Versailles, where she had an apartment at the Trianon Palace, and devoted herself to numerous charities with the same dedication and largesse she gave to her theatrical productions. She donated four ambulances to the American Hospital at Neuilly and funded and arranged an auxiliary hospital set up at the Hotel Carlton. She even saw to nursing duties herself, wearing, ever true to her sense of elegance, a uniform designed by Bakst. In early 1915 when Sarah Bernhardt needed her lame leg amputated, Ida, continuing her charitable gestures, quietly paid for the operation and her recuperation.

The Bolshevik Revolution of 1917 closed the doors of Ida's birthplace to her forever, and although the family for whom she held little sentiment was lost to her, her fortune was not. It had long been invested outside of Russia, and she remained after the war, as before, a very wealthy woman. In addition to her plane, her two-masted yacht the *Istar* (a gift from Walter Guinness), and her chauffeured motorcars, she bought, in 1920, a house at 7 place des Etats-Unis opposite that of the Duc de la Rochefoucauld. She employed Léon Bakst to advise on the decoration, and he thoughtfully arranged the garden "so that all the flowers were in trays," reported an amused Igor Stravinsky, "and the whole garden could be changed every few weeks" to match Ida's mood and outfit.[40]

Inside, the atmosphere was spare and meditative with soothing blue and white walls. The rehearsal studio was vast with a raked floor approximating the steep angles of the Paris Opéra stage. The drawing room was hung with full-length mirrors and heavy curtains with gold tassels, and the few articles of decoration were eclectic and exotic: a Senegalese instrument of torture, a statue from ancient Athens, a Japanese table displaying the works of D'Annunzio. "She has a gift, truly strange, for completely tasteful emptiness," commented Bakst. "Madame Rubinstein has a genius for laconicism."[41]

In keeping with her postwar theme of renovation and redecoration, Ida, now approaching forty, also appears to have done some on herself at this time, visiting a well-known surgeon for a face-lift. During the ensuing decade, the newly revitalized Ida went on to mount eleven major productions, all premiering in prestigious Parisian theaters. Never aligning herself again with an existing dance or acting company, she continued the habit, initiated with *St. Sebastian*, of being a theatrical world unto herself.

In 1920 she revisited Cleopatra, this time in Shakespeare's *Antoine et Cléopâtre* in a new translation she commissioned from André Gide, and two years later she performed, again on her toes, as the goddess of archery in *Artémis Troublée*, with unmistakable lesbian undertones between Artemis and her band of Amazon women. In 1923 Ida returned to dramatic acting with a lavish new production of *La Dame aux Camélias*, by Alexandre Dumas fils, in which Ida played the tubercular courtesan Marguerite Gautier, a role made famous by Bernhardt, who had died that same year. She was coached by Sacha Guitry, who found her vain and self-centered, but the audience embraced her performance and she played the consumptive courtesan over fifty times.

Adoring Dostoevsky, Ida commissioned a stage-play version of *The Idiot* in 1925 and played the courtesan Nastasya Filippovna Barashkov. In *L'Impératrice aux Rochers*, set to a long dramatic poem by Saint-Georges de Bouhélier and music by Arthur Honegger, she appeared in thirteen gowns designed by Alexandre Benois, who, like Bakst, was one of Diaghilev's great Russian scenic designers. This major display of couturier beauty was not enough to save the production from doom, and Ida managed to beat her own record for long evenings. The curtain was raised at 7:45 P.M. and did not descend until 4 A.M.

After five performances, which it is hard to imagine anyone saw in their entirety, *L'Impératrice aux Rochers* disappeared forever onto the already impressive list of stupendously extravagant, but ultimately unsuccessful, Rubinstein productions. She was making her mark not so much as an actress or dancer, but as a woman with relentless ambition, impeccable taste in collaborators, and the apparently bottomless financial coffers from which she could realize her elaborate fantasies. And British beer continued to pay.

Rather than retreating from the stage as she approached middle age, Ida merely changed course. In several of her recent productions she had appeared, for the first time in her life, as a ballerina on the tips of her toes. She clearly liked it up there and decided that her next project would be a ballet company with herself as its star ballerina. Common sense had never played a role in her choices, and the fact that she was now forty-five years old and not a classically trained ballet dancer proved no deterrent to this woman of determined nature and improbable self-image. If Ida wanted a tutu, she would have it.

Les Ballets Ida Rubinstein was a fast-formed company dedicated more to Narcissus than Terpsichore, though its roster of participants was culled from the elite of the ballet world. Bronislava Nijinska, sister of Nijinsky, who had choreographed for the Ballets Russes, was named chief choreographer and ballet mistress. Anatole Vilzak and his wife, Ludmilla Schollar, lead dancers from Diaghilev's company, were employed as principal dancers, and David Lichine, Nina Verchinina, and Frederick Ashton each made their professional debuts dancing behind Ida Rubinstein. Dancers were recruited from an amazing array of countries — England, Denmark, Rumania, Estonia, Yugoslavia, the United States, Bulgaria, Switzerland, and Poland, with most from Russia, including nine dancers lured from Diaghilev's company.

Between 1928 and 1934 the company presented four Paris seasons at the Paris Opéra, one European tour, and paid a visit to London's Covent Garden, premiering a total of thirteen new ballets. Ida employed, as always, the best artists of the time — music commissioned from Maurice Ravel, Igor Stravinsky, and Arthur Honegger; scenery and costumes from Alexandre Benois; choreography from Bronislava Nijinska, Kurt Jooss, Michel Fokine, and Léonide Massine; and texts from André Gide and Paul Valéry. Ida wanted to compete with the Ballets Russes; her audacity was astonishing. Casting was simple: Ida would star in every single ballet.

Among the unwritten rules of the company was Ida's decree that no dancer would upstage her, and so neither female nor male dancers were allowed any extended solo work. This false hierarchy engendered considerable bitterness. Nina Tikanova, a young Russian dancer, described a rehearsal with Ida in full ballerina flourish: "Vilzak turned with passionate élan toward someone who made her entrance with a grand jeté in a romantic tutu. . . . Horrified, we all turned as one. The view of Ida Rubinstein, carried by Vilzak, hanging like a package of wet washing, her back arched over, the legs badly extended, surpassed our most terrible expectations. . . . After months of throwing our hearts and exertions into work, the dancing of our 'patronne' reduced our efforts to nothing."[42]

Among Ida's commissions were several notable musical premieres.

In response to her request for a Spanish dance, Ravel composed *Bolero*, and she became the first dancer to swing and sway to that heady beat, on a tabletop in a Spanish tavern. Another piece by Ravel, *La Valse*, originally written for Diaghilev but dismissed as "a masterpiece not a ballet," received its first dance rendition in Ida's company.[43]

From Stravinsky came *Le Baiser de la fée*, based on themes by Tchaikovsky. The composer attributed to this commission from Ida his own final break with Diaghilev, who thought Stravinsky had "sold himself" to Ida. The Russian composer disliked Nijinska's choreography for the piece, although he did agree to conduct the orchestra for the premiere. As for Ida, Stravinsky was brutal: "No one in the artistic world," he stated, "is as mysteriously stupid as this lady."[44]

Diaghilev's interest in Ida's premiere season in 1928 was so intense that he had rushed back from Manchester, England, where the Ballets Russes was performing, to attend the first performances and recorded his impressions in a series of letters to Serge Lifar, his favorite dancer at the time. Referring to Ida as the "poor Russian woman" and her company as "Les Ballets Juifs" — "The Jewish Ballet" — he set the tone for his relentless invective.

> The worse thing we saw was Ida. . . . All bent, her red hair dishevelled, without any style, wearing ballet shoes. . . . She is incapable of dancing anything. . . . Her face appears to consist of nothing but an enormous gaping mouth with close-set teeth attempting to grimace a smile. It was frightful. She wore a pistachio-coloured toga (no doubt costing 1,000 francs a meter), and her figure is thicker then before, whereas her legs have grown thinner. She is as old as the devil.[45]

Beneath the acidity, Diaghilev was right: ballet is for the young in body, and Ida was far too old for tutus and tiaras and even, apparently, togas. Les Ballets Ida Rubinstein was an unprecedented display of aging vanity and warped judgment, and yet the company enjoyed considerable public success. Tickets sold out each evening, and the *Dancing Times* in London reported that "for sumptuousness of presentation these ballets have set a standard that will be difficult to surpass."[46]

Henry Prunières, an eminent music critic, stated in the *New York Times*, "Ida Rubinstein is treading in Diaghilev's footsteps." The impresario himself remained threatened by the competition, and verged on hysteria: "We need somebody, a Napoleon or the Bolsheviks, to explode a bomb under these old hovels [theaters] with their audiences, their sluts who think themselves dancers, their millions spent on buying musicians."[47]

In a more dignified tone for *La Renaissance*, a French Russian-language newspaper, he summarized, possessively, Rubinstein's betrayal: "Twenty years ago it was I who introduced an exotic, mysterious, hieratic Ida Rubinstein to choreography. How has she had the temerity to alter so mercilessly the image we had of her? To us that image seems unforgettable, but she has erased it forever."[48]

Within the year Diaghilev died, at the age of fifty-seven, in Venice, leaving the dance world without its visionary leader and Ida without her severest critic. Impervious to criticism, she was beholden to no one, not even Serge Diaghilev, and continued her pursuit of her own particular idea of beauty. She appeared blind to her physical limitations as a dancer, and few of her collaborators seemed willing to tell her the truth — most were in her pay.

Ida's final dance season took place in 1934. She was now fifty years old, and if the reception had been lukewarm before, this time the message was clear — Ida needed to get off pointe. But she ended her brief career as a ballerina in considerable style.

Several new works were premiered. The first, *Perséphone*, had music commissioned from Stravinsky, verse from André Gide, and choreography by the German Kurt Jooss, who had made his seminal ballet *The Green Table* only two years earlier. The production was vast, including three tableaux with a baritone, a full chorus, and a boys' choir accompanying Ida's recitation. There was trouble among the illustrious collaborators from the start. Stravinsky did not approve of Gide's prose, calling it "vers le caramel," and Gide, in turn, disliked Stravinsky's music, boycotting all three performances.[49]

The final premiere was an Egyptian-Assyrian extravaganza that poignantly, and unintentionally, illustrated just how far Ida had come, and fallen. *Sémiramis* had music by Arthur Honegger, a text by Paul Valéry, and dances by Fokine, still choreographing for Ida thirty years after her Russian *Salomé*. The ballet told the story of the amazon Babylonian goddess Sémiramis, who is seen as a warrior, a conqueror of empires, and a one-night-only lover whose handsome captive is rewarded for his sexual prowess with a dagger by which to kill himself. Sémiramis is immolated as an offering to the sun god.

With this production Ida revisited both the glory and power of Diaghilev's lusty Cleopatra, as well as the spiritual yearning for sacrificial martyrdom of D'Annunzio's St. Sebastian. But the poetic juxtaposition failed in the actualization, and the Egyptian style, so fashionable in 1910, was desperately outdated by 1934.

This final season presented the apotheosis of Ida's now deeply distorted self-image, and, at age fifty, gaunt, hunched, and severe, she fooled no one. Every performance verged on catastrophe as Ida bourréed on her long pointes and bent knees beneath her sagging tutu. She looked like an original Edward Gorey dancer — tall, aquiline, and epically morose. "If Art is what Man makes in God's image," commented Keith Lester, a dancer in the company, "then creating a ballet for Rubinstein must have been a choreographer's Purgatory."[50]

The critics dropped all pretense of admiration during this final season of Les Ballets Ida Rubinstein and became openly hostile. Ida had pushed herself beyond novelty, beyond decorum, even beyond tolerance. Called "La folie d'Ida" by the poet Paul Claudel,[51] Ida's productions presented the anomaly of the rich ballet dancer, that rare creature who had both the finances, and the temerity, to launch an entire ballet company as a personal showcase. No other professional ballet company would have hired her; she was unqualified.

When the curtain fell on the final performance on 21 May, it was her last appearance as a dancer before the Parisian public who had been her receptive audience for twenty-five years. A European tour was cancelled, as was a projected 1938 season. Ida's company had performed a total of only thirty-odd performances.

In a bittersweet footnote to Ida's ballet fiasco, the French government made her a Chevalier of the Legion of Honor in 1934 for her services to French culture. It was not unmerited, for as a patron of the arts alone, she had earned the honor and had kept many great artists well employed. But Ida did not persist in her folly and was to spend her remaining years in almost complete solitude.

Chapter Seventeen

Salvation

S her glory on the stage faded before her eyes, Ida looked up from the ashes of questionable honor and growing stage fright, and there she found God. Her interest in religion was not new, but her obsession with St. Sebastian in 1911 had stemmed more from his theatrical possibilities and his erotic mysticism than from his true spirituality. As she entered her sixth decade, the comfort and stability of a less tangible faith gradually came to supplant her need for theatrical display, and the last third of her life was devoted to the vast and invisible stage of God's work. Ida spent her youth as a femme fatale but her old age as a committed religious penitent.

While putting her allegiances in order she obtained French citizenship in early 1935, after living in France for twenty-six years. In September of the following year, with her hairdresser and maid in tow, Ida set off in her chauffeured motorcar to the Dominican Convent of Saulchoir in Tournai, where she was received into the Roman Catholic Church. She converted not from the Judaism of her birth but from the Russian Orthodoxy of her youth. She became a tertiary sister of the order, and, despite her rich trappings, her allegiance to Catholicism was real. It is not difficult to comprehend the transition of Rubinstein the theatrical diva to Rubinstein the pious Catholic. Her description some years earlier of the meditative process she underwent in preparing a role echoes that of spiritual pursuit: "I live my roles. By a sort of reflex psychological process I adapt myself to my role without being conscious of it. . . . Often I sit for hours at the piano and I dream. Nights and days I sit like that. I dream and come back to the world of realities perhaps after only forty-eight hours . . . the hours when I am seeking to rise higher and to exalt my soul."[52]

Not quite ready to leave the stage entirely, Ida had commissioned a new theatrical piece by Paul Claudel about France's patron saint, Joan of Arc. Claudel, a French diplomat, was a mystical poet of the first order and a man of deep Catholic faith who was idolized throughout France. Joan of Arc had been canonized in 1920 and much had been written on the subject of the female saint, but a work by Claudel would transcend the popular versions. Ida longed to portray her, just as Bernhardt had in 1873.

Claudel finished his play *Jeanne d'Arc au bûcher* in late 1935, but the eighty-minute oratorio, set to orchestral music by Arthur Honegger, had a difficult time reaching the public. It would be Ida's public declaration of her new Catholic faith as well as her new French nationality. It did not, however, pass unnoticed that both Rubinstein and Honegger were Jews creating a work about a Catholic saint.

Claudel presented Joan, tied to the stake, recalling in flashback the events, battles, betrayals, and trial that had led her young body into the flames of death. She sees her condemners as ferocious wild beasts, she watches her childhood pass before her, and finally, as fire engulfs her, she dies for love and immortality. Ida Rubinstein could wish for no greater role to complement her earnest love of both the theater and God.

On 10 May 1938 the work premiered in a concert-oratorio in Basel, Switzerland, under the baton of the distinguished conductor Paul Sacher. It was a total triumph and hailed immediately as a masterpiece. Even Claudel confided to his diary, "Immense success. 1000 in audience. Endless ovations."[53] It was Honegger's greatest success in more than fifteen years and even Ida's portrayal of Joan, voice and all, was highly praised.

The French premiere occurred, appropriately enough, in May 1939 in Orléans, as part of the saint's feast day celebrations and the audience comprised church, state, and army officials. The Paris premiere took place on 15 June 1939 at the newly inaugurated Palais de Chaillot. *Jeanne d'Arc au bûcher* was Ida's most important commission since *The Martyrdom of St. Sebastian* twenty-eight years earlier; not only did the lives of saints appeal to her spiritual sensibilities but they too, had been good to her.

As Joan of Arc, Ida had finally perfected the death scene she had been practicing all her life — from Salome's death by shields and St. Sebastian's death by arrows, to La Pisanelle's death by thorns and Sémiramis's death by fire. Her youthful promise "to come to the people with a full heart and exalted mind, to be mad for truth, then to sing this truth and light the whole world with my song," now rang strangely true. As she expires, Joan murmurs, "There is love that is the strongest. There is God that is the strongest."[54]

Ida's triumph as Joan of Arc, at the age of fifty-four, was absolution for her entire career. Tracing a unique arc, Ida had begun her search for identity in the pagan land inhabited by the nineteenth-century femmes fatales of Salome and Cleopatra and finished her self-definition with two androgynous saints, one male and one female. In an ironic gender twist, Sebastian, a beautiful boy, receives the phallic arrows, whereas Joan of Arc, a boyish girl, delivers them. This trajectory illustrates the very personal progression of Ida Rubinstein from a fatal woman to a phallic woman — the feminist of today with the glamour intact. "She is a projectile," the Comte de Montesquiou said of her, "who goes straight to the bullseye without bothering about anything else."[55]

During the next few years Ida commissioned several more theatrical works, all of a deeply religious nature, though they never made it to the stage with her in command. The latter half of the 1930s saw both a fading of Ida's career and the deaths of her collaborators and friends. With Montesquiou and Bakst long gone, she lost Ravel in 1937 and D'Annunzio and Astruc in 1938. Her life became increasingly devoted to charity and personal renunciation, and the advent of World War II in 1940 provided Ida with the opportunity to devote herself to causes less theatrical and more humane as well as providing a graceful exit from the public eye.

When the war began Ida set up convalescent homes, as she had during World War I, in both Paris and Etioles, as well as performing *Jeanne d'Arc au bûcher* for charity on Radio Paris, at the portal of the Lucerne cathedral, and on a tour of Belgium. The oratorio had become a rousing patriotic event against the oppression of Hitler and was even performed by amateur musicians in the French Free Zone.

Although she dedicated herself to the war cause, Ida was scared and for good reason. Despite her conversion to Catholicism, the Gestapo knew that Ida was both rich and Jewish. When Hitler unleashed his forces against Holland and Belgium and troops crossed the French border in May 1940, Walter Guinness, now appointed to a peerage as Lord Moyne, persuaded her to flee with her secretary to southern France. Proceeding perilously across the Mediterranean to Algeria and on to Casablanca, they caught a plane to Lisbon and then to London, where they arrived in spring 1941.

Without access to her own money, Ida lived out the remainder of the war at the Ritz Hotel, under the care of Guinness. She kept a low profile, not mixing in society or attending the theater but continuing her support of the war effort. She arranged dinners for officers in her suite at the Ritz, paid for the honeymoon of a soldier and his bride before he left for the trenches, and donated both her time and money to the Free French Forces.

Deeply involved in Winston Churchill's government, Guinness was sent to Cairo in 1942 as Deputy Minister of State where he became the target of Zionist revenge for the sinking of the *Struma* and its hundreds of Rumanian Jews. He was assassinated on 6 November 1944 while driving his car to work. His body was flown to England for his funeral and cremation. Ida did not attend. She had lost her single greatest supporter, a lifelong friend, and quite possibly the only man with whom she had experienced physical love. Guinness had stood by his promise that "there will always be, in a black bank of that black City, what it takes to satisfy all of your aspirations."[56] It is incalculable how much money he actually spent on Ida, but some estimates suggest as much as a third of his entire fortune.

With the war over, Ida returned to Paris in May 1945 to find that her house on the place des Etats-Unis had been ransacked by the Nazis. She packed her bags and left Paris, her beloved home for forty years, the site of her greatest triumphs and most dismal failures. She was now sixty-seven years old, "a long-eyed skeleton," recalled one acquaintance, "in an old dress made by Léon Bakst, a scarecrow left over from the Ballets Russes."[57] Her time in the City of Light was over; she had become a remnant from another time and place.

Settling in Biarritz in 1950, she rented a magnificent villa for several years before moving on to Provence, where she bought a house in Vence, a medieval walled town high above the Mediterranean where she would live out her remaining years. Several of the new works she had commissioned, including two by Claudel, were performed after the war, but Ida had no interest in seeing them and their producers had no interest in her contribution.

In Vence she lived a simple, ascetic life, sleeping little, taking midnight walks, contemplating the stars, reading her religious books, saying the rosary, and seeing no one. She visited Paris a few times and made pilgrimages to the Abbey of Cîteaux in Bourgogne but was otherwise reclusive. There was one person from her past whom Ida attempted to see, her old lover Romaine Brooks, who had a studio in nearby Nice. But Romaine was unsympathetic to Ida's religious devotion and refused to see her, saying only, "She's no longer like an orchid."[58] Romaine did, however, keep on her wall a full-length nude she had painted of Ida around 1917, *The Weeping Venus*.

The only luxuries Ida indulged from earlier times were silk lingerie and champagne. "The day that I no longer drink champagne it is finished for me," she told a friend.[59] She ate little, took a laxative each night, avoided self-pity, and slowly faded away.

The heart in the body D'Annunzio described as "a mystical skeleton" stopped on 20 September 1960.[60] Ida was buried, in a great black gown, in virtual secrecy at the local cemetery in Vence. The white marble slab that marks her grave reads simply "Ida Rubinstein 1960." The only decoration is a large engraved cross. What was left of her fortune went to the Catholic church. She had asked her secretary to wait for one month after her death before notifying the press of her passing, a final addition to her already growing obscurity.

Jean Cocteau, who as a very young man had been so obsessed with Ida's femme fatale, wrote in *Le Figaro*, "With Ida Rubinstein, once again a little of my youth slips away . . . there she is on her way on the River of the Dead, she who came from the Russian ghetto wrapped in Cleopatra's carpet."[61]

As an erotic icon, a bored bisexual, and a female dandy in the guise of dancer, actress, and orator, Ida Rubinstein had a magnificent career of self-glorification that has been, paradoxically, almost completely forgotten. She emerges from the great artistic shuffle of her life without real identity. Although she was patron to artists greater than herself, the most illustrious of her day, their work and fame have left hers in the wings of history's merciless memory of the fantastic, the bizarre, and the once-beautiful. In defying category for her talents she became an anomaly, and she has been ostracized from all.

Of the many ironies that Ida embodies, perhaps the most significant lies in her anachronistic aesthetics. She was a woman whose sensibilities and concepts of beauty were deeply entrenched in fin-de-siècle decadence where she found Salome. But by the second decade of the twentieth century, when grandiosity and mythology were already passé, she insisted on being Helen of Troy, Cleopatra, and Artemis, not to mention the men she played — St. Sebastian, David, and Orpheus — and the ones she didn't, but wanted to — Don Quixote and Christopher Columbus. She proceeded stubbornly with a dated sensibility, while simultaneously heralding modernism with her public narcissism and deeply defiant and eclectic approach to her own life as theater, both onstage and off. With a foot in the past and a foot in the future, she found no means of reference in her present.

As a true Hebrew princess of dark hair, almond eyes, flat chest, narrow hips, and ambiguous sexuality, Ida gave Salome a future beyond the vaudeville belly dancer and the voluptuous temptress who died in World War I with Maud Allan and Mata Hari. She transformed her into a flapper. Her Salome danced not for anyone's head — man or woman — she danced to keep her own intact. Legs closed, she embodied both sexes while being neither, thus attaining a kind of female freedom, a cold severity that lies beyond, or beneath, the world where lust leads. Her allure lay in her mystery, both contrived and real, a withholding that provided a camouflage for vanity and a throne for her perceived potency. Salome became a carapace for Ida's rejection of familial ties, and her "unknowable interiorness."[62]

There was one element beyond all others that allowed Ida to proceed as this transitional Salome — money. A wealthy woman with an even wealthier consort, Ida was able to choose her own life completely and to manifest her vision in reality. She bought her own stage and enjoyed the view. Her financial means added a unique element to the continuing destiny of Salome. She could now decapitate through mercenary means, an option not previously available to her. As a twentieth-century woman Salome became an agile, independent beauty no longer yearning for a saint's head on a platter to satisfy her. She had become the saint herself, carrying a platter piled high with cash.

PART V

Colette:
The Mental Hermaphrodite

I was secretly craving just then to be completely a woman. . . . I am alluding to a genuine mental hermaphroditism which burdens certain highly complex beings. . . . I happened to be making a particular effort at the time to rid myself of this ambiguity, along with all its flaws and privileges.

— Colette

□ □

Chapter Eighteen
_____

The Kiss

*T*HE Moulin Rouge, the most famous music hall in Belle Epoque
Paris, was filled to the rafters on the evening of 3 January 1907.
A well-distributed poster had recently announced a special addition to the regular program: a pantomime entitled *Le Rêve
d'Egypte* (Egyptian dream). The stars were Colette Willy and the
mysteriously named "Yssim." There would be only ten performances, but everybody who was anybody was there for the first night.
Among the elegant aristocrats were the marquis de Belbeuf and other
aristocrats of the empire, members of the Jockey Club led by the Prince
Murat, and various illustrious courtesans. Seated in a box was one of the
writers of the pantomime, Henri Gauthier-Villars, better known as Willy.
As husband to the show's star and presumed author of the four notori-
ously naughty *Claudine* books, the most successful novels produced in
France since the new century began, Willy was a celebrity of notable proportions. His new mistress sat beside him.

The curtain rose at 11 P.M. on a simple stage set. An archeologist
dressed in a blue velvet suit was looking through his scientific tomes in
search of a formula. Before him stood an Egyptian sarcophagus framing
a figure from the ancient world, swathed in layers of linen. As the ban-
dages were unwound from this particular mummy, a beautiful woman
emerged, wearing metal breastplates, snake arm bands, and a long diaphanous skirt draped from the hips (fig. 20). She proceeded to dance in
a distinctly Egyptian manner, undulating her arms and supplicating her
master while lying at his feet in obeisance.

The pantomime in its Oriental style was timely — only two years

FIG. 20. Colette in a publicity still for *Le Rêve d'Egypte,* Paris, 1907
(Bibliothèque de France)

earlier Mata Hari had unveiled herself at the Musée Guimet, and four
months hence Maud Allan would do the same at the Théâtre des Variétés,
both wearing similar Salome outfits. Two years later Ida Rubinstein
would be unwound from her own bandelets at the elegant Théâtre du
Châtelet. Unwrapping the fatal woman, on Parisian stages, was clearly
the fashionable foreplay of the new century.

Murmurs from the rowdy audience began from the moment the curtain rose. When the scientist rejuvenated the mummy from centuries of
slumber with a kiss on the mouth — long, deep, and passionate — the audience went half mad with outrage. Cascades of garlic bouquets tied with
yellow ribbons rained down on the two performers. Pandemonium en-
sued, and for the remaining minutes of the pantomime matchboxes, or-

anges, candy, and cigarette stubs were flung at the stage from the audience of fifteen hundred, while women in the front rows threw their seat cushions. Loud boos drowned out the orchestra of forty musicians. The two performers finished their mime amid the cacophony.

As the curtain lowered, all eyes turned to Willy, who was attempting a hasty exit with his mistress, only to be beaten with fists and umbrellas before the police escorted him to safety. The prefect of police closed down the show on the spot and evacuated the theater, and the press had a field day moralizing on the event — unanimously condemning the proceedings as "a spectacle of . . . audacious immodesty."[1] The episode became legendary as "The Scandal of the Moulin Rouge."

Why all the fuss? This was the very public declaration of lesbian love between two women in front of their husbands, their peers, and their social circle. The man in the blue velvet suit was a woman, the marquise de Belbeuf, recently divorced from the marquis, and the mostly naked mummy whom she kissed was her lover, the delectable Colette Willy, only recently estranged from her own husband. Resonating among the unruly catcalls during the pantomime was the cry, "Down with the dykes!"[2]

This was not the two women's first public appearance together. Less than three weeks earlier, they were seated in a loge box at the prestigious opening of the Théâtre Réjane in the company of the exotic Liane de Pougy, one of the Belle Epoque's most celebrated courtesans, who also took women as her lovers. The marquise — "Missy" to her intimates and the "Yssim" of the pantomime — was dressed in her usual full male attire, cigar in hand, while Colette's neck was provocatively encircled by a dog collar engraved with the words "J'appartiens à Missy" (I belong to Missy).[3]

While the kiss outraged the Moulin Rouge audience, it was the aristocratic lineage of the marquise that caused the most consternation. As the niece of Napoleon III through illegitimate couplings, great-granddaughter of Empress Josephine, and the daughter of the Duc de Morny and the Russian Princess Troubetskoï, a Romanov, Missy was of exceptionally blue blood. For aristocracy to appear onstage at all, not to mention in a depiction of inverted sexuality, was tantamount to blasphemy. The act threatened the very foundations of French social order — and once again, Salome, in the guise of an Egyptian mummy, in the amateur hands of Colette Willy, was onstage center for the provocation.

lette's appearance in *Le Rêve d'Egypte* in 1907 was the first time Sa-
ad appeared overtly as both a femme fatale and a lesbian, a curious
ination. The fatal woman who is lesbian offers the men who covet
hc. the ultimate dismissal, the ultimate challenge. She stands in a fortress
of self-protection from their desire, with her own desire focused not on
them, but on her own sex. Furthermore, she has the temerity to compete
with them for women. This juxtaposition of male and female attributes
was perfectly suited to Colette's experiments with her own complex sexuality.

Unlike Maud Allan, Mata Hari, and Ida Rubinstein, Colette appropriated Salome not as her identity but as her personal accomplice, her
transforming device, in searching out her own true identity as a woman
with a powerful male sensibility. This was a Salome who could look at
women with the desire of a man, and at men with the desire of a woman.
It all began with her formidable, exceptional mother.

Chapter Nineteen

Sido's Masterpiece

*T*HE Scandal of the Moulin Rouge was not the first indiscretion
of Colette's long life, nor the last — and all related to her defiant
acts of personal liberation. The seeds for this rebellion were
sown when her freethinking mother, Sido, baptized her fourth
child two months late. The neighbors were scandalized that this
woman did not rush to protect her child's soul from the devil,
but the pagan Sido wanted to protect her beloved baby's flesh from the
cold January winter air.

Later in her life Colette declared unequivocally that her mother was
the most important person in her whole life. Sido was an unconventional
woman for her time; she never took second place to a man, valued her
own mind, and cared little for the opinions of others. She counseled that
one should not marry the man one was in love with, for power was lost —
but as for lovers, well, she had had one of her own.

Born in Paris, Sido was orphaned early and spent her youth with her
two older brothers among the intelligentsia of Brussels. Married off at

twenty-one to a wealthy landowner twice her age, she took up residence with him in the small Burgundian town of Saint-Sauveur-en-Puisaye, where he was famous as the town drunk. When he beat his young wife in an alcoholic rage, she responded with headstrong vigor: "I hurled everything on the mantle at his head, a little lamp with sharp edges among other things. I hit him in the face and he carried the scar to his grave. I was very pleased with myself. That taught him."[4] This miserable alliance produced two children, a girl and a boy, though the second child was commonly considered to be the illegitimate son of Sido's lover, Captain Jules Colette.

The son of a naval officer, the captain had lost his left leg in military service under Napoleon III in Italy and, after being awarded the Legion of Honor, was given the job of tax collector in Saint-Sauveur, where he met Sido. When her husband conveniently died from his inebriate dissipation, Sido quickly married her lover, and they lived comfortably off his modest salary in addition to the money, houses, and land left to Sido by her first husband.

A second son, Leo, was conceived and then, in 1873, Gabrielle Sidonie Colette was born — with great difficulty. Sido believed that it was a deep and lasting attachment to the mother that produced such a protracted and painful labor — the child not wishing to leave the womb. This last daughter was adored by her mother who called her "Bel-Gazou," "Jewel-of-pure-gold," and "my Masterpiece."[5] Colette never had reason to doubt her mother's love.

Everyone in the Colette household read books, literary journals, and newspapers and played a musical instrument. Children's books were nowhere to be found, and young Gabrielle was reading Honoré de Balzac and Victor Hugo by age seven. Intellect aside, nature in the form of food, animals, and vegetation was Sido's god and her youngest daughter absorbed a love of these sensual pleasures that would guide and dominate her life. Raised in an atmosphere of few rules, the children were allowed to come and go as they pleased, and eat when and what they pleased. The only thing forbidden in the household was "to forbid."

When it came time for formal schooling, Sido did not send her daughter to a classical boarding school but, wanting to keep her close to home, sent her to the local school with the village children. Sido, however, made sure Colette knew that she was superior to Saint-Sauveur and its simple way of life. This school, its teachers, and its pupils would be immortalized, and scandalized, some years later in the Claudine tales. Colette enjoyed the Catholic ceremonies that all schoolchildren attended, and, while Sido had a bemused tolerance of such ritual, she taught her own form of spirituality. When young Colette proudly presented a posy "blessed" at the May Day service, Sido responded, "Do you think it wasn't already blessed before?"[6]

Sido passed on to her daughter an abiding suspicion of the male sex. Her cynicism even extended to male animals. When Colette found her mother shooing the male hunting dog away from his litter of puppies, she asked Sido, where would he go? "To the tavern, or to play cards with Landre, or to flirt with the washerwoman," was her mother's cool reply. Sido championed women, even taking in, to the town's dismay, unmarried pregnant girls to see them through their predicament. She taught her daughter, in no uncertain terms, that she was not only equal to any man but perhaps something better. "You are a girl, a female beast," she counseled, "my equal and my rival."[7]

As a child, Colette dreamed of being a courtesan, not a writer. As a provincial Salome-in-progress, she was enamored by the lives of the Parisian cocottes she read about in the gossip sections of the newspapers. These magnificent, larger-than-life creatures presented the little country girl with the image of "an admirable, unknown race."[8] While Colette stopped just short of becoming one herself, these sexual sirens would later become her friends, as well as the heroines of her literary explorations.

The trail of Colette's sexual fascination with women can be traced to her childhood from a "first seduction," as she later termed it, by one of her mother's friends whose great breasts with their "violet and hard" tips intrigued her.[9] Later she developed a crush on her piano teacher, Augusta Holmes, a magnificent blond beauty, daughter of the poet Alfred de Vigny and mistress to Richard Wagner. After enough men and children, Holmes had become entirely lesbian.

While women in Colette's childhood and adolescence were clearly the stronger and more attractive sex, men had their place as husbands. Colette soon found a colorful one of her own who would lead her to Belle Epoque Paris, to the power of her pen, and to the lesbian underground where Salome awaited her.

Chapter Twenty

Willy's Ghost

"WILLY was not huge, he was bulbous," wrote Colette of her first husband — he was all curves at the edges, rounded shoulders and hips, with a soft face and drooping eyes standing on a neck the size of Scarlett O'Hara's waist. "It has been said that he bore a marked resemblance to Edward VII," wrote his wife. "I would say that, in fact, the likeness was to Queen Victoria."[10] Despite this unattractive physique, Henri Gauthier-Villars — "Willy" — had considerable success with women: he was a dandy, importing his shirts from London and sporting a monocle and a full, well-curled mustache. Willy oozed charm and adored intrigue.

Called by one biographer the "most accomplished scandal-monger of the Belle Epoque" and by another one of the era's "most putrid wrecks," Willy derived from an intellectual family who published the work of such thinkers as Louis Pasteur, Albert Einstein, and Marie Curie. Though a highly educated man and editor of several journals himself, Willy had little use for rational thought; his interest was illusion, and his credo stated that all art is both autobiographical and erotic. He was best known as the popular music critic for the paper *L'Echo de Paris*, where he championed Wagner, Debussy, and Fauré and later Stravinsky and Poulenc. "In music," he wrote of himself, "he possessed deliciously vague notions."[11] Publicity of any variety was Willy's passion above all else, though even he had little inkling just how much he would receive thanks to the young provincial virgin he chose as his bride.

In 1889 Willy's beloved mistress gave birth to a son, and when she died two years later, he was bereft and took his progeny to Châtillon-sur-Loing, where the Colette family now lived. Willy's father and Captain Colette were old friends, and Willy thought Sido could find a wet nurse for his motherless son. That was not all he found.

Colette was now eighteen, a lively, literate, but inexperienced young lady with a chiseled face, mischievous eyes, and a braid of hair extending to her feet. She had been reading articles in journals for years signed by the estimable Willy and, at fourteen years her senior, he presented an impressive figure of Parisian elegance and sophistication. Sido plotted: her daughter was without a dowry to attract a husband, and while Willy was of better family, the match was evened out by the shame of his illegitimate child. Colette fell in love as only virgins can, even begging one night to be his mistress, but to her later chagrin, he wanted to marry her and make the alliance respectable. After a two-year, long-distance engagement, they were married in 1893, several months after her twentieth birthday, in a small ceremony in Châtillon. Only days before the wedding it was rumored in *Gil Blas*, a Parisian publication, that the young woman from Châtillon was already his mistress, and Willy, always ready to meet scandal head on, promptly challenged the editor to a duel, wounding him in the abdomen and salvaging his bride's honor.

Willy confided to a friend that this was not for him a marriage of love — that was buried in the cemetery with his son's mother — nor of money, but of affection. And sexual initiation. "Next day," the bride wrote fifty years later of her wedding night, "I felt separated from that evening by a thousand leagues, abysses, irremediable metamorphoses."[12] There was not only sex, there was Paris, and Willy was her guide to both.

Moving first into the crowded "Venusberg" bachelor pad Willy had named in honor of Wagner, and then to an apartment in the heart of the Latin Quarter on the rue Jacob, Colette and Willy employed a cook, a maid, and a valet. In her memoirs Colette left the impression that she was a martyred young wife, following her famous husband on a tightly held leash, bored, lonely, and somewhat disregarded. The truth was otherwise. She may well have been Galatea to Willy's Pygmalion, but in filling that role she received the education from which she was to draw a lifetime of experience.

Within the first several years of her marriage Colette met, via Willy, *le tout Paris*. They frequented musical concerts and salon gatherings where she listened to Anatole France, Paul Valéry, and Léon Daudet propound their philosophies. She exchanged correspondence with Marcel Proust and Claude Debussy, while Gabriel Fauré developed a crush on her, sending both gifts and compositions. She was painted, caricatured, and photographed incessantly, usually in some subservient position to Willy in top hat and sweeping mustache (fig. 21). She developed close friendships with numerous young writers and novelists of the day. In 1896 Colette began her own Sunday salon.

Willy also took his young wife to the music halls, clubs, and cafés

FIG. 21. Colette and Willy, ca. 1905
(Collection Jouvenel, Musée Colette)

where she met the sexual misfits of Paris — aristocratic lesbians, bisexual
courtesans, heterosexual dandies, celibate homosexuals, cross-dressers,
anorexics, sadists and masochists, and addicts of various persuasions
from alcohol and sex to opium and morphine. A year and half into her
marriage, Colette, led by an anonymous letter, came face to face with the
dark underbelly of her own marriage — a Mlle. Charlotte Kinceler, a five-
foot-tall wild girl with lower-class charm and a fast tongue whom men
adored and who lent her favors generously.

Colette caught Willy with Charlotte, engaged not in lovemaking but in an act even more intimate for Willy — going over his account books. Distraught, Colette was enveloped by an extended and somewhat mysterious illness. While some biographers suggest syphilis caught from Willy (Colette never admitted to it), most conclude this was a nervous breakdown. Either way, Willy's infidelity was the cause and she descended into three months of scorching hot baths, headaches, dark rooms, and despairing doctors. She wrote later of this episode as her "punishment" for "becoming the show, the plaything, the licentious masterpiece of some middle-aged man."[13] Only when Sido was summoned to Paris to nurse her did she begin to show a willingness to live again and arose, like a phoenix, from her sickbed to meet her nemesis — in more ways than one.

"From her [Kinceler] I got my first notions of tolerance and concealment and the possibility of coming to terms with the enemy. Concentration, humility — it was an instructive time." Befriending Charlotte, who sold erotic toys among her herbs and teas, Colette began to take charge of her own sexual life by learning from those déclassé women who made sex their profession. Present at the arrival of one of Willy's lovers in her home, she watched, perversely fascinated, as the passionate woman lay languorously across the bed, untying her bodice, while describing exactly how she liked to make love. Colette embraced her jealousy and called Willy's mistresses "my 'monsters.'"[14] She also learned complicity, on one occasion entertaining one of her husband's mistresses while he entertained another.

Heterosexual sex was, for young Colette, a curious mélange of bittersweet disconnection. "It would seem that for him," she wrote, "sexual pleasure is made up of desire, perversity, lively curiosity and deliberate licentiousness . . . whereas it shatters me and plunges me into a mysterious despair that I seek and also fear." This despair took the form of a lover, and the lesbian tendencies of young Colette found their object of desire. In May 1901 she began an affair with a rich, beautiful, and married American woman. Georgie Raoul-Duval mesmerized Colette, who followed her about Paris from dress shops to her boudoir like a lovesick puppy, a prisoner of her passion. Willy, his voyeurism piqued, encouraged the liaison, a perverse logic Colette understood: "Certain women need women in order to preserve their taste for men."[15] He insinuated himself even further into the affair by finding a love nest on the avenue Kléber where the two women could meet undisturbed — but he kept a key.

In August the three met in Bayreuth to attend Wagner's *Ring* cycle, and shortly thereafter Colette discovered the devastating truth: Georgie had seduced Willy as well, and was fond of receiving her married lovers in hourly succession. Not only did Colette feel the humiliation of being a mere diversion for Georgie, but she had been deeply betrayed by Willy yet again, as well as by her own lover, a woman. She took swift revenge by recording the whole fiasco on paper.

Several years earlier, in his guise as a soft-core pornographer, Willy had suggested to Colette that she write down her adolescent adventures, and thus was born the titillating tale of the young libertine, Claudine, Colette's subversive alter ego. The books were published under Willy's name. In Claudine's third installment, appearing in 1902, Colette told the extraordinary tale of her complex triangle with Willy and Georgie, and the book was hailed as "the *Liaisons dangereuses* of the twentieth century."[16] The Claudine books became one of the biggest publishing successes in French literature, and Claudine went onstage, leading the way to Colette's own stage debut a few years later.

On 22 January 1902 *Claudine à Paris* premiered in a play adapted by Willy and Lugné-Poë, the actor who had directed the first stage production of Wilde's *Salome* in 1896. The production launched the career of a petite Algerian actress from the music hall stage named Polaire. "Tear it apart favorably," Colette wrote to the drama critic of *L'Echo de Paris*. "It has nothing to do with either art or literature, of course. It's idiotic, and you should say so. But please also say that it will be a 'box-office hit.' It has to be because we need the money."[17]

The show was indeed an enormous hit, playing for a hundred and twenty-three performances, and Polaire, with her sixteen-inch waist, enormous soulful eyes, and schoolgirl outfits, became a star. Willy's fame soared to such an extent that the actor Sacha Guitry commented, "As far as I can see only God and perhaps Alfred Dreyfus are more famous than Willy these days." Capturing the public's imagination, the Claudine craze initiated an early example of modern celebrity, and her schoolgirl image was marketed, American-style, in lotions, socks, collars, dresses, hats, perfume, powder, cigarettes, postcards, statues, and even ice cream. By 1904 there were no less than five biographies written about Willy and Colette, and he became inundated with young women all claiming to be Claudine. Surmised his wife, "the whole lot of them long for my death."[18]

Relishing the publicity, Willy bought Polaire and Colette several identical outfits and marched them out in public together as twins, his "two kids," inviting rumor as to the true nature of this incestuous three-some. Once again, as with Georgie, Colette was in a triangular scenario with another woman and her husband. Willy also orchestrated a private showing of his two protegées. The Spanish painter José Maria Sert was hosting a party at the restaurant Paillard, and for dessert a giant cake was wheeled out from the kitchen. From the depths of the whipped cream, to the delight of all, emerged Colette and Polaire, stark naked.

About this time Colette, in a bold act of self-reinvention, cut off her floor-length hair, twenty years of Sido's careful cultivation, and emerged as a modern woman with a racy, androgynous bob. No longer Rapunzel waiting in her tower to be saved, Willy's wife was opening her eyes from marital disillusion and rejecting her submissive stance. Her rebellion soon took on dimensions both radical and original for a wife of her social standing in turn-of-the-century France.

In addition to her now well-toned literary discipline, Colette had been attending to another form of toning — that of her physical body. In early 1902 the Willys moved to 177 bis rue de Courcelles, where Colette installed a symbolic white balustrade dividing the living room into two equal halves. As she entered her tenth year of marriage to Willy, signs of separation abounded in proportion to betrayals and affairs. Upstairs she inaugurated her garconnière — a bachelor pad — to which she alone kept the key, and here she received her lovers and friends in private.

Designed as a small gymnasium, the room sported a horizontal bar, trapeze rings, and a knotted climbing rope where Colette practiced daily. Working out in 1902 was an uncommon venture for a woman. "Thinking about it later," she wrote, "it seemed to me that I was exercising my body in just the way prisoners do, who are not exactly planning to escape, but who nevertheless cut up a sheet and plait it, sew coins inside a lining, and hide chocolate under the mattress."[19]

In 1905, as an extension of her gymnastics routine, she began taking lessons from Georges Wague, a professional mime. The woman of words was now intent on entering the world of three dimensions. She was readying herself for the stage, for public seduction, for Salome. But it was not a man who would provide Colette with her first audience; it was a woman.

In June 1905, one month after the Willys legally separated their ma-terial possessions and finances, *La Vie Parisienne* announced that Colette would be performing a pantomime in the private salon of Miss Natalie Clifford Barney, an American heiress. Barney was born in Dayton, Ohio, and had installed herself permanently in Paris in 1894 at the age of eighteen. A notorious lesbian seductress, she proceeded to become the center of a circle of Sapphic sisters who lived for love, conquest, and art. No sexual liaison developed between the two women — Barney found Colette far too attached to Willy, who initially introduced them — but they did develop a lifelong friendship.

Living at the time in a house in the Parisian suburb of Neuilly, Barney invited Colette to perform at one of her famous afternoon gatherings where, according to one male visitor, "young women, transported by literature and champagne, danced madly about in each other's arms."[20] Colette made her amateur debut in a male role as the shepherd Daphnis in love with a beautiful wood nymph. Mata Hari, whose debut at the Musée Guimet three months earlier had thrust her into the spotlight, had also been invited to perform her Hindu dance.

Later that summer Colette was summoned several more times to Barney's, performing as a faun in a piece by Willy inspired by Debussy's *Afternoon of a Faun,* and again in a short play by Pierre Louÿs, a writer of sophisticated erotica. *Dialogue au soleil couchant* found Colette, again *en travestie,* in a short crepe de chine tunic, Roman buckskins, and a Tahitian-style wreath courting Eva Palmer, a beautiful red-haired American and Natalie Barney's lover.

This last occasion was a performance for women only, and Mata Hari was to perform in the nude. These half-dressed Salome sisters were now convening under lesbian edict. Defying her husband's protest, Colette attended, appearing in a few revealing rags, and found refuge in an underground world where women loved women openly and passionately. Colette's own femme fatale, her Egyptian mummy, was not a response to the male gaze, but to the female gaze. Salome would turn lesbian in Colette's incarnation.

Chapter Twenty-One

The Barrier of Light

H AVING lived Willy's life for twelve years, Colette was ready to try a life of her own and, at the age of thirty-three, with a very public switch in sexual orientation, Colette began her descent into the music hall where the femme fatale resided. Colette's lesbian foray and her newfound profession were intertwined experiments in a kind of veiled self-protection that would allow for a radical liberation of both her body and her mind. The exhibitionist would perform and the writer would watch.

Colette's sexual interest in women had begun long ago with her childhood crushes and schoolgirl trysts. Two years into her marriage with Willy, Colette admitted to suffering "a sharp but brief infatuation for a great, red-haired horse of a woman,"[21] and several years later she indulged her first outright love affair with Georgie. Once her marriage with Willy had settled into an arrangement, more public and professional than private and intimate, Colette found comfort, support, and sex not with another man but in the maternal arms of a woman — a woman who had established herself as one of the most remarkable lesbians of the time.

Sophie-Mathilde-Adèle de Morny, Missy to her friends, was ten years Colette's senior and a child of the uppermost aristocracy. After an isolated and unhappy childhood with a deeply critical mother, she was married off by her wealthy family to the equally wealthy marquis de Belbeuf. She had slept twice with men and did not care to repeat the ordeal. After six years of marriage she separated from the marquis, and they finally divorced in 1903.

Missy was one of the Belle Epoque's notable cross-dressing lesbians. She comported herself as a man, padding out her small feet with socks to fit her men's shoes, and wearing overalls and three-piece suits, a short haircut, and a rounded center that betrayed no breasts. She even tried making herself a mustache from her poodle's tail. So convincing was her masculine appearance that on the rare occasion she wore a dress even members of her own family thought "she looked like a man dressed up as a woman."[22] She hosted dinner parties at her Paris mansion where she gave generously to her extended family, a glamorous mixture of courtesans, handsome heterosexual men (her "sons"), and lively young actresses. This eclectic group called their hostess "Monsieur le marquis," and "mon oncle." Evenings would end with various couples disappearing into dark corners indulging in morphine, opium, and sex.

The Napoleonic Code of 1805 had made no provision for the punishment of homosexuality, and Paris had become, during the turn of the twentieth century, a center for lesbian freedom. Public cross-dressing was, however, forbidden by law, and so the women's affairs were conducted in the privacy of their homes and salons. Exhibitionism was key to their self-expression, and private theatrical performances provided the ideal entertainment. This international Paris-Lesbos community which Colette now entered included a colorful array of aristocratic women like Missy herself: "Baronesses of the Empire, canonesses, lady cousins of Czars, illegitimate daughters of grand-dukes, exquisites of the Parisian bourgeoisie, and also some aged horsewomen of the Austrian aristocracy."[23]

Missy was present at Natalie Barney's afternoons where Colette performed her first amateur steps, and soon the ingenue dancer came under the protective embrace of the marquise de Belbeuf, living with her by late 1906. If, as a grown woman, she could not go home to Sido, she could at least have Missy. Colette's own admitted "virility" was once again cushioned in the soft, rounded feminine edges common to both her husband and her new female lover (fig. 22).

Colette wrote of Missy's "overwhelming gaze," and in her short story "White Night," published in 1907, she referred to her lover as granting "me sensual pleasure as relief, as the sovereign exorcism which drives from me the demons of fever, anger and anxiety." Years later she explained her experience of lesbianism in her very personal examination of sexual inversion, *The Pure and the Impure:* "In no way is it passion that fosters the devotion of two women, but rather a feeling of kinship. . . . A woman finds pleasure caressing a body whose secrets she knows, her own body giving her the clue to its preferences."[24]

Her new lover was not only devoted but generous with her money, paying the rent on Colette's pied-à-terre on the rue Villejust, giving her five hundred francs a month — two hundred more than Willy had given his wife for her writing services — and even buying her a beach house in Normandy where the ladies spent their summers. On occasion Willy and his mistress were invited to join them. Colette had made the transition

FIG. 22. Sem, *Claudine en ménage* (Colette and Missy, the marquise de Belbeuf),
1906 (Collection Viollet)

from a betrayed wife to a kept woman — kept by a woman — and never
had she felt more liberated. Her self-regard had grown in an ironic and
sinuous manner.

Emboldened by her new stability with Missy, Colette launched her
stage career with ferocious ambition, backed by Willy's formidable publicity machine. Though she continued to write, her reputation was not yet
established, and any money she might make from her pen was both small
and intermittent. Besides, she never really enjoyed the act of writing. She
was down to basics, and displaying her body was her first choice for a

new career. The current popularity of the Eastern femme fatale provided the model for this dancing declaration of her new sexual autonomy, and she had a ready audience of both male voyeurs and lesbian peers.

After her initial amateur appearances in Barney's salon, she continued to study mime with Wague to perfect her new craft and performed several new salon pieces — "La Danse du Sphinx" and "La Danse du serpent bleu" — both in the current fashion of Oriental-style dancing. She found herself on occasion in the curious position of dancing at soirées where her husband's mistresses, present and former, as well as their husbands, were her audience, while she was the evening's "entertainment." Musing on the precarious juxtaposition of class to which she now subjected herself, she wrote: "Packed closely together they crane forward with that curiosity, that cynical courtesy which men of the world display towards a woman who is considered 'déclassée,' the woman whose finger-tips one used to kiss in her drawing-room and who now dances, half-naked, on a platform."[25]

The theater became Colette's refuge. "The modern convent," she called it, and her dressing room, full of mirrors, makeup, and costumes, became her "cloister." The music hall provided Colette with a venue for a very public reinvention of herself. "There came to me that odd sensation," she explained, "that only on the stage was I really alone and safe from my fellow-creatures, protected from the whole world by the barrier of light." Onstage she found relief, and she cheerfully described herself as "a lady of letters who has turned out badly."[26]

The music hall — with its frequent tours, arduous rehearsals, unpredictable conditions and late-night shows — was a good teacher for a woman searching out independence. It provided one of the few venues at the time where a woman could earn her own living with her body that was not outright prostitution. On matters financial Colette claimed that the theater converted her into "a tough but honest little businesswoman," and within a few years she would haggle over her contracts with new-found self-worth, claiming, "I have a name with proved box-office value, [so] why should I contract myself to never get more than five louis?"[27]

She came to value her body as her instrument: "I began to take care of myself, to worry about my bowels, my stomach, my skin, with the tetched vigilance of a devoted landlord." Life in the music hall also allowed Colette to indulge in her devotion to makeup, the layers of illusion. "It's useful," she explained. "I am made up for life. I'll have nothing to add

when I'm twenty years older."[28] But most of all, her theater life provided
her with an experience of backstage life which she would reveal and re-
examine in her novels during the ensuing four decades. Her heroines
would remain actresses, dancers, courtesans, and ingenues, her peers
from her days in the music hall.

By 1906 Colette had become a paid professional. Performing in four
entertainments, all of an ambiguous sexual nature, she appeared in various Paris theaters for the general public. On 6 February she reprised her
faun image in a short tunic with two horns embedded in her hair in *Le
Désir, l'amour et la chimère,* by Francis de Croisset at the Théâtre des Ma-
thurins. The show received huge publicity thanks to Willy's efforts and
toured to Brussels. By the end of the month she was performing in Monte
Carlo accompanied by her estranged husband. Despite their separation,
Willy remained for several years as the manager and producer of her
growing stage career, and they saw each other daily. In late March she
appeared at the small Théâtre Royale in Paris in a one-act play entitled
Aux innocents les mains pleines by Sacha Guitry, another protegé of Missy's.
This piece showcased Colette as a playboy in a Saville Row suit exchang-
ing a long kiss with a woman.

By October Colette was appearing at the enormous Olympia music
hall, where Mata Hari had recently starred, in a mimed drama entitled *La
Romanichelle.* Once again, refusing the usual body stocking, she was
shockingly nude under her skimpy costume. One critic claimed that "the
debut of Colette Willy will certainly lure all of Paris to the Olympia. The
famous name, the literary and social reputation, the talent and beauty of
the young debutante make her one of the most important stars discovered by a music-hall director in a long time."[29]

The following month she performed at the Théâtre Marigny in *Pan*
directed by Lugné-Poë. *Pan* was a philosophic piece in three acts that
praised the senses and attacked sexual taboos. Colette as Paniska danced
hedonistically among various vines wearing a tattered gypsy costume
that showed "her leg and thigh naked to the hip. Accompanied by string
instruments, she struck some ceremonial poses, during which her skirt
rose still higher." It was reported that the Sapphic section of the audience
"became delirious."[30] One critic even announced that "la nature," her
sex, was momentarily revealed. Indeed, Colette was diving into her new
profession with considerable abandon — and notoriety.

On tour in Brussels she was angry when she was compelled by the town authorities to wear a body stocking under her costume. She declared her rebellion in the journal *La Vie parisienne:* "I've had enough of it! I want . . . I want . . . I want to do as I please! . . . I want to play in pantomime and even in comedy. If I find tights uncomfortable and degrading to my body, I want to dance naked."[31]

Colette believed she had two complementary gifts, one on the stage, the other on the page — the words of her pen giving voice to her mime, both basking in the marriage of sound and rhythm. Exhibitionism was not only a literary attitude for Colette; it was her manifest destiny. While Marie Curie was breaking ground as a Sorbonne professor, the thirty-three-year-old Colette was breaking barriers of a different nature by baring her body for all of Paris, and she used her pen to describe, and defend, the life she sought in the theater, behind the "barrier of light."

> I'll never go to a first night again, except on the other side of the footlights. Because I mean to go on dancing in the theatre, and I shall dance naked or clothed for the sheer pleasure of dancing, of suiting my gestures to the rhythm of the music and spinning round ablaze with light, blind as a fly in a sunbeam. And I shall invent beautiful slow dances with a veil; sometimes it will cover my body, sometimes it will envelop me with a spiral of smoke, and when I run it will billow behind me like the sail of a ship.[32]

By January 1907 Colette was ensconced in her veils and jeweled breastplates, kissing Missy for the outraged public at the Moulin Rouge. Contrary to her fears, she did not have to leave the country to earn her living; in fact, her salary increased as a result of the scandal. Her success as a performer reached its summit seven months later when she starred in a new mimed drama where an unprecedented show of nudity grabbed headlines and audiences and didn't let them go for four years.

This pantomime was entitled *La Chair* (The flesh), and the melodramatic tale explored the subject of the power of female nudity. Hokartz, a smuggler, played by Georges Wague, discovers that his beautiful wife, Yulka, played by Colette, has been unfaithful with a dashing young officer. In a fit of rage, Hokartz lunges at his wife with his dagger, but instead of killing her, he tears her dress and reveals a breast. Overwhelmed by her beauty, and consumed with guilt over his murderous intent, he kills himself. Yulka looses her mind in madness. The flesh is triumphant, and, as in Salome's tale, a woman's naked beauty results in a dead man.

Rehearsals for the drama provoked an intense breast debate. Initially there was merely a ripped dress, but the director was not pleased,

"It's not naked enough there!" Colette, standing in her shredded dress, replied, "Not naked enough! What more do you want?" After a few moments he declared, "Let out a breast!" and thus Colette's bosom was exposed.[33] It was the first use of nudity in serious pantomime for the time, and once again Colette was at the center of a sexually scandalous exposé and everyone had an opinion.

While rival performers criticized Colette's flagrant display, her male audience was ecstatic. One Belgian critic described the "admirable gesture, this violent ripping of the tunic that lets gush out the tasty fruit of the bosom," while another rhapsodized, "When one knows her breasts one adores them." Her "cups of alabaster" mesmerized the shy Maurice Chevalier, then an unknown eighteen-year-old music hall performer. Autographing a photograph for him, she wrote: "Hide discreetly . . . what I am displaying with such generosity."[34]

An unqualified hit, *La Chair* went on the road. After Paris the troupe traveled to Nice and Monte Carlo with its drama, and again caused trouble as a brief postcard from Colette to a friend indicates — "Quick success, although the Prefect of the Alpes Maritimes veiled the left breast."[35]

Colette's easy acquiescence to exposing herself onstage was the culmination of an uninhibited and proud attitude toward her naked body that had been evident long before. Only three years into her marriage she had posed topless for a bust by a sculptor that was featured in the Paris Salon of 1896. Several years later, an acquaintance told of visiting Willy at home and catching sight in a mirror of a reclining naked Colette in the next room. "Do you know Séché sees you in the mirror?" asked Willy, amused. Without moving from her position, Colette quipped, "I hope that he is pleased." "She emitted," wrote another friend, "an indefinable and troubling odour of sensuality."[36]

For the next four years, in more than two hundred and fifty performances, Colette's bosom pleased audiences from Grenoble, Brussels, and Geneva, to Lyon, Marseille, and Montpellier, where it had the ability on every occasion to silence an unruly crowd and satisfy its expectant viewers. Missy often toured with Colette, easing the trials of frequent moves with her chauffeured car and first-class accommodations. Keeping Sido apprised of her accomplishments, Colette sent her mother more than one hundred postcards from her travels — from Nancy she reported that the crowd at Reims "cried the name of your daughter throughout the theater!"[37] These missives always ended with regards sent from Missy. The liberal Sido thoroughly approved of her daughter's lesbian liaison, knowing she was well cared for.

On 4 June 1909, while Ida Rubinstein was being unraveled for the first time from her sarcophagus in Diaghilev's *Cléopâtre* for the nobility of Paris, Colette Willy was in Marseille baring her breast at the Eldorado music hall in *La Chair* for a somewhat less chic but no less appreciative audience — two Salomes hard at work revealing their bodies to the eager French public both north and south.

With the success of *La Chair*, Colette's salary rose to equal those of the great music-hall stars of the day. She was now a self-supporting woman, and her bare bosom had done much to get her there. Having learned from Willy the value of publicity, she had herself photographed numerous times in various states of undress as a faun, as a showgirl, as an Egyptian dancer, wrapped in a revealing toga, reclining nude on a lion skin. Some of these images became popular postcards of the time, giving Colette yet another identity — she became a French pin-up.

While Colette focused on her celebrity, serious critics offered their divergent opinions on her actual talents as a mime. André Rouveyre recalled the young performer with disdain: "She danced pantomime, and she danced naked. It was a sorry sight. Although Colette already possessed wings of the spirit, they were not in evidence on her body in the theater. . . . After each jump, her naked feet would hit the floor with a thud."[38]

Critic Louis Delluc writing in the popular *Comoedia illustré*, however, sang her praises: "For me the most original of the mimes, and the most true, is Colette. . . . La Chair! She would willingly name the whole of her lived and living work by this title. . . . Her plastic poses are those of an intellectual woman. . . . Then she reveals her uplifted bosom . . . we feel that in all this there is something inexplicable and something very pure."[39]

By June 1910 Colette's divorce from Willy was final, though their literary vengeance continued. Willy's "factory" of ghost writers published numerous books with titles like *The Perverted Peasant* and *The Imprudences of Peggy* wherein Colette was derided. In *Lélie, the Opium Addict* of 1911, he requested of his ghost writer that the Baronne de Bize "resemble — blatantly . . . Mme. Colette Willy." The result was brutal: "Not that Mme. de Bize was any spring chicken. Her forty years were all-too evident from

the bitter creases in her sunken cheeks . . . her exaggerated hips that had
in bygone days been praised . . . for their arrogant curves were now, un-
fortunately, turned to fat. Her short, thick waist revolved above those
hips, reminiscent of a gourd."[40] Brutal, but bad literature. Colette, however, produced in her novel of vengeance a masterpiece.

Despite immersion in her ongoing stage life, Colette, using the discipline Willy had taught her, continued to chronicle her own life in autobiographical novels. In 1910 *The Vagabond* was published to enormous acclaim, receiving three votes for the prestigious Prix Goncourt. The
heroine of this book, Renée Néré, "dancer and mime," is a music hall performer living a celibate life following a painful marriage of betrayal to
Adolphe Taillandy — Willy — who is manipulative, untalented, and degenerate. The story details the pain of disillusion with love and Renée's
ambivalence when offered it again by an eager lover: "I cease to belong to
myself when he puts his mouth on mine. . . . He is my enemy, he is the
thief who steals me from myself."[41] She chooses, despite her erotic desires, to let the man go, wanting, beyond even love, to hold onto herself.
The novel is a treatise on female liberation, and the price is the renunciation of love and sex and thereby the slavery so often intrinsic in female attachment.

The rejected man in *The Vagabond* was based on an affair Colette had
during her years with Missy, who had blessed the relationship — the man
was one of her "sons." Auguste Hériot, a rich, eligible, and handsome
young man and heir to a department store fortune, adored Colette and
wanted to marry her. Despite a keen maternal affection for him, she considered him a boy and too shallow in his nature to be her match.

Within a year of the publication of *The Vagabond,* at the height of her
fame, Colette met another man who was her match and, proceeding beyond Renée Néré's rejection of love, fell deeply in love. She was now
thirty-nine years old, and her years of the music hall, breast baring, and
lesbian refuge had run their course. While healing from the betrayals of
Willy under Missy's tender gaze, she had established her own identity as
both an actress and a dancer as well as a writer. She now took this power
and self-confidence back into the precarious arena of heterosexual nego-
tiation to meet a man on her own terms. Colette's six years in the land of
Lesbos came to an abrupt end.

Chapter Twenty-Two

The Mature Seductress

*T*HE object of Colette's new passion was Baron Henry de Jouvenel des Ursins, an editor at *Le Matin*, the Parisian newspaper
that hired Colette as a journalist at the end of 1910 following her
success with *The Vagabond*. The affair began with considerable
drama in April of the following year during an evening of bo-
hemian couple-swapping at a house party attended by Colette
and Auguste Hériot, and Jouvenel and his current mistress, Isabelle de
Comminges, known as "La Panthère." A fire was ignited between the
scandalous music-hall star and the ambitious, dynamic editor.

By the end of May, Colette in her confusion decided to marry the
wealthy Hériot at the urging of both Missy and Sido and traveled to
Switzerland to perform in *La Chair*. Jouvenel sent a telegram declaring
that he could not, and would not, live without her and proceeded to show
up dramatically on her doorstep direct from his latest journalistic duel,
one arm in a sling. Colette hurriedly wired Hériot to cancel his imminent
arrival, ending the brief engagement and making her choice.

The Panther was furious and declared she would kill the "other
woman," whereupon Colette marched straight to her door and introduced herself as the "other woman." Jouvenel placed his new lover under armed protection until the threat had passed. His rejected mistress
reconciled herself by sailing off with Colette's ex-lover, Hériot, on his
yacht for a debauched few weeks of revenge and recovery.

Missy was "glacial and disgusted" at the swift turn of her lover's af-
fections and promptly moved out of the house in Brittany that she had
bought for Colette barely a year earlier. Natalie Barney, who had watched
approvingly Colette's transition from Willy to Missy, commented dis-
dainfully, "Colette loves seascapes and open horizons, little dogs, being
backstage, and having one man at a time to keep her in slavery."[42]

Jouvenel was from a aristocratic though cash-poor family who
owned a castle in central France. He was an intelligent, arrogant, wom-
anizing, and very attractive man a few years her junior, and Colette called
her new lover alternately Pasha, Sultan, and Sidi — "Lord" in Arabic.
She set up house with him almost immediately and married him the fol-

lowing year. He was, she told a friend, "a love as never before!" and she described her newfound sexual happiness to a girlfriend with sly intent. "But who told you I have been neglecting physical culture? I just have a new method, that's all. The Sidi Method. It's excellent. But no public courses. Only private lessons . . . extremely private."[43]

Within two short years, Colette had completely changed her life to its own opposite. She gave up autonomy, women, sexual freedom, the music hall, and even, briefly, writing novels, for the more conventional experience of monogamy, marriage, and motherhood. Her freedom established, she now gravitated to new circumstances, perhaps to test its strength. Colette proudly described her husband as "the master of all, . . . His presence relieves me of the need to think, to plan, to act other than to arrange the bedroom or arrange my figure. The rest is his domain."[44] The outrageous rebel appeared tamed, if not enslaved, by what was probably the first good heterosexual sex she had ever known — Willy certainly had not shown her that side of love.

"Are you a feminist?" she was queried in an interview only a year earlier. "Ah! No!" she replied with gusto. "The suffragettes disgust me. And if some women in France decide to imitate them, I hope they will understand that these customs do not have a place in France. Do you know what the suffragettes deserve? The whip and the harem."[45] Seemingly conservative words from a woman whose life traces a clear, though complex, trajectory toward her own emotional and physical liberation. But Colette was sly and knew the lure of "the whip and the harem" — they could be another route to sexual freedom.

For the next ten years Colette played the bourgeois wife and hostess to her powerful husband, who became increasingly interested in a political career for himself, a world for which Colette had little interest. Giving birth to a daughter, little Bel-Gazou, in 1913, she attempted motherhood in her own style, but the role did not come naturally to her. Bel-Gazou was shipped off to several boarding schools and spent more time with her nurse than her mother. When the child was stung by a bee one day, Colette berated her daughter for exciting the bee. Bel-Gazou grew up to marry, only to discover on her wedding night that she had a physical revulsion to men. The marriage was quickly dissolved.

Despite her circumstances, the rebel in Colette was not dead, only in hibernation experimenting with convention. She reemerged in grand style when Colette embarked upon a two-year affair with Bertrand de

Jouvenel, the seventeen-year-old son of her husband by his first wife, an act that precipitated the end of her marriage. Like Willy, Jouvenel was a notorious womanizer, and her affair with his son was perhaps the ultimate revenge for his adulteries. But it was much more.

Uncannily replicating fiction, the affair was very similar in circumstance to Colette's 1920 novel *Chéri*, which told of the passionate love affair between a middle-aged courtesan, Léa, and her beautiful boy lover. Art was now predicting life. "I made up Léa with foreboding," she wrote of her heroine. "Everything one writes comes to pass."[46]

The affair with Bertrand began during the summers of 1920 and 1921 at the seaside house in Brittany where Colette spent blissful summers in a matriarchal world of close female friends, her daughter, and brief visits from her husband. In the time-tested French tradition of a young man being initiated into the world of love by one of his mother's friends, Bertrand was ripe. Colette, his stepmother, took on the job and opened up to this attractive and intelligent young man not only the world of lovemaking but her whole world, Sido's world, the world of plants, animals, food, and books. Young Bertrand was smitten and adored this short, stocky, dynamic woman thirty years his senior.

Morally, of course, the dynamics were questionable. Colette was not only sleeping with her husband's son, but with her own daughter's halfbrother. This nearly fifty-year-old Salome had lost neither her lust, nor her powers of seduction, nor her desire for the impossible love. When Henry de Jouvenel discovered the affair, the couple separated and divorced after twelve years together. Even under this obvious distress, young Bertrand, in a defiant act of parental disengagement, chose to stay faithful to his mistress and not his own father. Colette reclaimed her autonomy once again by going back on the stage from which she had been absent for ten years, boldly playing Léa herself in a theatrical version of *Chéri*.

Colette's life — and the novels that accompanied the life — traces a profound progression in the growth of a woman becoming herself: from the schoolgirl Claudine under the vigilant eye of Willy, to the independent, lesbian Salome of her music hall years, to her years of accommodation to Henry de Jouvenel. In yet another turnabout, she returns as an aging heterosexual Salome in her incestuous affair with Bertrand, the beautiful boy.

There was one last stop in the quest toward completion for Colette, and it came in the debonair form of a thirty-five-year-old Parisian named

Maurice Goudeket. They met only a few years after her affair with Bertrand, and in 1935 he became her third and final husband. Goudeket was her lover, her friend, and her anchor, and they lived together in harmony for almost thirty years until her death. When asked by a friend in later years what drew Goudeket to her, she replied, "My male virility. Sometimes I shock him, and yet I'm the only one he can live with. When he wants to sleep with someone, he chooses a very womanly woman; he likes to surround himself with that kind of woman, but he couldn't live with them."[47]

Colette, always in need of money, never ceased to put pen to paper, producing journalism, novels, theater criticism, plays, screenplays, and even publicity for her own line of beauty products. Ever interested in female fashions, and always in search of an escape from her desk, Colette opened, in June 1932, her Institut de Beauté in Paris on the rue de Miromesnil. In one of her more cryptic personal descriptions, the great French novelist introduced herself thus: "I am called Colette and I sell scents." Her passion for makeup and "busying herself in the human face" began in her music hall days, but neither fame nor age decreased her fascination. On a trip to America in 1935 Goudeket recalled that his wife displayed "a real intoxication" for Woolworth's,[48] spending hours in the aisles, while the museums, parks, and historic sites of New York took a decidedly second place. Living life had always been for Colette a superior occupation to the act of writing, and in her short-lived beauty shop she was able to mingle with her audience — most of whom arrived for autographs, not lipstick.

She explained this curious adventure in *Vogue* magazine by referring to her music hall days: "I have turned from writing novels to manufacturing products for increasing, creating and preserving beauty. I too am amused. . . . I had scarcely earned a bit of fame as an author than I turned to the stage, 'went on the boards,' as one said in those days. I did a little mime, a little dancing, a little acrobatics, and I was harshly criticized."[49]

Several years later, in one last appearance for her public, Colette went onstage for four weeks, at the age of sixty-three, singing the Burgundian folk songs of her youth. During World War II she remained in Paris and was accused in some circles of collaboration by selling articles to publications controlled by the German occupation, prompting *Les Lettres françaises* to title an article "Colette, Burgundy and Mr. Goebbels." But the war hit Colette close to home. Goudeket, a Jew, was taken to a

camp by the Nazis while his desperate wife did all she could to communi-
cate, send care packages, and secure his release. When told that Maurice
might receive preferential treatment should he inform on friends, Colette, without pausing for breath, replied that if that was the only recourse then "We choose death."[50] He was returned to her, pale and thin,
but alive.

After enduring years of debilitating arthritis, Colette died in Paris at
the age of eighty-one in 1954 with Goudeket by her side. She had written
more than fifty novels, was president of the Académie Goncourt and was
a recipient of the Grand Cross of the Legion of Honor. "The life of Colette," wrote her friend Jean Cocteau, was "scandal upon scandal. Then
everything [is] over and she joins the ranks of the idols. She concludes
her life of pantomimes, beauty parlors and old lesbians in an apotheosis
of respectability."[51]

In death Colette became the first woman in France to be honored
with a state funeral; she was declared a national treasure. But even here
her scandalous past followed her to the grave. The Catholic Church refused to sanction a religious funeral for a woman who was twice divorced, bisexual, and had bared her breast on a music hall stage. The Association of Music Halls and Circuses, however, sent pink lilies to its
former member and literary patron saint.

Salome for Colette was a transitional character whom she essayed
during her six years in the music hall, the years of recovery from her role
as subservient wife. The Eastern femme fatale provided this provincial
French woman with one of her many identities, but unlike her sister
dancers — Maud Allan, Mata Hari, and Ida Rubinstein — Colette then
moved forward.

She alone carried Salome into middle age, whereas the others were
so deeply identified with Salome that they became entrapped by her image, relegated to tragedy or obscurity. Colette integrated the fatal woman
in a way few others could or would do. She tried on her shape to find its
fit and then used this sexual portrait as a rite of passage into both financial and emotional independence.

Colette brought Salome into maturity with dignity and grace, and
the naughty virgin child of Herod's court finally had a representation that
still proclaimed her lethal sexual attraction, but now her sharp edges
were softened by the compassion, even wisdom, of a mature seductress.

Salome, so brutally destroyed with Maud Allan and Mata Hari, so forgotten with Ida Rubinstein, was given new life. While they removed her
veils to reveal their flesh attached to a chosen identity, Colette removed
them to reveal her self. She alone was Salome's equal, using the femme fatale's image as a means, not an end, to her own iconoclastic identity — the
archetype of a brilliant, beautiful, fearless woman who managed to actually live a life while documenting it. She gave the daughter of Herodias
something more than a theatrical existence behind a protective proscenium. Inside Colette, Salome became a real woman.

Notes

Introduction: Colette's Breast

1. Flem, *Casanova*, 78.
2. Alain Bernardin, interview by author, Paris, 7 December 1990.
3. Flem, *Casanova*, 177.
4. Quoted in *Women's Wit and Wisdom*.
5. Quoted in ibid.
6. Friday, *Women on Top*, 293; Friday, *Forbidden Flowers*, 107, 223.
7. Baker and Bouillon, *Josephine*, 49–50.

Part I. *Salome: The Daughter of Iniquity*

Note to epigraph: Heinrich Heine, in Praz, *Romantic Agony*, 300. Some artists of the late nineteenth century, including Heine, wrote, more in line with the gospels of Mark and Matthew, of the desire of Salome's mother, Herodias, for John the Baptist's head, while Salome, the daughter, remains her passive pawn.

1. In 45–44 B.C., more than seventy years before the death of John the Baptist, Cicero mentions in *De Senectute* the story of a Roman governor of Gaul named Lucius Flaminius, who in 184 B.C. beheaded a prisoner at a banquet at the request of a courtesan he wished to impress. For his brash action he was expelled from the Senate. Livy in his *History of Rome*, Seneca in *Declamations*, and Plutarch in *Parallel Lives* all retell and elaborate on this morality tale, which may well have been familiar to Mark and Matthew when writing the gospels.

2. For an in-depth analysis of the sexologists' findings, see Bram Dijkstra, *Idols of Perversity*; William R. Greg, "Why Are Women Redundant?" *Westminster Review*, quoted in Showalter, *Sexual Anarchy*, 19–20.

3. Edmond de Goncourt, Journal of 14 July 1883, quoted in Showalter, *Sexual Anarchy*, 148.

4. Quoted in Said, *Orientalism*, 186–187; Flaubert, *Three Tales*, "Herodias," 102.

5. Huysmans, *Against the Grain*, 53–54.

6. Maurice Krafft cited in Michel Décaudin, "Un Mythe 'Fin de Siècle': Salomé," *Comparative Literature Studies* 4, nos. 1–2 (1967): 109.

7. *Letters of Oscar Wilde,* 834; quoted in Ellmann, *Oscar Wilde,* 372.

8. Quoted in Jullian, *Oscar Wilde,* 253; quoted in Ellmann, *Oscar Wilde,* 342.

9. *Letters of Oscar Wilde,* 319; in private productions *Salome* was performed in London on 10 and 13 May 1905 by the New Stage Club at the Bijou Theatre, Bayswater; 10 June 1906 by the Literary Stage Society at King's Hall; 27 February 1911 by the New Players at the Royal Court Theatre (*Times Literary Supplement,* Karl Beckson, letter 1994); and 9 April 1918 at the Kennington Theater.

10. Quoted in Ellmann, *Oscar Wilde,* 374.

11. Quoted in Pressly, *Salome: La belle dame sans merci,* 19, 39.

12. The historical Salome was born about 15 A.D. Sometime after the imprisonment of John the Baptist in 30 A.D., she married Philip, Tetrarch of Trachonitis, who was both half-brother of her father, Herod Philip, and half-brother of Herod Antipas, her mother's second husband. These connections made Philip, Salome's husband, both her uncle on her father's side and great-uncle on her mother's side. Considerably older than Salome, Philip ruled for thirty-seven years before his death in 33/34 A.D., indicating that Salome was widowed after only a few years of marriage. She then married Aristobulus, her first cousin, and had three sons by him. According to Tacitus, in 54 A.D. when Salome would have been about forty years old, the Roman Emperor Nero appointed her husband king of Armenia in Asia Minor (Lesser Armenia). In 72 A.D., when Armenia became part of the Roman Empire, Aristobulus was given the royal throne of Chalcis, which he held until his death in 92 A.D. There is in existence a coin that exhibits the profile of Aristobulus on one side and Salome, his queen, on the reverse, tangible proof of Salome's real-life existence.

13. Quoted in Ellmann, *Oscar Wilde,* 343; quoted in Jullian, *Oscar Wilde,* 245.

14. *Letters of Oscar Wilde,* note, 348.

15. Quoted in Wilhelm, *Richard Strauss: An Intimate Portrait,* 102.

16. Quoted in ibid., 100.

17. Strauss, *Recollections and Reflections,* 154.

18. *St. Louis Post Dispatch,* quoted in Carlton, *Looking for Little Egypt,* 79; *New York World,* quoted in ibid., 76.

19. Maria Louise Pool's 1893 novel *The Two Salomes* tells of a repentant Salome who forges a check and pays for her sin by retiring to Miami Beach with her mother. In Bret Harte's 1898 novel *Salomy Jane's Kiss,* Salome redeems Jack, a horse thief, with her kiss, and they live happily ever after on the ranch. The Reverend Isaac K. Loos, in his 1869 treatise entitled *Salome, the Dancer,* cautioned parents against allowing their daughters to dance, finding "it far better to dwell with saints on earth in the house of God than with Salome in the festal halls of Herod" (66).

20. Quoted in Pressly, *Salome,* 15; quoted in Bizot, "Turn-of-the-Century Salome Era," 73.

21. *Theatre Magazine,* quoted in Kendall, *Where She Danced,* 74.

22. *Hartford Courant,* 21 October 1908, quoted in Bizot, "Turn-of-the-Century Salome Era," 78.

23. Quoted in Buonaventura, *Serpent of the Nile,* 102.

24. *New York Times,* 24 August 1908.

25. *New York Times,* 16 August 1908.

26. Garden and Biancolli, *Mary Garden's Story,* 124.

27. Ibid., 211.

28. Quoted in Harris, *Loie Fuller, Magician of Light,* 20.

29. St. Denis, *An Unfinished Life,* 52.

Part II. *Maud Allan: The Cult of the Clitoris*

Note to epigraph: Quoted in Cherniavsky, *Salome Dancer,* 16.

1. Quoted in Kettle, *Salome's Last Veil,* 20.

2. Quoted in Cherniavsky, *Salome Dancer,* 244.

3. Quoted in ibid., 281.

4. 15 April 1895, quoted in ibid., 92, note 5.

5. Quoted in ibid., 51.

6. William Durrant letter to Maud Allan, quoted in ibid., 115.

7. Isabella Durrant letter to Maud Allan, 1 April 1899, quoted in ibid., 128–129, note 11.

8. Allan diary entry, 12 November 1895, quoted in ibid., 69.

9. Isabella Durrant letter to Maud Allan, 7 November 1895, quoted in ibid., 71.

10. Allan diary entry, 25 July 1895, quoted in ibid., 33.

11. Isabella Durrant letter to Maud Allan, early 1899, quoted in ibid., 118.

12. Allan diary entries 1896, quoted in ibid., 81–82; Allan diary entry 17 May 1897, quoted in ibid., 90.

13. Allan diary entry 8 January 1898, quoted in ibid., 110.

14. *Illustriertes Wiener Extrablatt,* 1903, quoted in Cherniavsky, "Maud Allan," Part I, 30.

15. Isabella Durrant letters to Maud Allan, 1 December 1903, and 26 March 1904, quoted in Cherniavsky, *Salome Dancer,* 134–136.

16. *Labour Leader,* 26 June 1908, quoted in ibid., 165.

17. 4 July 1908, *Saturday Review,* quoted in Cherniavsky, "Maud Allan," Part III, 138.

18. Allan, *My Life and Dancing,* 127.

19. *Herald,* Augusta, Georgia, 30 June 1907, quoted in Cherniavsky, *Salome Dancer,* 145–146.

20. *Magyar Szinpad,* Budapest, quoted in Cherniavsky, *Salome Dancer,* 144.

21. Sir Frederick Ponsonby, *Recollections of Three Reigns* (London, 1951), quoted in Cherniavsky, *Salome Dancer,* 153.

22. Simmons and Holland, "Salome and the King," 1967, 52.

23. Ibid., 53.

24. Publicity pamphlet from the Palace Theatre, February 1908, quoted in Cherniavsky, *Salome Dancer,* 162.

25. Quoted in ibid., 291.

26. Quoted in ibid., 175.

27. *San Francisco Examiner,* 26 April 1908, quoted in ibid., 168.

28. Duncan, *My Life,* 218.

29. Percival Pollard, "'Salome Craze' Raged in Europe Long Before It Came Here; Some History of Famous Dancers, from Lola Montez to Isadore [*sic*] Duncan," *New York Times,* 23 August 1908.

30. Allan, *My Life and Dancing,* 73, 114, 112.

31. Carl van Vechten, 30 January 1910, *Dance Index,* vol. 1, 148.

32. *San Francisco Chronicle,* April 1910, quoted in Cherniavsky, *Salome Dancer,* 197.

33. Quoted in ibid., 202.

34. Kitty Kelly, *Chicago Daily Tribune,* 5 July 1915, quoted in Weigand, "Rugmaker's Daughter," 246.

35. Allan, *My Life and Dancing*, 36.

36. *Imperialist*, 26 January 1918, quoted in Kettle, *Salome's Last Veil*, 8.

37. *Vigilante*, 23 March 1918, quoted in Kettle, *Salome's Last Veil*, 21; Arnold White, *Vigilante*, quoted in ibid., 5.

38. *Imperialist*, 26 January 1918, quoted in Kettle, *Salome's Last Veil*, 9.

39. All quotes from the court proceedings derive from the Proceedings at the Central Criminal Court, Rex v. Noel Pemberton-Billing, 29–31 May; 1, 3, 4 June 1918: the Official Record (British Museum). Also: Proceedings at Bow Street Police Court, Maud Allan, J. T. Grein v. Noel Pemberton-Billing, 6, 13 April, 1918: the Official Record (British Museum). Page numbers cited parenthetically in text refer to pages where proceedings are quoted in Kettle, *Salome's Last Veil*.

Part III. *Mata Hari: The Horizontal Agent*

Note to epigraph: Spoken to Dutch painter Piet van der Hem, quoted in Waagenaar, *Murder of Mata Hari*, 45.

1. Emile Massard, *Les Espionnes à Paris* (Paris, 1922), 36, quoted in Wheelwright, *Fatal Lover*, 90.

2. Quoted in Waagenaar, *Murder of Mata Hari*, 30.

3. Quoted in ibid., 26.

4. Quoted in Wheelwright, *Fatal Lover*, 9; Macleod letter to Margaretha 24 April 1899, quoted in Waagenaar, *Murder of Mata Hari*, 36.

5. Quoted in Wheelwright, *Fatal Lover*, 9.

6. Charles S. Heymans, *La Vrai Mata Hari, Courtisane et Espionne* (Paris, 1930), 42–43, quoted in Wheelwright, *Fatal Lover*, 10, 12.

7. Berenson, *Trial of Madame Caillaux*, 106; quotation in Skinner, *Elegant Wits and Grand Horizontals*, 23.

8. Cocteau, *Paris Album 1900–1914*, 63–64.

9. Quoted in Waagenaar, *Murder of Mata Hari*, 41.

10. Interview in *Nieuwe Courant*, September 1905, quoted in ibid., 67.

11. Quoted in Newman, *Inquest on Mata Hari*, 10.

12. *La Presse*, 18 March 1905, quoted in Waagenaar, *Murder of Mata Hari*, 50.

13. *Le Gaulois*, 17 March 1905, quoted in ibid., 53.

14. *Courrier Français*, quoted in Keay, *Spy Who Never Was*, 47–48.

15. Quoted in Ostrovsky, *Eye of Dawn*, 72.

16. Quoted in Castle, *Folies Bergère*, 54.

17. Frances Keyzer in London magazine *The King*, February–March 1905, quoted in Keay, *Spy Who Never Was*, 45.

18. Quoted in Janet Flanner interview in Wickes, *Amazon of Letters*, 268.

19. Colette, *My Apprenticeships*, 129–130.

20. Léon Bizard in *Souvenirs d'un Médecin* (Paris, 1923), quoted in Waagenaar, *Murder of Mata Hari*, 57

21. de Pougy, *My Blue Notebooks*, 98–99.

22. Quoted in Waagenaar, *Murder of Mata Hari*, 75, 77.

23. Quoted in ibid., 81.

24. Quoted in Wheelwright, *Fatal Lover*, 27.

25. Newman, *Inquest on Mata Hari*, 55.

26. Misia Sert, *Misia and the Muses: The Memoirs of Misia Sert* (New York, 1953), 114, quoted in Ostrovsky, *Eye of Dawn*, 87.

27. Quoted in Ostrovsky, *Eye of Dawn*, 85.

28. Quoted in Waagenaar, *Murder of Mata Hari*, 116.

29. Memorandum entered 9 December 1915, Aliens Registry, London, quoted in Keay, *Spy Who Never Was*, 125–126.

30. Quoted in ibid., 147.

31. Memorandum entered 22 February 1916, Aliens Registry, London, quoted in ibid., 153.

32. Quoted in ibid., 154.

33. Quoted in Howe, *Mata Hari*, 211.

34. Exchange on first day of trial 24 July 1917, quoted in Ostrovsky, *Eye of Dawn*, 180.

35. Quoted in Waagenaar, *Murder of Mata Hari*, 140.

36. London Public Record Office PRO MEPO file 3–2444, quoted in Wheelwright, *Fatal Lover*, 51.

37. Quoted in Waagenaar, *Murder of Mata Hari*, 150.

38. Letter from Sir Basil Thomson to the Netherlands Minister in London, 16 November 1916, quoted in ibid., 155.

39. Quoted in Wheelwright, *Fatal Lover*, 60.

40. Order of Arrest, 13 February 1917, Service Historique de l'Armée de Terre, Château de Vincennes, Dossier Mata Hari, quoted in ibid., 67.

41. Quoted in Howe, *Mata Hari*, 194–195.

42. Pierre Bouchardon, *Souvenirs* (Paris, 1935), quoted in Keay, *Spy Who Never Was*, 227.

43. Letter to Bouchardon 9 March 1917, Service Historique de l'Armée de Terre, Château de Vincennes, Dossier Mata Hari, quoted in Wheelwright, *Fatal Lover*, 74.

44. Quoted in Keay, *Spy Who Never Was*, 235.

45. Quoted in Waagenaar, *Murder of Mata Hari*, 174.

46. Quoted in ibid., 229.

47. Quoted in Keay, *Spy Who Never Was*, 242, 230.

48. Quoted in Waagenaar, *Murder of Mata Hari*, 187; letter to Bouchardon, 31 May 1917, quoted in Howe, *Mata Hari*, 222.

49. Quoted in Howe, *Mata Hari*, 226.

50. Quoted in Keay, *Spy Who Never Was*, 253.

51. Quoted in ibid., 259; Newman, *Inquest on Mata Hari*, 38.

52. Lieutenant André Mornet, quoted in Waagenaar, *Murder of Mata Hari*, 254.

53. Quoted in Keay, *Spy Who Never Was*, 263–264.

54. Quoted in Howe, *Mata Hari*, 248.

55. Quoted in Wheelwright, *Fatal Lover*, 90; Emile Massard quoted in ibid., 85.

56. Quoted in Waagenaar, *Murder of Mata Hari*, 259.

57. Quoted in ibid., 235.

58. Quoted in ibid., 266.

59. Quoted in Howe, *Mata Hari*, 214.

60. Interrogation with Bouchardon 31 May 1917, quoted in Wheelwright, *Fatal Lover*, 81.

61. Quoted in Howe, *Mata Hari*, 6.

62. Quoted in Wheelwright, *Fatal Lover*, 120; in *Geschichte des Weltkriegs und Nachkriegsspionage (History of World War and Postwar Espionage)*, quoted in Howe, *Mata Hari*, 284.

63. Quoted in Wheelwright, *Fatal Lover,* 68.

64. Emile Massard, *Les Espionnes à Paris* (Paris, 1922), 36, quoted in Wheelwright, *Fatal Lover,* 90.

65. Coulson, *Mata Hari, Courtesan and Spy,* 142, 258, 26, 14.

66. Singer, *World's Thirty Greatest Women Spies,* 150; Newman, *Inquest on Mata Hari,* 13.

67. Wighton, *World's Greatest Spies,* 81, 67.

68. On 15 October 2001, eighty-four years to the day after Mata Hari's execution, an official demand to reopen her case was presented to the French minister of justice.

69. Quoted in Waagenaar, *Murder of Mata Hari,* 239.

70. Coulson, *Mata Hari, Courtesan and Spy,* 87.

Part IV. *Ida Rubinstein: The Phallic Female*

Note to epigraph: Quoted in Tom Antongini, *D'Annunzio* (London: Heinemann, 1938), 443, quoted in Cossart, *Ida Rubinstein,* 37.

1. Alexandre, *Decorative Art of Léon Bakst,* 29–30.

2. Benois, *Reminiscences of the Russian Ballet,* 296.

3. Smith, *How Paris Amuses Itself,* 106–107..

4. Quoted in Garafola, "Circles of Meaning," 33.

5. Ibid., 42, note 1.

6. Quoted in Cossart, *Ida Rubinstein,* 9.

7. Garafola, "Circles of Meaning," 42, note 6.

8. Quoted in ibid., 33.

9. Quoted in ibid., 32.

10. Quoted in ibid., 32.

11. Cossart, *Ida Rubinstein,* 7.

12. Thomas, "Le peintre Bakst parle de Madame Ida Rubinstein," 94, 95.

13. Valerian Svetlov, *Le Ballet Contemporain* (Paris, 1912), 78, quoted in Mayer, "Ida Rubinstein," 34.

14. Quoted in Cossart, *Ida Rubinstein,* 18; quoted in Alison Settle, "The Birth of Couture: 1900–1910," in *Couture,* ed. Ruth Lynham, 68.

15. Quoted in Jullian, *D'Annunzio,* 224.

16. Vreeland, *D. V.,* 17.

17. Quoted in Steegmuller, *Cocteau,* 75.

18. Quoted in Jullian, *Prince of Aesthetes,* 37.

19. Jullian, *Prince of Aesthetes,* 223.

20. Natalie Barney quoted in Jullian, *D'Annunzio,* 245; Romaine Brooks quoted in Winwar, *Wingless Victory,* 246.

21. Quoted in Chadwick, *Amazons in the Drawing Room,* 90; Alan Dale, "The Only Girl Who Ever Broke D'Annunzio's Heart," *New York American,* 23 June 1912.

22. Quoted in Winwar, *Wingless Victory,* 242; quoted in Cossart, *Ida Rubinstein,* 27.

23. Quoted in Depaulis, *Ida Rubinstein,* 72.

24. Quoted in Secrest, *Between Me and Life,* 245.

25. Quoted in ibid., 236.

26. Quoted in Jullian, *D'Annunzio,* 223.

27. Quoted in Secrest, *Between Me and Life,* 204.

28. Quoted in Garafola, "Circles of Meaning," 39.

29. Quoted in Pierre Van Paassen, *New York Evening World*, 23 June 1926.

30. Quoted in Garafola, "Circles of Meaning," 39.

31. Quoted in ibid., 31, 40; quoted in Jullian, *D'Annunzio*, 231; quoted in Cossart, *Ida Rubinstein*, 41.

32. Alexandre, *Decorative Art of Léon Bakst*, 41–42.

33. Quoted in Winwar, *Wingless Victory*, 249.

34. Quoted in Buckle, *Nijinsky*, 185.

35. Quoted in Nijinska, *Bronislava Nijinska: Early Memoirs*, footnote 406.

36. Bernhardt letter 1912, quoted in Cossart, *Ida Rubinstein*, 53.

37. Dale, "Only Girl Who Ever Broke D'Annunzio's Heart."

38. Benois quoted in Kochno, *Diaghilev and the Ballets Russes*, 12.

39. Quoted in Dale, "Only Girl Who Ever Broke D'Annunzio's Heart."

40. Quoted in Cossart, *Ida Rubinstein*, 84–85.

41. Quoted in Thomas, "Le peintre Bakst parle de Madame Ida Rubinstein," 101.

42. Tikanova, *La Jeune Fille en Bleu*, 98–99.

43. Quoted in Garafola, *Diaghilev's Ballets Russes*, 239.

44. Quoted in Brody, *Paris, The Musical Kaleidoscope 1870–1925*, 221.

45. Quoted in Lifar, *A History of Russian Ballet*, 272, 270.

46. *Dancing Times*, January 1929, 569.

47. Quoted in Cossart, *Ida Rubinstein*, 145; quoted in Lifar, *Serge Diaghilev*, 240.

48. Quoted in Kochno, *Diaghilev and the Ballets Russes*, 287.

49. Quoted in Cossart, *Ida Rubinstein*, 169.

50. Lester, "Rubinstein Revisited," 26.

51. Paul Claudel, *Claudel, Homme de Théâtre: Correspondance avec Copeau, Dullin, Jouvet* (Paris: Gallimard, 1966), 198, quoted in Mayer, "Ida Rubinstein," 39.

52. Quoted in Van Paassen, *New York Evening World*, 23 June 1926.

53. Quoted in Cossart, *Ida Rubinstein*, 195.

54. See note 9; quoted in Depaulis, *Ida Rubinstein*, 464.

55. Quoted in Winwar, *Wingless Victory*, 251–252, letter dated 1911.

56. See note 23.

57. Bettina Bergery quoted in Secrest, *Between Me and Life*, 326.

58. Quoted in ibid., 327.

59. Quoted in Depaulis, *Ida Rubinstein*, 506–507.

60. Quoted in ibid., 545.

61. *Le Figaro*, 17 October 1960, quoted in Cossart, *Ida Rubinstein*, 212.

62. Romaine Brooks quoted in Depaulis, *Ida Rubinstein*, 548.

Part V. *Colette: The Mental Hermaphrodite*

Note to epigraph: Colette, *Pure and Impure*, 60.

1. Félicien Pascal, *L'Eclair de Montpellier*, 7 January 1907, quoted in Sarde, *Colette, Free and Fettered*, 200.

2. Quoted in Thurman, *Secrets of the Flesh*, 171.

3. Francis and Gontier, *Colette*, 203.

4. Letter to Colette, 24 February 1909, quoted in Sarde, *Colette, Free and Fettered*, 25.

5. Colette, *Sido*, 14.

6. Ibid., 22.

7. Colette, *En Pays Connu*, quoted in Mitchell, *Colette: A Taste for Life*, 24; Colette, *La Maison de Claudine*, quoted in Francis and Gontier, *Colette*, 50.

8. Quoted in Francis and Gontier, *Colette*, 74.

9. Quoted in ibid., 68.

10. Colette, *My Apprenticeships*, 54–55.

11. Sarde, *Colette, Free and Fettered*, 105; Raymond Escholier quoted in Richardson, *Colette*, 8; *Lettres de l'Ouvreuse* (Paris: Vanier, 1890), 152, quoted in Lottman, *Colette: A Life*, 24.

12. Colette, *Earthly Paradise* (from "Noces"), 87.

13. Colette, *My Apprenticeships*, 23.

14. Ibid., 31; Colette, *Pure and Impure*, 148.

15. Colette, *Complete Claudine (Claudine Married)*, 375, 439.

16. Jean de la Hire, quoted in Sarde, *Colette, Free and Fettered*, 169.

17. Colette to Lucien Muhlfeld, January 1902, *Letters from Colette*, 1.

18. Sacha Guitry, 1904 quoted in Phelps, *Belles Saisons*, 51; Colette, *Creatures Great and Small*, 108.

19. Quoted in Dormann, *Colette: A Passion For Life*, 101.

20. Matthew Josephson, quoted in Rogers, *Ladies Bountiful*, 44.

21. Colette, *My Apprenticeships*, 109.

22. Quoted in Massie, *Colette*, 58

23. Colette, *Pure and Impure*, 69.

24. Colette, *Sido*, "Nuit Blanche," 107; Colette, *Pure and Impure*, 111.

25. Colette, *Vagabonde*, 47–48.

26. Quoted in Verne, *Aux usines du plaisir, La Vie secrete du Music Hall*, 236; Colette, *Vagabonde*, 82, 32, 14.

27. Colette, *Vagabonde*, 28; Colette to Georges Wague, 1909, *Letters from Colette*, 12.

28. Colette, *Vagabonde*, quoted in Sarde, *Colette, Free and Fettered*, 250; Colette, *Music Hall Sidelights*, 158.

29. Maurice-Edmond Sailland (Curnonsky) in *Paris qui chante*, quoted in Lottman, *Colette: A Life*, 69.

30. *Le Rire*, 15 December 1906, quoted in Francis and Gontier, *Colette*, 201.

31. Colette, "Toby-Dog Speaks," 27 April 1907, in *La Vie parisienne*, originally in *Vrilles de la Vigne*, 1908, *Creatures Great and Small*, 106–107.

32. Ibid., 111.

33. Colette, *Sido*, "Music-Halls," 239–240.

34. *Le Messager de Bruxelles*, 6 February 1910, *Colette en Tournée*, 59; *La Presse*, 5 November 1907, quoted in Francis and Gontier, *Colette*, 221; Phelps, *Belles Saisons*, 88.

35. Colette, *Colette en Tournée*, 19.

36. Alphonse Séché, *La Mêlée littéraire, 1900–1930* (Société française d'éditions, 1935), 37, quoted in Francis and Gontier, *Colette*, 177; Sylvain Bonmariage, *Willy, Colette et Moi* (Paris: Froissart, 1954), quoted in Mitchell, *Colette: A Taste for Life*, 86.

37. Colette, *Colette en Tournée*, 63.

38. André Rouveyre, *Mercure de France*, 1 June 1926.

39. Louis Delluc, *Comoedia illustré*, 5 January 1913, quoted in Pichois, *Colette Oeuvres* I, CIX–CX.

40. Willy, *Lélie, fumeuse d'opium* (Paris: Albin Michel, 1911), quoted in Sarde, *Colette, Free and Fettered*, 208–209.

41. Colette, *Vagabonde*, 215.

42. Colette, *Letters from Colette*, 20; Natalie Barney, *Aventures de l'esprit* (Paris, 1929), quoted in Lottman, *Colette: A Life*, 51.

43. Colette to Georges Wague, September 1912, *Letters from Colette*, 27; Colette to Christiane Mendelys, 29 August 1911, ibid., 22.

44. Quoted in Chalon, *Colette, l'éternelle apprentie*, 183.

45. *Paris Théâtre*, 22 January 1910, quoted in Pichois, *Colette Oeuvres* II, X.

46. Quoted in Sarde, *Colette, Free and Fettered*, 351.

47. Quoted in Lottman, *Colette: A Life*, 242.

48. Quoted in Goudeket, *Close to Colette*, 70, 89.

49. *Vogue*, September 1932, quoted in Sarde, *Colette, Free and Fettered*, 395–396.

50. Quoted in Goudeket, *Close to Colette*, 178.

51. Jean Cocteau, *Le Passé défini*, vol. 2 (Paris: Gallimard, 1985), 41–42, quoted in Lottman, *Colette: A Life*, 300.

Bibliography

Introduction: Colette's Breast

Baker, Josephine, and Jo Bouillon. *Josephine*. Translated by Marianna Fitz-patrick. New York: Harper and Row, 1977.

Flem, Lydia. *Casanova: The Man Who Really Loved Women*. New York: Farrar, Straus and Giroux, 1997.

Friday, Nancy. *Forbidden Flowers*. New York: Pocket, 1975.

———. *Women on Top*. New York: Pocket, 1991.

Women's Wit and Wisdom. Philadelphia: Running Press, 1991.

Part I. *Salome: The Daughter of Iniquity*

Apostolos-Cappadona, Diane. "Scriptural Women Who Danced." *Dance as Religious Studies*, edited by Doug Adams, 95–108. New York: Crossroads, 1990.

Aubyn, F. C. "The Redemption of Salome in American Literature." In "Salome Dossier." Compiled by Richard Bizot. Dance Collection, New York Public Library, 1993.

Bade, Patrick. *Femme Fatale*. London: Mayflower, 1979.

Baron, Magda. "In Search of Salome." *Arabesque* (March–April 1983): 18–21.

Barthes, Roland. "Striptease." In *Mythologies*. New York: Hill and Wang, Farrar, Straus and Giroux, 1972.

Becker-Leckrone, Megan. "Salome: The Fetishization of a Textual Corpus." *New Literary History* (Spring 1995): 239–260.

Bizot, Richard. "Salome in Modern Dance." *Israel Dance*, 1980 (also complete notes from 5–9 August 1979 conference).

———. "When Salome Came to Town." *North Florida Living* (June 1985): 12–15.

———. "The Turn-of-the-Century Salome Era: High-and Pop-Culture Variations on the Dance of the Seven Veils." *Choreography and Dance 1992*, vol. 2, part 3, Harwood Academic Publishers, 71–87.

Bizot, Richard, comp. "Salome Dossier." Dance Collection, New York Public Library. New York, 1993.

Brandstetter, Gabriele, and Brygida Maria Ochaim. *Loie Fuller Tanz/Licht-Spiel/ Art Nouveau*. Freiburg,: Rombach Verlag, 1989.

Bucknell, Brad. "On 'Seeing' Salome." *ELH* 60 (Summer 1993): 503–526.

Buonaventura, Wendy. "Salome and the Seven Veils of Ishtar." *Arabesque* (March–April 1984): 5, 17.

———. *Serpent of the Nile*. New York: Interlink, 1994.

Carey, John, ed. *Eyewitness to History*. Cambridge, Mass.: Harvard University Press, 1987.

Carlton, Donna. *Looking for Little Egypt*. Bloomington, Ind.: IDD, 1994.

Carter, Randolph. *Ziegfeld*. London: Bernard, 1988.

Castle, Charles. *The Folies Bergère*. New York: Franklin Watts, 1985.

Croutier, Alev Lytle. *Harem: The World Behind the Veil*. New York: Abbeville, 1989.

Current, Richard Nelson, and Marcia Ewing Current. *Loie Fuller: Goddess of Light*. Boston: Northeastern University Press, 1997.

Delevoy, Robert L. *Symbolists and Symbolism*. New York: Rizzoli, 1978.

Derval, Paul. *Folies-Bergère*. New York: E. P. Dutton, 1955.

Dijkstra, Bram. *Idols of Perversity*. New York: Oxford University Press, 1986.

Di Mario, Phillipe. "Death Kiss." *Bedtime Stories* (July 1933).

Ellmann, Richard. *Oscar Wilde*. New York: Alfred A. Knopf, 1984.

Flaubert, Gustave. *Flaubert in Egypt*. Translated and edited by Francis Steegmuller. London: Michael Hagg, 1972.

———. *Salammbô*. Translated by J. C. Chartres. New York: Dutton, 1931.

———. *Three Tales*. Translated with introduction and notes by A. J. Krailsheimer. Oxford: Oxford University Press, 1991.

Fuller, Loie. *Fifteen Years of a Dancer's Life*. Introduction by Anatole France. 1913. Reprint, New York: Dance Horizons, 1977.

Garden, Mary, and Louis Biancolli. *Mary Garden's Story*. New York: Simon and Schuster, 1951.

Gilliam, Brian, ed. *Richard Strauss and His World*. Princeton, N.J.: Princeton University Press, 1992.

Gilman, Richard. *Decadence*. New York: Farrar, Straus and Giroux, 1975.

Girard, René. "Scandal and the Dance: Salome in the Gospel of Mark." *Ballet Review* (Winter 1983): 67–76.

Gold, Arthur, and Robert Fizdale. *The Divine Sarah*. New York: Alfred A. Knopf, 1991.

Gray, Piers. "The Comedy of Suffering." *Critical Quarterly*, 33, no. 4 (Winter 1991): 41–57.

Hadas-Lebel, Mireille. *Flavius Josephus*. Translated by Richard Miller. New York: Macmillan, 1993.

Hanna, Judith Lynne. *Dance, Sex and Gender*. Chicago: University of Chicago Press, 1988.

Harris, Margaret Haile. *Loie Fuller, Magician of Light*. Exhibition catalogue, Virginia Museum, Richmond, Virginia, 1979.

Higham, Charles. *Ziegfeld*. Chicago: Henry Regnery, 1972.

Huysmans, Karl Joris. *A Rebours (Against the Grain)*. 1884. Reprint, New York: Dover, 1969.

Hyde, H. Montgomery. *Oscar Wilde*. New York: Farrar, Straus and Giroux, 1975.

Josephus, Flavius. *Complete Works*. Translated by William Wiston. Grand Rapids, Mich.: Kregel, 1960.

Jullian, Philippe. *Oscar Wilde*. Translated by Violet Wyndham. New York: Viking, 1969.

———. *Dreamers of Decadence*. New York: Praeger, 1971.

———. *The Symbolists*. London: Phaidon, 1973.

———. *The Orientalists*. Oxford: Phaidon, 1977.

Kendall, Elizabeth. *Where She Danced*. New York: Alfred A. Knopf, 1979.

Kirstein, Lincoln. *Dance: A Short History of Classic Theatrical Dancing*. New York: Dance Horizons, 1935, 1977.

Knapp, Bettina L. "Flaubert: Dance and the Archetypal Harlot, Wife, and Castrator." *Arabesque* (November–December 1985): 8–9; (January–February 1986): 6, 25.

———. "Wilde: The Erotic Dancer Archetype." *Arabesque* (March–April 1986): 4–5, 16–17.

Knox, Melissa. *Oscar Wilde: A Long and Lovely Suicide*. New Haven: Yale University Press, 1994.

Laver, James. *The First Decadent*. New York: Citadel, 1955.

Leeming, David, and Jake Page. *Goddess: Myths of the Female Divine*. New York: Oxford University Press, 1994.

Loos, Rev. Isaac K. *Salome, The Dancer*. Philadelphia: S. R. Fisher, 1869.

Mascetti, Manuela Dunn. *The Song of Eve*. New York: Simon and Schuster, 1990.

Michel, Artur. "Salome and Herodias, from the Bible to Martha Graham." *Dance Magazine* (February 1946): 8–10, 47–49; (March 1946): 18–20, 48–49.

Minkin, Jacob S. *Herod, King of the Jews*. New York: Thomas Yoseloff, 1936.

Nochlin, Nina. *Women, Art and Power and Other Essays*. New York: Harper and Row, 1988.

Parker, Brian. "Strindberg's 'Miss Julie' and the Legend of Salome." *Modern Drama* (December 1989): 469–484.

Parker, Derek, and Julia Parker. *The Natural History of the Chorus Girl*. London: David and Charles, 1975.

Praz, Mario. *The Romantic Agony*. London: Oxford University Press, 1951.

Pressly, Nancy L. *Salome: La belle dame sans merci*. Exhibition catalogue. San Antonio Museum Association, San Antonio, Texas, 1983.

Rodney, Nanette B. "Salome." *Metropolitan Museum of Art Bulletin* (March 1953).

Sacher-Masoch, Leopold von. *Venus in Furs*. 1870. Translated by Ewe Moeller and Laura Lindgren. Reprint, New York: Blast, 1989.

Said, Edward W. *Orientalism*. New York: Pantheon Books/Random House, 1978.

Saretta, Phyliss. "Salome." *Arabesque* (January–February 1976): 8–9.

Schurer, Emil. *A History of the Jewish People in the Time of Jesus Christ*. Edited by Nahum Glatzer. New York: Schocken, 1961.

Showalter, Elaine. *Sexual Anarchy: Gender and Culture at the Fin de Siècle*. New York: Penguin, 1990.

Smith, A. William. "References to Dance in Fifteenth-Century Italian Sacre Rappresentazioni." *Dance Research Journal*, 23, no. 1 (Spring 1991).

Sobel, Bernard. *A Pictorial History of Burlesque*. New York: G. P. Putnam's Sons, 1956.

St. Denis, Ruth. *An Unfinished Life*. New York: Harper and Brothers, 1939.

Strauss, Richard. *Recollections and Reflections*. Edited by Willi Schuhm. London: Boosey and Hawkes, 1949.

Studlar, Gaylyn. "'Out-Salomeing Salome': Dance, the New Woman, and Fan Magazine Orientalism." *Michigan Quarterly Review* (Fall 1995): 486–510.

Sudermann, Hermann. *John the Baptist*. Translated by Beatrice Marshall. London: John Lane, 1909.

Troyat, Henri. *Flaubert*. Translated by Joan Pinkham. New York: Viking, 1992.

Wilde, Oscar. *Salome*. Introduction by Steven Berkoff. First English translation 1894. London: Faber and Faber, 1989.

———. *The Letters of Oscar Wilde*. Edited by Rupert Hart-Davis. New York: Harcourt, Brace and World, 1962.

Wilhelm, Kurt. *Richard Strauss: An Intimate Portrait*. New York: Rizzoli, 1989.

Wood, Leona. "Danse du Ventre: A Fresh Appraisal." *Arabesque* (January–February 1979): 8–13; (March–April 1979): 10–13, 20–21.

Part II. *Maud Allan: The Cult of the Clitoris*

Allan, Maud. *My Life and Dancing*. London: Everett, 1908.

Cherniavsky, Felix. "Maud Allan, Part I: The Early Years, 1873–1903." *Dance Chronicle* 5 (1983): 1–36.

———. "Maud Allan, Part II: First Steps to a Dancing Career, 1904–1907." *Dance Chronicle* 6 (1983): 189–227.

———. "Maud Allan, Part III: Two Years of Triumph, 1908–1909." *Dance Chronicle* 7 (1984): 119–158.

———. *The Salome Dancer*. Toronto: McClelland and Stewart, 1991.

Cocteau, Jean. *Paris Album, 1900–1914*. Translated by Margaret Crosland. London: A Comet Book, 1956, 1987.

Cohen, Barbara Naomi. "Gertrude Hoffman, Salome Treads the Boards." *Dance Research Journal* (1978): 23–32.

Duncan, Isadora. *My Life*. New York: Liveright, 1927.

Hoare, Philip. *Oscar Wilde's Last Stand*. New York: Arcade, 1997.

Kettle, Michael. *Salome's Last Veil: The Libel Trial of the Century*. London: Granada, 1977.

Koritz, Amy. "Dancing the Orient for England: Maud Allan's 'The Vision of Salome.'" *Theatre Journal* (March 1994): 63–78.

McDearmon, Lacy. "Maud Allan: The Public Record." *Dance Chronicle*, 2, no. 2 (1978): 85–105.

Seroff, Victor. *The Real Isadora*. New York: Dial, 1971.

Simmons, E. Romayne, and D. J. Holland. "Salome and the King." *Dance Magazine* (November 1967): 52–53.

Weigand, Elizabeth. "Maud Allan and J. T. Grein." *Proceedings of Society of Dance History Scholars* (11–13 February 1983): 233–238.

———. "The Rugmaker's Daughter, Maud Allan's 1915 Silent Film." *Dance Chronicle* (1986): 237–251.

Part III. *Mata Hari: The Horizontal Agent*

Berenson, Edward. *The Trial of Madame Caillaux*. Berkeley: University of California Press, 1992.

Coulson, Major Thomas. *Mata Hari: Courtesan and Spy*. New York: Harper and Brothers, 1930.

"Danses Brahmaniques." *Le Matin*, 14 March 1905.

"Les Danses Brahmaniques au Musée Guimet." *L'Illustration*, 18 March 1905.

de Pougy, Liane. *My Blue Notebooks*. Translated by Diana Athill. New York: Harper and Row, 1979.

Ferrare, Henri. "Les Mystères Bouddhiques." *La Presse*, 16 March 1905.

Hester, Al. "Mata Hari: Dancer of Illusion." *Arabesque*, part I (May–June 1982): 12–13, 24, 33; part II (July–August 1982): 6–7, 18–19.

Howe, Russell Warren. *Mata Hari: The True Story*. New York: Dodd, Mead, 1986.

Keay, Julia. *The Spy Who Never Was*. Large type edition. Oxford: Clio, 1989.

Montardon, Marcel. "Mata-Hari et sa Légende." *Marianne*, 2 November 1932.

Nadaud, Marcel, and André Fage. "La Danseuse espionne." *Le Petit Journal*, 15–16 July 1925.

Newman, Bernard. *Inquest on Mata Hari*. London: Robert Hale Limited, 1956.

Ostrovsky, Erika. *Eye of Dawn: The Rise and Fall of Mata Hari*. New York: Macmillan/Dorset, 1978.

Rearick, Charles. *Pleasures of the Belle Epoque*. New Haven: Yale University Press, 1985.

Roberts, W. Adolphe. "The Fabulous Dancer." *The Dance Magazine* (July 1929): 13–16, 60; (August 1929): 18–21; (September 1929): 24–27, 51; (October 1929): 40–41.

Roob, J. D. "Mata Hari." *TV France*, 14 January 1964.

Rowan, Richard Wilmer. *The Story of the Secret Service*. New York: Literary Guild of America, 1937.

Shapiro, Barbara Stern. *Pleasures of Paris: Daumier to Picasso*. Exhibition catalogue. Museum of Fine Arts, Boston, in association with David R. Godine,
Publisher, 1991.

Singer, Kurt. *The World's Thirty Greatest Women Spies*. New York: Wilfred Funk,
1951.

Skinner, Cornelia Otis. *Elegant Wits and Grand Horizontals*. Boston: Houghton
Mifflin, 1962.

Svetloff, Valerian. "The Execution of Mata-Hari." *The Dancing Times* (November 1927): 193–197.

Waagenaar, Sam. *The Murder of Mata Hari*. London: Arthur Barker, 1964.

Wheelwright, Julie. *The Fatal Lover*. London: Collins and Brown, 1992.

Wickes, George. *The Amazon of Letters*. New York: G. P. Putnam's Sons, 1976.

Wighton, Charles. *The World's Greatest Spies*. New York: Taplinger, 1962.

Part IV. *Ida Rubinstein: The Phallic Female*

Alexandre, Arséne. *The Decorative Art of Léon Bakst*. Notes by Jean Cocteau,
translated by Harry Melvill. London: The Fine Arts Society, 1913. Reprint,
New York: Dover, 1972.

Baer, Nancy Van Norman. *The Art of Enchantment: Diaghilev's Ballets Russes, 1909–
1929*. Fine Arts Museum of San Francisco. New York: Universe, 1988.

Beaumont, Cyril W. *Michel Fokine and His Ballets*. London: C. W. Beaumont, 1935.

Benois, Alexandre. *Reminiscences of the Russian Ballet*. Translated by Mary Brit-
nieva. London: Putnam, 1941.

Breeskin, Adelyn D. *Romaine Brooks*. Washington, D.C.: Smithsonian Institu-
tion Press, 1971, reprint 1986.

Brody, Elaine. *Paris, The Musical Kaleidoscope, 1870–1925*. London: Robson, 1988.

Buckle, Richard. *Nijinsky*. London: Weidenfeld and Nicolson, 1971.

Chadwick, Whitney. *Amazons in the Drawing Room: The Art of Romaine Brooks*. With
an essay by Joe Lucchesi. Exhibition catalogue. Berkeley: University of
California Press, 2000.

Chalon, Jean. *Portrait d'une Seductrice*. Paris: Editions Stock, 1976.

de Cossart, Michael. "Ida Rubinstein and Diaghilev: A One-Sided Rivalry."
Dance Research, 1, no. 2 (Autumn 1983): 3–20.

———. *Ida Rubinstein*. Liverpool: Liverpool University Press, 1987.

Depaulis, Jacques. *Ida Rubinstein: Une inconnue jadis*. Paris: Editions Honoré
Champion, 1995.

Fokine, Michel. *Memoires of a Ballet Master*. Boston: Little, Brown, 1961.

Furie, Kenneth. "Honegger's 'Joan,' Timeless yet Timely." *New York Times*, 3
April 1994.

Garafola, Lynn. *Diaghilev's Ballets Russes*. New York: Oxford University Press,
1989.

———. "Bronislava Nijinska's Bolero." *Proceedings of Society of Dance History
Scholars* (8–10 February 1991): 251–259.

————. "Circles of Meaning: The Cultural Contexts of Ida Rubinstein's *Le Martyre de Saint Sebastian*." *Proceedings of Society of Dance History Scholars* (10–13 February 1994): 27–47.

Gullace, Giovanni. *Gabriele D'Annunzio in France*. Syracuse, N.Y.: Syracuse University Press, 1966.

Haskell, Arnold. *Diaghileff: His Artistic and Private Life*. London: Gollancz, 1955.

Jullian, Philippe. *Prince of Aesthetes*. Translated by John Haylock and Francis King. New York: Viking, 1968.

————. *D'Annunzio*. Translated by Stephen Hordman. New York: Viking, 1972.

Kochno, Boris. *Diaghilev and the Ballets Russes*. Translated by Adrienne Foulke. New York: Harper and Row, 1970.

Krasovskaya, Vera. *Nijinsky*. New York: Dance Horizons, 1979.

Lester, Keith. "Rubinstein Revisited." *Dance Research*, 1, no. 2 (Autumn 1983): 21–31.

Levinson, André. *The Story of Léon Bakst's Life*. New York: Brentano's, 1922.

Lieven, Prince Peter. *The Birth of the Ballet Russes*. London: George Allen and Unwin, 1936, reprint, 1956.

Lifar, Serge. *Serge Diaghilev, His Life, His Work, His Legend*. New York: G. P. Putnam's Sons, 1940, 1950.

————. *A History of Russian Ballet*. Translated by Arnold Haskell. London: Hutchinson, 1954.

Malmstad, John E. *Times Literary Supplement*. Letter, 7 October 1994.

Massine, Léonide. *My Life in Ballet*. London: Macmillan, 1968.

Mayer, Charles S. "Ida Rubinstein: A Twentieth-Century Cleopatra." *Dance Research Journal*, 20, no. 2 (Winter 1989): 33–51.

Munhall, Edgar. *Whistler and Montesquiou: The Butterfly and the Bat*. New York: Frick Collection, 1995.

Nijinska, Bronislava. *Bronislava Nijinska: Early Memoirs, 1891–1972*. Translated and edited by Irina Nijinska and Jean Rawlinson. Introduction by and in consultation with Anna Kisselgoff. New York: Holt, Rinehart and Winston, 1981.

Nijinsky, Romola. *Nijinsky*. New York: Grosset and Dunlap, Simon and Schuster, 1934.

Secrest, Meryle. *Between Me and Life*. New York: Doubleday, 1974.

Severn, Margaret. "Dancing with Bronislava Nijinska and Ida Rubinstein." *Dance Chronicle* (1988): 333–364.

Smith, F. Berkeley. *How Paris Amuses Itself*. New York: Funk and Wagnalls, 1903.

Spencer, Charles. *Léon Bakst*. New York: St. Martin's, 1973.

Steegmuller, Francis. *Cocteau*. Boston: Little, Brown, 1970.

Thomas, Louis. "Le peintre Bakst parle de Madame Ida Rubinstein." *Revue Critique des Idées et des Livres* (Paris), February 1924.

Tikanova, Nina. *La Jeune Fille en Bleu*. Lausanne: L'Age d'Homme, 1991.

Vaughan, David. "A Peruvian in Paris." *The Dancing Times* (October 1974): 16–17.

Vreeland, Diana. *D. V.* New York: Alfred A. Knopf, 1984.

Wickes, George. *The Amazon of Letters*. New York: G. P. Putnam's Sons, 1976.

Winwar, Frances. *Wingless Victory: A Biography of Gabriele D'Annunzio and Eleanora Duse*. New York: Harper and Brothers, 1956.

Part V. *Colette: The Mental Hermaphrodite*

Barney, Natalie Clifford. *Souvenirs indiscrets*. Paris: Flammarion, 1960.

Benet, Mary Kathleen. *Writers in Love*. New York: Macmillan, 1977.

Benstock, Shari. *Women of the Left Bank*. Austin: University of Texas Press, 1986.

Calmette, Gaston, and Alfred Delilia. "Le Scandale du Moulin-Rouge." *Le Figaro* (Paris) 4 January 1907.

Chalon, Jean. *Colette, l'éternelle apprentie*. Paris: Flammarion, 1998.

Cocteau, Jean. *My Contemporaries*. Edited by Margaret Crosland. Philadelphia: Chilton, 1968.

Colette, *Sido*. Paris: Livre de Poche, Hachette, 1901.

―――. "Les Dames Nues." *Paris-Soir,* 26 December 1938.

―――. *Cheri and The Last of Cheri*. Translated by Roger Senhouse. New York: Farrar, Straus and Giroux, 1951.

―――. *Creatures Great and Small*. Translated by Enid McLeod. New York: Farrar, Straus and Giroux, 1951.

―――. *The Vagabond*. Translated by Enid McLeod. New York: Farrar, Straus and Young, 1955.

―――. *My Apprenticeships and Music Hall Sidelights*. London: Secker and Warburg, 1957.

―――. *Earthly Paradise*. Edited by Robert Phelps. New York: Farrar, Straus and Giroux, 1966.

―――. *The Pure and the Impure*. New York: Farrar, Straus and Giroux, 1966.

―――. *The Complete Claudine*. New York: Farrar, Straus and Giroux, 1976.

―――. *Letters from Colette*. Translated by Robert Phelps. New York: Farrar, Straus and Giroux, 1980.

―――. *Colette en Tournée, Cartes Postales à Sido*. Preface by Michel del Castillo. Paris: Editions Persona, 1984.

―――. *Lettres, Sido Lettres à sa Fille*. n.p.: Des Femmes, 1984.

―――. *Colette Oeuvres*, I–II. Edited by Claude Pichois. Bibliothèque de la Pléiade. Paris: Editions Gallimard, 1984, 1986.

―――. *Nudité* (1943). In *Belles Saisons I et II*. Paris: Flammarion, 1985.

―――. *The Evening Star*. Translated by David Le Vay. London: Women's Press, 1987.

Cottrell, Robert D. *Colette*. New York: Frederick Ungar, 1974.

Crosland, Margaret. *Madame Colette: A Provincial in Paris*. London: Peter Owen, 1954.

―――. *Colette: The Difficulty of Loving*. New York: Bobbs-Merrill, 1973.

Dormann, Geneviève. *Colette: A Passion for Life*. New York: Abbeville, 1985.

"Fin d'un scandale." *Le Matin* (Paris) 5 January 1907.

Francis, Claude, and Fernande Gontier. *Colette*. Paris: Perrin, 1997.

Goudeket, Maurice. *Close to Colette*. New York: Farrar, Straus and Cudahy, 1957.

Jouve, Nicole Ward. *Colette*. Bloomington: Indiana University Press, 1987.

Lottman, Herbert. *Colette: A Life*. Boston: Little, Brown, 1991.

Marks, Elaine. *Colette*. New Brunswick, N.J.: Rutgers University Press, 1960.

Massie, Allan. *Colette*. London: Penguin, 1986.

Mitchell, Yvonne. *Colette: A Taste for Life*. New York: Harcourt, Brace and Jovanovich, 1975, 1977.

Phelps, Robert. *Belles Saisons: A Colette Scrapbook*. New York: Farrar, Straus and Giroux, 1978.

Remy, Tristan. *Georges Wague, Le Mime de la Belle Epoque*. Paris: George Girard, 1964.

Richardson, Joanna. *Colette*. New York: Franklin Watts, 1984.

Rogers, W. G. *Ladies Bountiful*. New York: Harcourt, Brace and World, 1968.

Rouveyre, André. "Theatre: Colette actrice." *Mercure de France*, 1 June 1926.

Sarde, Michèle. *Colette, Free and Fettered*. Translated by Richard Miller. New York: William Morrow, 1980.

"Soirée tumultueuse au café concert." *Le Matin* (Paris) 4 January 1907.

Thurman, Judith. *Secrets of the Flesh: A Life of Colette*. New York: Ballantine, 1999.

Verne, Maurice. *Aux Usines du Plaisir, La Vie Secrete du Music Hall*. Paris: Editions des Portiques, 1929.

de Vieilleville. "Nos Fiches, Yssim et Colette." *Fin de Siècle* (Paris) 17 January 1907.

Index